To Merwyn and Dorothy, whose love for these mountains was,
and is, a gentle inspiration

Black Mountain, from Mile 8.4 on Garden Gulch Trail

Marble   Mountain

Wilderness

David Green

Wilderness Press

BERKELEY

Acknowledgments

Any person wishing to debate knowledgably on the question of whether Forest Service personnel, as employees of the Federal Government, are indeed public servants should undertake the research for a trail guide. I found support for the project at every turn—people taking time to answer the most trivial and obscure questions, and opening their files to offer copies of pertinent documents on various facets of wilderness management. The number of such contributors is too great to list completely; however, David Devine, Curt Marsik, Bill Roberts, Jim Rock, Bob Schiowitz, Chuck Smith and Harry Taylor were particularly responsive to my needs. Linda Barker, Kenneth Coop and Juan de la Fuente of the Forest Service performed an additional service in reading sections of the natural-history chapter. And it is with special warmth and fondness that I mention Doug Andrews and Max Creasy, who became friends as well as sources of information.

It takes more than mere information to make a trail guide, however. This acknowledgment can in no way repay the kindness of Doug and Laurie Andrews, Merwyn and Dorothy Rickey, Bill Jenney and Laura Leather, Neil Berg, and the Ashland family, who opened their homes to me as sanctums for writing and friendship. And I owe a particular debt also to Tom Winnett and Jeff Schaffer of Wilderness Press, who guided me to the realization that trail description must be understandable to the reader as well as the author.

David Green
Berkeley, California
November 1979

Contents

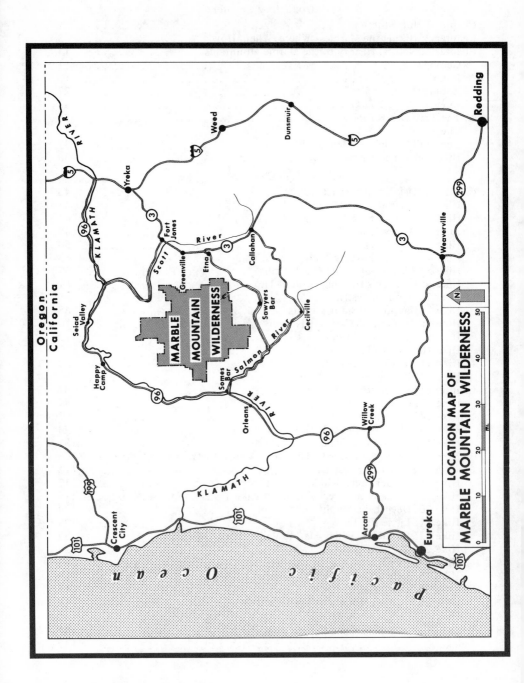

LOCATION MAP OF
MARBLE MOUNTAIN WILDERNESS

Chapter 1

Introduction

The whole wide landscape appears to have been formed by some mighty convulsion of the earth that has thrown up numerous spurs or broken ranges of mountains to the height of from 7,000 to 9,000 feet, and piled them together in strange confusion . . . . [There are] craggy heights, towering upward from amid deep, dark forests of evergreens, that hang like shadows around their bases and sides—lonely and unfrequented lakes hemmed in by beetling walls of rocks—nameless and untrodden valleys, where the deer, bear, and elk still roam in all their native freedom—and wild and foaming streams, winding downward from their native tarns, now plunging over steep and rocky cliffs, forming lofty cascades, whose voices awaken the echoes far and near, and again winding in solemn murmurs through the deep recesses of the mountains . . . . and valley glade and glen robed in a mantle of verdure, in which are mingled the choicest of wildflowers.

> I.A. Reynolds,
> in the *Yreka Journal*, December 1, 1875

There has been little change in the small corner of wilderness known as the Marbles since Reynolds so richly praised it over a century ago. True, the elk no longer roam there, and the lakes are not quite so lonely and unfrequented as they once were, the valleys not so untrodden. Yet, for the backcountry traveler grown jaded by the John Muir Freeway in the High Sierra, or by the alpine lakes decoratively hemmed by tents of many colors in the Cascades, Marble Mountain Wilderness offers a setting bountiful with natural wonders and the indefinable magic of wilderness.

It has long been this way in the Marbles. Nearly encompassed by the Scott, Salmon and Klamath rivers in the northwestern corner of California, it was largely the province of miners and Indians at the time that Reynolds wrote of it. Even then, activity was primarily restricted to the river areas, and the mountainous region in the interior was visited largely in late summer and autumn for hunting and wild food gathering. By the late 19th century, the burgeoning cattle industry in Scott Valley, along the eastern edge of these mountains, began to use the high meadows as wet range. The timber industry also was making inroads into the forests, although not until the mid-20th century did it become much more than a small-scale, local industry.

As a recreational resource, however, the Marbles were a forgotten wilderness. Without a large metropolitan area to draw on or a Sierra Club to promote it, it remained a backyard preserve for the locals of Scott Valley and the river communities. Trails were built for largely utilitarian purposes: to aid fire control, to provide access to the wet range meadows for the ranchers, and occasionally to reach a favorite fishing lake. That it became a wilderness at all was, to some degree, a fortuitous occurrence. Had Herbert Hoover not often enjoyed the pleasures of Wooley Creek in the southwestern part of the Marbles during the 1920s, it is unlikely that this mountain region would have been singled out for primitive-area designation during his administration. The Marble Mountain Primitve Area was established on April 18, 1931. Wilderness designation came much later, in December of 1953.

Yet, even with federal recognition, Marble Mountain Wilderness went largely neglected. Then came the backpacking mania of the late '60s and, as the crowds grew in the better-known Sierra Nevada and Cascades, the search for a wilderness experience stretched farther afield. Backpackers began "discovering" the Marbles, and its usage multiplied.

To a great extent, this trail guide is a byproduct of the increased popularity of Marble Mountain Wilderness. Obviously, the guide would not have been written in the first place if there had not already been a good deal of interest in the area. However, the value of this book lies in its potential for affecting the usage patterns within the wilderness. On the whole, the Marbles remain a relatively litte-used wilderness: although the fourth largest federal wilderness in California, it registers just one third as many annual visitor-days as Desolation Wilderness, in the South Lake Tahoe area, and less than one tenth the annual visitor-days of John Muir Wilderness in the High Sierra (based on Forest Service data for 1974-78).

Within Marble Mountain Wilderness, however, usage is severely skewed. The high-access Scott River district on the east side of the wilderness receives over half of the backcountry travelers, though it has less than one third of the trail miles. Indeed, of the 25 trailheads described in this guide, there are two in this district that alone serve as entry point for close to half of the wilderness visitors. While Sky High Valley, the Marbles' most popular area, will be aswarm with several dozen visitors on any given summer weekend, there are pristine lakes, panoramic ridgecrest vistas and flower-hued meadows elsewhere in this wilderness that won't be seen by that many people in a full year.

Thus, this guide is more than an introduction to Marble Mountain Wilderness. It is a guide to the wilderness *within* the wilderness.

Chapter 2

Hiking the Marbles
—Where, When, How
Where

The Marble Mountain Wilderness lies within the grand jigsaw of ranges of the Klamath Mountains, which includes the Trinity Alps to the south and the Siskiyou Mountains on the Oregon border to the north. It was named for Marble (6880′) and Black (7442′) mountains, the gleaming marble jewels that crown the juncture of the two major ranges within the wilderness: the Marble Mountains, which extend north from these peaks, and the Salmon Mountains, which describe a great horseshoe with southward-pointing arms and an apex at Marble Mountain.

If you were to draw a diagonal line from Eureka on the coast through the heart of Klamath National Forest to Yreka in the valley on Interstate 5, Marble Mountain Wilderness would rest just above the line. For most hikers headed for the Marbles, Yreka and Eureka are the likely points of departure from the major north-south highways serving northern California. From a junction with Interstate 5 at the southern end of Yreka, State Highway 3 travels southwest just over 15 miles through Fort Jones to the Scott River Ranger Station, near the northeast corner of the wilderness. North of Eureka 8 miles—and just north of Arcata—State Highway 299 leaves coastal US 101 to travel inland 38 miles to Willow Creek, from which it is another 45 miles north on State Highway 96 to the Ukonom Ranger Station in Somes Bar, near the southwest corner of the Marbles.

There is a 167-mile "loop road" that encircles the wilderness. Along this road you'll find four of the five district ranger stations, several small communities in which you can make last-minute purchases, a host of National Forest campgrounds, and all the trailheads—or at least Forest Service roads feeding trailheads—for the wilderness (see map, p. vi). Going clockwise from Somes Bar, the loop follows the Klamath River and State Highway 96, then meanders along the curvaceous Scott River Road to Fort Jones and State Highway 3. Highway 3 makes a short, straight shot south to Etna, from which the Somes Bar-Etna road completes the circuit. The Somes Bar-Etna road is a county road that winds excessively in places and is completely paved only for its first 17½ miles southeast from Somes Bar. The primitive nature of this road is the reason why the Salmon River district, in the southern part of the wilderness, receives a disproportionately low number of weekend visitors.

From the loop road, Forest Service and logging roads head up toward the wilderness and the trailheads. These are generally all-weather roads, well-graded and evenly surfaced, though there are a few roads paved at least part way, and a few shocks-destroying dirt roads in various stages of disrepair. In all but the Scott River district, these roads traverse public lands. However, on the east side, there is a broad band of private land between the wilderness and State Highway 3. Several of the roads feeding the trailheads of this district are subject to the managerial whims of principal owner International Paper Co., since they are not within the jurisdiction of the Forest Service. This situation is discussed more fully in the **Access** section of the introduction to the Scott River district.

When

The heavy-use season in the Marbles is between Fourth of July and Labor Day, with a small surge from late September through mid-October during deer-hunting season. Summer is an ideal time to be mountaining here, for it is the dry season: hot days and pleasantly warm nights, with little more than an occasional spate of afternoon thunderstorms in the high country. Indeed, at the lower elevations, it becomes uncomfortably hot during these months, with temperatures nearing 100°. The high meadows are ablaze with floral color by mid-July, and the highly deciduous low- to mid-elevation forests are brilliant with autumn hues by late September. The winter snowpack is gone from all but a few north-slope pockets by mid-July.

However, there is more than one hiking season. True, this area has a thoroughly wet winter: the high country receives upward of 80 inches of precipitation, primarily from November through March, with a winter snowpack often exceeding 10 feet. Nevertheless, there are several trails that provide the finest hiking spring has to offer. The North Fork and Little North Fork trails in the Salmon River district, the Kelsey Creek Trail in the Scott River district, the Grider Creek Trail in the Oak Knoll district and the Elk Creek Trail in the Happy Camp district all have trailheads below 3000 feet, and normally are free of winter snowpack for several miles by April or May. And the Wooley Creek Trail, with a trailhead elevation of 650 feet, and Fowler Cabin 10.2 miles up-trail at under 1400 feet, is a bona-fide four-season hike. Furthermore, with a network of unplowed Forest Service roads leading to its borders, the wilderness is widely accessible to—and largely ignored by—cross-country skiers and winter campers.

A word to the wise about the seemingly benign summer season: Though spring comes to the low valleys by April or May, and has climbed to the peaks by June, winter is never entirely banished from the mountains. The Scott River Ranger Station, at 2720 feet, has recorded freezing temperatures in every month of the year, and the high country has experienced fresh snowfall in every month. The threat of hypothermia to the backcountry traveler is perhaps greater during the summer than in any other season for the very reason that it is least expected then. The author recommends you carry wet-weather gear and a full change of wool clothing, regardless of season.

An additional note: you can get up-to-date weather information at the ranger stations, for they receive regional weather service reports about 10:30 a.m. and 4:00 p.m. every day. Don't simply inquire about the weather, however, for you'll likely be told only that it'll be "'bout the same as it has been." Ask specifically for the latest weather report transmitted from the Supervisor's Office in Yreka.

How

There are Rules of the Road for the off-road walker. You will receive a sheet of them when you visit a ranger station, or write for a wilderness permit. Indeed, obtaining a wilderness permit is Rule #1. Marble Mountain Wilderness' Rules for Use are reproduced here, since several of them can benefit from annotation.

1. Obtain a Wilderness Permit before entering the Wilderness. Permits are obtainable from any Ranger Station or the Supervisor's Office.

Wilderness permit is a misnomer, for it in no way is a license for wilderness use. One doesn't have to submit his equipment to inspection or have a ranger accompany him on a test walk. Yet 10-15% of wilderness users neglect to pick up a permit, because of the inconvenience of fitting a business-hours stop at a ranger station into a tight weekend schedule, or out of resentment at "just another government regulation."

Yet the wilderness-permit system can be an aid to the wilderness traveler rather than a hindrance. From the stack of permits issued that day, the ranger station can tell you if that little-used lake you have your eyes on is hosting a Boy Scout troop for the weekend. At present the ranger stations don't keep an ongoing tally at the front desk that would take into account permits issued earlier in the week or written in for, but they have the resources to do so and, if enough people begin asking for this information, perhaps the Forest Service will respond.

Unlike California's Desolation Wilderness or Oregon's Rogue River, where usage is so great that a quota system has been instituted and advance registration is recommended and often required, Marble Mountain Wilderness has no population-control measures—yet. So there is no need to write for a permit in advance except to avoid the necessity of a stop at a ranger station. But by applying for your permit in person before heading into the wilderness, you'll be able to ask for current information on trail conditions, remnant snowpack, weather, ornery bears, etc.

Listed below are the addresses and phone numbers of the five district ranger stations and the Supervisor's Office in Yreka. During the winter season—variable, but generally about October 1 to May 15—office hours are 8:00-4:30, weekdays only. During the summer season, the district stations are open seven days a week. Their hours, which vary, are listed below with their addresses. All the districts but Happy Camp have guard stations at separate locations, where wilderness permits may be obtained; specifics on the whereabouts of these work centers are included in the Access section of each chapter introduction.

Supervisor's Office
Klamath National Forest
1215 S. Main Street
Yreka, CA 96097

Oak Knoll Ranger Station
Klamath River, CA 96050
(916) 465-2241
summer hours: 8:00-6:00

Happy Camp Ranger Station
Happy Camp, CA 96039
(916) 493-2243
summer hours:
    7:00-6:00, weekdays
    9:30-6:00, weekends

Ukonom Ranger Station
Somes Bar, CA 95568
(916) 469-3331
summer hours: 8:00-6:00

Salmon River Ranger Station
Sawyers Bar, CA 96027
(916) Ft. Jones toll station 4600
summer hours: 7:00-6:30

Scott River Ranger Station
Fort Jones, CA 96032
(916) 468-5351
summer hours: 8:00-4:30

2. Respect the solitude of others who come in search for quiet and serenity. Provide for camping privacy.

3. Pack out all unburnable refuse; burn or pack out burnable refuse.

There are customary reasons for packing out your garbage: the esthetic blemish of rusted cans and garish Mountain House freeze-dried foil, and the tendency of bears to begin haunting campsites, and campers, where they've found rewards before. But there is also a

Black bear ambling along Portuguese Peak Trail

less-recognized argument. Each summer, the Forest Service hires six to eight wilderness rangers to roam through the Marbles backcountry. These rangers have generally been schooled in various facets of natural history and are a tremendous resource for wilderness interpretation. Yet far too much of their time is spent removing garbage; much too often they must interact with the public on matters of campsite location and fire use, rather than bird identification and forest types. It's a shameful waste of talent.

4. Use of motors and motorized equipment is prohibited by law.

5. Protect live vegetation; do not cut tree boughs for bedding.

6. Dispose of human waste at least 200 feet from any water source, campsite or trail. Stay within the "biological disposal layer" by digging a hole no deeper than 6-8 inches.

Beginning in 1979, the Forest Service's *Marble Mountain Wilderness* maps were stamped with the following message: "Water quality testing is not performed on open water sources, such as lakes, streams, and springs. Boil or treat water before using." This warning is in compliance with the Federal Water Quality Act, passed a few years back, which requires such an advisory statement whenever specific tests have not been completed to ascertain the purity of a water source.

Actually, specific tests have been carried out at a number of lakes and streams in the wilderness, and they have generally found an unsafe level of coliform bacteria. Coliform bacteria thrive in the intestinal tracts of animals. Their presence in a water source means someone—man, packstock, bovine, bear—has been unloading its intestines in or around the water.

To lessen the impact of teeming humanity, the Forest Service has constructed several pit toilets. Presently, these are located at Granite Meadows in the Happy Camp district, at Timber Hotel, Tom Taylor Cabin, English and Hancock lakes in the Salmon River district, and at Campbell Lake and Marble and Sky High valleys in the Scott River district. In most instances, the Forest Service has attempted to avoid the esthetic taint of the pit toilet's presence by hiding it so well as to subvert its benefits. This guide pinpoints their locations in the appropriate trail descriptions.

7. Locate campsites a minimum distance of 100 feet from water sources, meadows, trails and other campsites.

During 1973-4 the Forest Service made a survey of the campsites in the Marbles, preparatory to writing a management plan for the wilderness. Their findings were not unexpected: most, and the most favored, campsites were located on stream banks and lake shores. With the recreational boom in the backcountry that began in the late '60s, these sites were becoming overused and highly impacted: delicate vegetation was being trampled into oblivion and regeneration was impossible due to the compacted soil and continued use. Vegetationless soil was then washing into lakes and streams.

In response to this situation, the Forest Service considered several courses of action. One was to establish a quota system for high-use areas based on a study of the estimated carrying capacity of each area. Another was to implement a rest-rotation schedule for overused areas by roping off the most abused sites and perhaps closing off entire lakes to camping. A third proposal was to create guidelines for campsite location.

The first two plans were tabled. However, the above rule for campsites was established. The guideline is more specific regarding lakes: campsite distance restrictions were created for each lake of up to 200 feet from shore. The Rules for Use sheet issued with the wilderness permit lists the lakes of the wilderness and the camping distance regulations for each. The lake chart in Chapter 4 also lists the distance restrictions for the 52 lakes discussed in this book.

Although the campsite location guidelines were adopted with the best of intentions in mind, their application is sometimes quite impractical. Nestled in deep-dish glacial cirques, many lakes simply do not lend themselves to observing the guidelines: 100 feet from the lakeshore can put you up on a 30° slope. And the quirks of topography can sometimes allow for perfectly acceptable campsites to be located inside the distance regulation: at Pine Lake in the Salmon River district, for instance, a slight rise along the southwest shore places the campsite located nearby in another drainage; hence erosion from the camp is not washed immediately into the lake but is effectively trapped by surrounding foliage before reaching the outlet creek.

Thus the best rule for campsite location is to use your common sense. The wilderness rangers are empowered to issue fine-bearing citations for blatant disregard of the guidelines. However, their concern is that you heed the *spirit* of the law. Use previously established campsites, rather than clearing away brush and vegetable litter to create a new site. Use sites with established firerings rather than building new rings. Destroying fresh firerings and rehabilitating newly created campsites is yet another burden with which the wilderness rangers find themselves continually saddled. Make an effort to choose campsites that cause minimal impact on the natural and esthetic environment—the trail descriptions in this book often make recommendations in this respect. In short, live with nature rather than above it.

8. Dispose of waste water, bathe and wash dishes in a suitable location away from the water source.

Simply because one uses soap made from the essence of bee pollen does not mean that this regulation can be ignored. *All* soaps are biodegradable eventually; *all* soaps are a pollutant until they biodegrade.

9. Limit party size to 25 people or less.

The Forest Service made an additional decision about campsites with regard to large groups (groups of more than 10 people): large groups should altogether avoid camping at a lake. The Forest Service's wilderness map suggests nearly two dozen areas for large group camping, all in valleys or meadow areas. A comment on these recommended camping locations: many are located *only* on that map because there is no established campsite; in some instances, there is not even a trail to the area. The suggested areas are meant to serve as much as guidelines for large group camping as they are as actual recommendations.

The last five Rules for Use concern the management of packstock. Until the late '60s, the use of packstock was prevalent in the wilderness and, though backpackers outnumber horsepackers now by an increasingly large margin, packstock is still a popular mode of travel, particularly in the Scott River district, with its neighboring ranchlands. For the most part the commercial packers with permits to work the Marbles are located in the Scott Valley area. The list of currently approved commercial packers is available from the Scott River Ranger Station and the Supervisor's Office.

Scott Valley—the homeland for most of the Marble's cattle

10. Graze livestock AFTER July 1 only. Because native vegetation is generally not ready before this date, pack in hay, grain or pelletized feed.

There is one area for which the horsepacker needs to pack in feed regardless of the season. In the Salmon River district, in the high meadows along the North Fork Trail between Tom Taylor Cabin and English Peak, grazing is always prohibited.

Between Tom Taylor Cabin (above) and English Peak, grazing is always prohibited.

11. Overnight pasturing of pack and saddle stock in areas not restricted to this use.

In addition to the restriction near English Peak, overnight pasturing of stock is prohibited in the following areas:

Ukonom district:	Pleasant Lake
Scott River district:	Angel Lake (off trail)
Happy Camp district:	Rainy Lake
	Tickner Hole
	Ukonom Lake
	Blue and Green/Gold Granite lakes
	Independence Lake (off trail)

12. Control pack and saddle stock by means other than a picket pin; hobbling is the preferred method.

13. Tie pack and saddle stock no closer than 200 feet from any water source, campsite or trail.

14. Lead unridden saddle and pack stock when on the trail.

There are also regulations regarding hunting and fishing, established by the California Department of Fish and Game. Hunting is mentioned here more for the protection of the nonhunter than for the information of the hunter. There is little to fear during bow-hunting season—spanning approximately the first three weeks of September—as bow-hunters generally move close enough to their prey to be able to distinguish between deer and backpacker. Gun-hunting season is another matter; the newspapers regularly report the bagging of the first hunter of the season at dawn of opening day. Wilderness status does not exclude the Marbles from the invasion; during the last couple of days before the season's opening, the commercial packers seemingly do enough business to support them through the winter. Although it is not necessary to consider the wilderness hazardous to your health during the entire gun-hunting season—generally from the next-to-last weekend of September through mid-October

—it might be best to avoid the backcountry during the highly charged first and last weekends of the season. There is also a bear-hunting season in the Marbles, which usually extends from the last weekend of October to just beyond mid-December.

Fishing is a much more widely practiced activity, indeed, the prime motivation for many visits to the wilderness. The following pertinent information, culled from the Department of Fish and Game regulations booklet, is included to aid you in engaging in the sport legitmately.

A fishing license is required of any person over age 15.

In addition to the basic license, a stamp is required for fishing in inland waters and another stamp is needed for fishing for trout, salmon or steelhead in inland waters.

License fees:

Resident license	$4
Nonresident license	$15
Special 10-day nonresident license	$5
Inland water license stamp	$2
Trout and salmon license stamp	$3

Fishing hours pertaining to Marble Mountain Wilderness and vicinity: from one hour before sunrise to one hour after sunset.

Lake fishing: season is all year; limit is ten trout from the last Saturday in April through November 15, and five trout through the rest of the year.

Stream fishing: season is from the Saturday preceding Memorial Day through November 15; limit is ten trout or salmon in combination.

—Exception to stream fishing season and limits: Wooley Creek is closed to all salmon fishing from August 1 to November 15.

Chapter 3

Natural History
of the Marble Mountains

If there is anything that typifies the natural scene of the Marble Mountain Wilderness, it is its atypicality. At the bottom of it all is a melange of rock types whose range of ages and compositions represents a veritable family tree of California geology. In addition, the Marbles are a botanical melting pot, reflecting the influence of both ocean and mountain, mixing plants of the Sierra and the Cascades, and even harboring several plant species that occur naturally only in northwestern California. Although the faunal community does not exhibit quite the variety of its floral counterpart, the flitting, scurrying, dashing, soaring and lumbering about of its members are integral parts of the wilderness experience. Given such bountiful complexity, the following discussion of the geology, botany and zoology can be no more than the merest introduction to the natural wonders of the Marbles.

GEOLOGY

The Marble Mountain Wilderness lies within the Klamath Mountains geologic province, which also includes the Siskiyou Mountains to the north and the Trinity Alps to the south. Through radiometric dating and the presence of certain fossilized radiolarians—single-celled marine lifeforms—the "birth" of the Klamath Mountains has been placed in the area of 380 million years ago, during the Devonian period of the Paleozoic era (see Geologic Time Table). These mountains began as ocean floor, which received sediments such as clay, silt, and sand from the western edge of the North American continent. Minute skeletons and dead remains of marine animals and plants also added to these sediments. As all these deposits increased in thickness and weight, they were transformed into sedimentary rocks such as shale, sandstone and limestone. In addition, sporadic volcanic activity produced lava flows and other volcanic rocks that intermixed with the sedimentary deposits.

As the accumulation of these various deposits continued beneath the ocean depths, another ongoing process—instrumental in mountain-building along the Pacific coast—was also at work. The recently evolved theory of plate tectonics posits that the earth's major land and ocean masses rest on massive plates floating on the earth's mantle, and that the collision of two plates results in the formation of mountain ranges. Along the west coast of North America, the oceanic Pacific plate was diving under the western edge of the more bouyant, continental North American plate. As it did so, the several-mile-thick layer of ocean-floor deposits and volcanic rocks was being "scraped off" along the edge of the continental plate and compressed by the movement of the plates against each other. Under the heat and pressure produced in the process, the oceanic sedimentary and volcanic rocks were metamorphosed into a melange of slate, quartzite, schist, gneiss, metachert, soapstone and marble—the metasediments and metavolcanics found in such great quantity throughout the Klamath Mountains.

GEOLOGIC MAP OF
MARBLE MOUNTAIN WILDERNESS

METAMORPHIC ROCKS   INTRUSIVE ROCKS

Marble   Mostly granodiorite
                      and quartz diorite
                      ("granite")

All other meta-   Mostly diorite
morphic rocks   and gabbro

                      Ultramafic rocks,
                      mostly serpentinite
                      (altered peridotite)

N

0   1   2   3
        miles

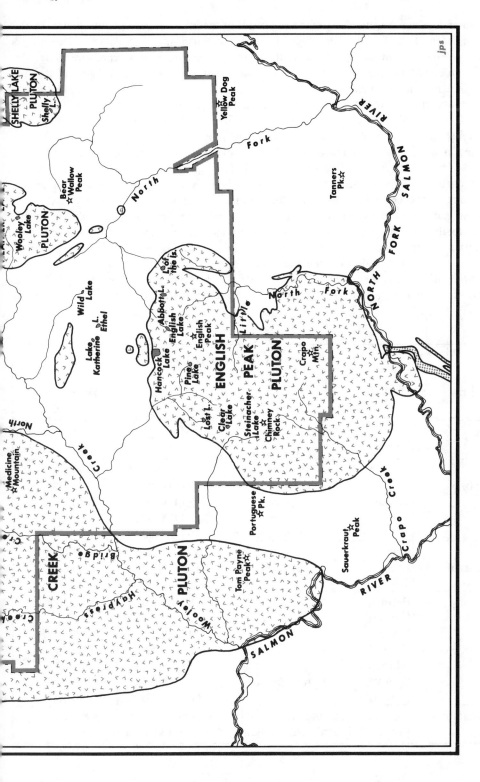

Other rock types were also formed as a result of the interaction of the two plates. As the leading edge of the Pacific plate slipped beneath the North American plate and descended a couple of hundred miles toward the earth's core, the extreme heat and pressure melted the rock, producing magma—molten subsurface rock—that gradually ascended toward the surface. The magma that reached the surface and cooled above ground formed volcanic rocks, mostly andesite and basalt, which have since metamorphosed into meta-andesite and green-schist. The magma that cooled and hardened while still underground formed large bodies (plutons) of igneous rock, the granitic rocks. The most extensive granitic bodies in Marble Mountain Wilderness are the English Peak and Wooley Creek plutons, which are largely composed of two kinds of granitic rocks, quartz diorite and granodiorite (see Geologic Map).

A distinctive type of intrusive igneous rock also formed as a byproduct of the under-thrusting of the oceanic plate. Under the extreme pressures produced, major thrust faults formed parallel to the edge of the Pacific plate and extended down through the earth's crust to the superheated mantle. From this iron- and magnesium-rich molten mass, sheets of ultramafic rock squeezed up into these rents in the earth's crust. ("Mafic" is a corrupted contraction of "Ma" and "Fe", the chemical symbols for magnesium and iron, respectively; an *ultra*mafic rock is even richer in these elements.) The original rock was a dark, dense plutonic rock called peridotite, but the metamorphic process transformed much of the ultra-

GEOLOGIC TIME TABLE				
Era	**Period**	**Epoch**	**Began** (years ago)	**Duration** (years)
	Quaternary	Holocene	10,000	10,000
		Pleistocene	1,800,000	1,800,000
Cenozoic		Pliocene	5,200,000	3,400,000
		Miocene	21,700,000	16,500,000
	Tertiary	Oligocene	35,000,000	13,300,000
		Eocene	49,000,000	14,000,000
		Paleocene	64,000,000	15,000,000
	Cretaceous	*Numerous*	135,000,000	71,000,000
Mesozoic	Jurassic	*epochs*	195,000,000	60,000,000
	Triassic	*recognized*	225,000,000	30,000,000
	Permian		280,000,000	55,000,000
	Carboni-ferous	*Numerous*	345,000,000	65,000,000
Paleozoic	Devonian	*epochs*	400,000,000	55,000,000
	Silurian		435,000,000	35,000,000
	Ordovician	*recognized*	500,000,000	65,000,000
	Cambrian		600,000,000	100,000,000
Precambrian	No widely accepted time units; oldest known rocks are 3.8 billion years old; Earth's crust solidified 4.6 billion years ago.			

mafic rock found in the Klamath Mountains to serpentinite. This rock, which weathers to a rich, burnt-sienna color due to its high iron content, forms the ruddy bulk of the Red Mountain massif and of Red Rock in Marble Mountain Wilderness. (There are also mafic granitic rocks, with somewhat lesser concentrations of iron and magnesium. The gabbro-and-diorite mass cut by the lower reaches of Kelsey Creek is an example of a mafic granitic body.)

A long, geologically quiet period existed before 230 million years ago, and it was during this period that the crown jewels of the wilderness, Marble and Black mountains, had their origins. Over uncounted millenia a coral reef grew in tropical waters, forming a thick limestone bed. Later, this bed underwent metamorphism, and it was changed to a layer of marble several miles long and several hundred feet thick. The dark cap on the pinnacle of Black Mountain is composed of sediments that were deposited atop the coral reef, probably near the time of renewed geologic activity. Like the coral limestone, these deposits were then converted through heat and pressure to metasedimentary rocks.

Forces can build up within the earth which can literally move mountains. One such time of significant mountain-building—called an *orogeny*—occurred from about 170 to 130 million years ago, during the mid-to-late Jurassic period. The extreme pressures created by the plate movement during the Nevadan orogeny, as this period of mountain building is called, led to severe thrust-faulting, renting the earth's crust. In these rents great slabs of ultramafic rock were emplaced. The main intrusions of granitic masses also occurred during this time: the Wooley Creek and English Peak plutons, mentioned earlier, are dated as 147 to 157 million years old. These rising masses shouldered aside the overlying sedimentary, volcanic and ultramafic rocks, and contributed to the forces of metamorphism that have so altered the older, overlying rocks in the Klamath Mountains. The Nevadan orogeny was a period of widespread disruption; the alignment of major thrust faults and the correlation of dates of granitic intrusions indicate that the Klamath Mountains are in fact an extension of the Sierra Nevada that were later displaced to the west through further fault movement.

Following the Nevadan orogeny, the Klamath Mountains found themselves surrounded by a shallow ocean whose shoreline waters lapped against the hills east of the Sacramento Valley and related valleys to the north. The mountains continued to be uplifted by the powers below and eroded away by the forces above. Eroded sediments from the Klamath Mountains were deposited in the floor of a sea that covered the continental shelf. Today, you can see these uplifted Cretaceous rocks along the hills on the western edge of the Sacramento Valley.

Around the beginning of the Tertiary period, some 60 million years ago, the ocean receded and the Klamath Mountains were reunited with the mainland. There were continued periods of significant uplift, one near the close of the Eocene epoch, and another that approximately spanned the Pliocene epoch. These periods of uplift further catalyzed erosion and stream-cutting in the Klamath Mountains, producing deep canyons whose lower portions were quite similar to those of today.

However, the upper portions then underwent dramatic change during the Pleistocene glaciation. For hundreds of thousands of years, glaciers—particularly on north and east slopes—robed the high peaks and extended down-canyon to below the present 4500-foot-level. Near the beginning of the Holocene epoch, 10-12,000 years ago, the glaciers receded, leaving behind them broadened, gracefully U-shaped canyons, with clusters of moraine-dammed lakes in deep-sculpted bowls, or cirques, at the heads of the canyons. Deposits from glacial streams can still be seen today in several places along the North Fork of the Salmon River and its Right Hand Fork. At present there are no living glaciers in Marble Mountain Wilderness, but they could reappear in the near future. The only alpine glacier remaining in the Klamath Mountains clings to the north face of Mt. Thompson in the Trinity Alps.

The glaciers not only contributed to the natural beauty of the Marbles, but they were also a factor in the gold fever that swept through California in the mid-19th century. Granitic rock is a source rock for several metallic minerals—gold, silver, copper, lead, zinc, tungsten, molybdenum—which are generally formed near the perimeters of granitic bodies, perhaps as a result of chemical interaction with the surrounding rock. The glaciers swept over the granitic bodies, harvesting mineral-laden rocks and depositing them in the streambed gravels of the outwash. In the Marbles area, the Scott, Salmon and Klamath rivers and their major tributaries were all hotbeds of placer mining activity. Today, with the price of gold soaring, there has been a small resurgence of placer mining, mostly along the Salmon River; the North Fork Trail passes two placer mining claims in its lower reaches outside the wilderness.

Also of special interest at the present are the caves found in the marble mass at the center of the wilderness. As groundwater percolates through the marble, it washes the rock's calcium carbonate into solution and carries it away, leaving a sinuous system of underground caverns and tunnels. A spelunking organization, calling itself the Klamath Mountains Conservation Task Force, has been mapping the caves in the Marble Mountains for the past several years. Thus far, they have mapped over 8 miles in the cave system which, due to the tilt of the marble layer, descends over 1250 vertical feet from the cave openings. They have found the skeletons of elk, timber wolf and bighorn sheep, and subterranean lakes whose temperatures hover just above freezing.

Sound exciting, does it? Although this brief description may have whetted your appetite for spelunking, this trail guide will not help you satisfy it; none of the cave entrances are identified. This is because the marble caves in this wilderness do not lend themselves to idle wandering. For the most part, they require rock climbing skills and equipment, and cold weather gear (wetsuits for traversing standing water). Even more, they require experience. If you are sufficiently intrigued and don't have any spelunking friends familiar with the caves of the Marbles, the author suggests you contact the Klamath National Forest offices in Yreka for current information regarding the Klamath Mountains Conservation Task Force.

BOTANY

The botanical community of the Marble Mountain Wilderness, indeed, of the entire Klamath Mountains region, is a wonderland of extraordinary diversity and singularity. Well over 500 species of plants have been identified within the wilderness and several are endemic to the Klamath Mountains, occurring naturally nowhere else in the world.

It appears that we have the quirks of geologic history in the Klamath Mountains to thank for the complex mosaic of plant life supported by the area. While other regions of the coastal states were submerged beneath a more inland-reaching ocean, inundated by great basaltic lava flows, or choked off by more extensive glaciation, the Klamath Mountains enjoyed more stable conditions, which permitted the existence of a floral island that provided asylum for plant communities that were being eliminated elsewhere. Several of the endemic plants found here are relict species that were far more widespread in prehistoric times. Too, the floral multiplicity of the Klamath region derives from the numerous source areas that have fed it. The Klamath Mountains' flora are influenced by the Cascades to the north, the Sierra

Nevada to the south, the humid coast to the west and the hot Modoc plateau to the east. One study of the Marbles identified 535 plants, of which approximately 420 species are common to the Cascades and a like number to the Sierra Nevada.

On the other hand, extreme variation in topography, climate, and even soil type within the Marbles has created a wide range of habitats in this relatively compact area. Plants that customarily inhabit alpine environments, for instance, have adapted and evolved subspecies and varieties that are quite at home on the north face of a middle-elevation peak or in the perpetually shaded confines of a narrow ravine.

The diversity in influences and the variety of habitats make the botanical community of the Marble Mountains difficult to categorize. In recent years the "plant communities" system of classification has come into favor among botanists. This system sets aside the variegated influences acting on the flora and looks first at the results of those influences, namely, readily identifiable groupings of plants that repeatedly occur together regardless of apparent nonconformities in habitats. A noted California botanist, Philip Munz, has identified 29 plant communities in his study of California flora.

The Marble Mountains include seven distinct plant communities: mixed-evergreen forest, mixed-conifer forest, red-fir forest, subalpine forest, mountain meadows, montane chaparral and alpine fell-fields. Occasionally, a particular ecological factor—soil type or sun exposure, for instance—will take precedence over all other factors, resulting in an association of plants that will be found in several different plant communities, but always occupying a particular niche determined by that overriding factor. Such plant groupings in the Marbles are the ultramafic soil grouping, streamside grouping, shade-tolerant grouping and sun-tolerant grouping.

Before we start listing trees and wildflowers and shrubbery, a few words need to be said about plant identification and the Name Game. For most of us, a rose is a rose is a rose. If we wanted to get picky and pulled out a field guide, we would discover that the rose growing beneath the conifers of the Marbles is a Wood's rose, but we would still be speaking English. Botanists, on the other hand, talk in tongues. Latin, to be exact. It is not a Wood's rose, it is *Rosa woodsii*. *Rosa* is the name of the genus, and *woodsii* is the name of the species, a member of the genus. Thus, in one trip of the tongue, the plant is both identified and classified.

The advantage of the scientific name is that it is understood around the world by those who have worked and studied in the particular field, whereas the common name for a given species of plant may differ from state to state. Take the shrub *Ceanothus veluntinus*. In California, its English moniker is tobacco brush. In the Pacific Northwest, however, it commonly goes by snowbush, and is also called sticky laurel and white lilac.

The variation in common names occurs in all types of plants: the endemic shrub Sadler oak also goes by the name of deer oak, and loggers refer to white fir as piss fir in reference to its acrid odor when cut. But it is with the wildflowers that the Name Game seems to have the fewest rules. If you intend to try your hand at flower identification and use the flower lists here as an aid, it will help you to know that, for the most part, the common names used in this trail guide were taken from *A Field Guide to Pacific States Wildflowers*, a Peterson guide by Niehaus and Ripper.

Even with all the answers on a sheet of paper in front of you, identifying wildflowers is a tricky business. Mother Nature is forever tinkering in her workshop, changing the color of a blossom here, the shape of a pistil there, the lobular pattern of a leaf over yonder. It is this ongoing evolution in the natural world that keeps the scientific language in a state of flux. The plant mentioned in this guide as "scarlet gilia" was once known to the botanists as *Gilia aggregata* but underwent a generic name change in recent years to *Ipomopsis aggregata.* Such name changes are often initiated by one botanist specializing in a particular family of plants. S/he may even use the new name in authoring books and field guides. Yet it may be several years before the change is recognized and standardized by the entire scientific community, during which time the botanists can be victims of the same Tower-of-Babel confusion we lay-folk are subject to with common names.

The result of evolution and the scientists' penchant for nitpicking is several genera that include dozens of species distinguished by the most minute and intricate of details. In his most nearly definitive work, *A California Flora*, Philip Munz lists over 300 different members of the genus *Lupinus*, the lupines. The Neihaus and Ripper flower guide, prepared for the lay person and much less complete than Munz, identifies only 27. And your trail guide differentiates only between broadleaf lupine and elegant lupine, often referring simply to lupine. You'll also find that the plant keys, particularly of wildflowers, are only seasonally useful, and the flowers don't keep the same season. By June the bloom is gone from the violet's cheeks, while the explorer's gentian is yet prepubescent. Nor do wildflowers rigidly keep to their habitats; they are prone to appear in several. The wildflower lists included here generally mention each plant in its most common habitat.

So, by all means, carry a wildflower field guide with you on your next trip to the Marbles; it will add another facet to your involvement with the wilderness. But remember that it is the flower's beauty not its identity, that brought you to the mountains in the first place. The following description of the Marble Mountain plant communities is based on the work of Munz, on adaptations of his system made by several botanical studies conducted in the wilderness, and on the author's own field work.

Plant Communities

1. Mixed-Evergreen Forest

Trees: Douglas-fir, madrone, tanbark-oak, golden chinquapin, hazelnut, canyon live oak, Pacific dogwood, bigleaf maple, California black oak, Oregon white oak

Shrubs: deer brush, western azalea, poison oak, red huckleberry, raspberry

The mixed-evergreen forest is the lowland forest in the Marbles. With the exception of along the trails in the Salmon River district, you will usually be in this ecosystem while driving to the trailhead, for it rarely grows above 3000 feet. Only along the Wooley Creek Trail will you travel through an extended stretch of mixed-evergreen forest within the wilderness.

Many of the broadleaf trees of this forest association—golden chinquapin, canyon live oak, Oregon white oak—are also found at higher elevations in other plant communities, such as the mixed-conifer forest and montane chaparral, but there they exist in scrub form, not as trees. Although wildflowers are discussed later under a slightly different system of classification, there are a few flowers that are rarely found outside this plant community. These include star thistle and Klamath weed, found in forest openings, in cutblocks and along roads, and woodland madia and long-tube iris, found in forest shade.

Another plant that is largely restricted to this lower-elevation forest is poison oak. This plant takes many forms, from low-lying clumps to head-high shrubs, and its leaves are variously colored from spring's bright green, through summer's mottled yellow-green-red to autumn's brilliant red. It is most easily identified by the triple-leaf clusters of its variably lobed leaves, which are glossy with skin-irritating oils. The district ranger stations have a small, free brochure on this plant with excellent color photographs.

2. Mixed-Conifer Forest

Trees: white fir, Douglas-fir, ponderosa pine, sugar pine, knobcone pine, incense-cedar, California black oak, mountain maple

Shrubs: tobacco brush, currant, gooseberry, greenleaf manzanita, Sadler oak, huckleberry oak, wood rose, golden chinquapin, baneberry, snowberry

Ferns: lady fern, sword fern, bracken fern

Most hikes in the Marbles begin in the dense, lush forests of this plant community. The conifers tower above one like monuments to the Creator; an incense-cedar in Devils Canyon in the Salmon River district is touted as the largest of its species in the world. The few deciduous trees in this community are altered either in form—smaller size than at lower elevations —or in habitat—they are restricted to streamside and gulch environments.

Though the mixed-conifer forest extends nearly continuously between 3000 and 6000 feet, it has a varied constituency. In the cool, moist microclimate of a canyon bottom, all the conifers are likely to be present, with incense-cedar, Douglas-fir and white fir the dominant species. In the warmer, drier environs farther upslope, you'll find the pines, particularly ponderosa pine, in greater concentrations. At the higher elevations of this community, nearly pure stands of white fir tend to form, with a characteristically scant understory of wintergreens—white-vein pyrola and one-sided pyrola, western prince's pine—and saprophytes—pinedrops, sugarstick, Merten's coralroot and spotted coralroot.

As the mixed-conifer forest begins to phase into the next "higher" plant community, you will often pass through a distinctive *ecotone*—the interface between two plant communities —of red fir and white fir. This ecotone is most readily recognized by the lack of cones on the ground, since true firs do not naturally drop their cones as do the pines, incense-cedars and Douglas-firs.

3. Red-Fir Forest

Trees: Shasta red fir, noble fir, western white pine, mountain hemlock, mountain maple, weeping spruce, Pacific silver fir

Shrubs: wood rose, Sadler oak, greenleaf manzanita, tobacco brush, baneberry, red elderberry, blue elderberry, gooseberry, currant, huckleberry

Ferns: cliff brake, holly fern, brittle fern, lady fern, bracken fern, sword fern

The red-fir forest is the highest-elevation full-bodied forest in the Marbles. The next higher community, the subalpine forest, is a timberline association, with isolated pockets of growth. But then, the red-fir forest also exists in pockets outside its usual horizontal belt between 5500 and 7000 feet. On north-facing slopes, where the limited exposure to the sun results in a greater retention of winter snowpack and hence a cooler, moister microclimate than on slopes of other orientations, the red-fir forest may extend down to 4500 feet or less. It is generally on these north-facing slopes that the endemic weeping spruce occurs. A similar phenomenon occurs in valley and canyon bottoms, where the night air grows cold and, being more dense, descends downslope to settle in the "cold air well" of the bottom. There are several river bottoms in the Marbles where red-fir forest constituents can be found, while trees of the generally lower elevation mixed-conifer forest are growing higher upslope. The most impressive example of this inversion is located in the Haypress Meadows area, where the meadows are bordered by red fir, mountain hemlock, western white pine and lodgepole pine, while sugar pine, ponderosa pine, white fir and Douglas-fir cover the hillocks only 50 vertical feet higher.

Although this plant community is entitled the red-fir forest, it's unlikely that you'll see a simple red fir in this wilderness. Where the northern Sierra Nevada fades into the southern Cascades, roughly midway between Lake Tahoe and Mt. Shasta, a variety of red fir known as the Shasta red fir begins to appear. The Shasta red fir becomes more common northward and quite overwhelms the common variety by the time it reaches the Marbles. The distinction between the two varieties is mainly in the cones. The Shasta red fir has protruding bracts, which partly cover the surface of the cone, but the red fir has none. The bracts serve as the distinction also between the Shasta red fir and the closely related noble fir, which grows as far south as northern California. On the noble-fir cone, the bracts are so numerous that they produce a shingle effect and completely hide the cone's scales. Outside of the cones, the similarities between these three trees are so close that even professional botanists are often at a loss to distinguish among them. Since these trees are all true firs and hence don't shed their cones until after the seeds have been distributed, amateur botanists are at a loss to distinguish one type from another (you will occasionally find green cones on the ground that have been harvested by Douglas squirrels). To simplify matters, this trail guide refers to all three firs as red fir, though noble firs probably make up 15-25% of this total, and increase toward the western edge of the wilderness.

Also starting its range in northern California is the Pacific silver fir, its two locations in the Marbles representing the southernmost known appearances of this tree. Only one of these locations is passed by trail: the stand on the slopes south of Hancock Lake in the Salmon River district. Here they are found mostly with mountain hemlocks, though also with some red firs and western white pines.

Often the ecotone between the red-fir and mixed-conifer forests is a simple joining of ranks, referred to by some as an "enriched conifer forest." One noted example of this is near the junction of the Shackleford Creek and Red Mountain trails, near Log Lake. In addition to the collection of white fir, red fir, Douglas-fir, sugar pine, western white pine and incense-cedar here, there is also Jeffrey pine from the ultramafic-soil association and lodgepole pine from the nearby meadow border.

At its ecotone with the subalpine forest, often near the top of a canyon headwall, the red-fir forest consists of pure stands of red fir (and noble fir). What makes these groves noteworthy is the extensive growth of staghorn lichen that coats the trunks. The scraggly, yellow-green robe generally starts on the trunk 3-8 feet above the ground, indicating the level of the snow surface during the winter.

4. Subalpine Forest

Trees: mountain hemlock, weeping spruce, whitebark pine, foxtail pine, western white pine, Shasta red fir, dwarf juniper, curl-leaf mountain mahogany

The subalpine forest is the timberline forest in the Marbles. In most areas in the wilderness, it appears very similar to the red-fir forest except that mountain hemlock is the dominant species and its most substantial stands are generally limited to north-facing slopes. In the Scott River district, particularly in the area of Boulder Peak, the subalpine forest is more diversified, adding white-bark pine and foxtail pine. Foxtail pine, like weeping spruce, was first "discovered" and named in the Shasta and Scott valleys area by English botanist John Jeffrey in 1852, and is found outside the Klamath Mountains region only in isolated stands in the southern Sierra Nevada. The most easily accessible displays of whitebark pine and foxtail pine are along the Wright Lakes Trail.

Somewhat similar to the way that deciduous trees of the mixed-evergreen forest grow only in a stunted, scrub form at higher elevations, conifers from lower-elevation forests grow as *krummholz*—literally, "crooked wood"—at timberline, the result of bitter cold and snow-driving winds. Gnarled, dwarfish western white pines grow along the ridge above Monument Lake in the Ukonom district, for instance, and a contorted Douglas-fir grows amid scattered weeping spruces near the outlet of Hancock Lake.

5. Mountain Meadow

Trees: incense-cedar, lodgepole pine, quaking aspen

Shrubs: bilberry in wet meadows, sagebrush and rabbitbrush in dry meadows

Wildflowers, moist meadow: angelica, arrowhead butterweed, death camas, red clover, white clover, leafy daisy, common dandelion, mountain dandelion, coast delphinium, explorer's gentian, nettle-leaved horsemint, corn lily, yellow fawn lily, coiled lousewort, lovage, broadleaf lupine, giant red paintbrush, self heal, sidalcea, Bigelow sneezeweed, cluster thistle, tinkers penny, western tofieldia, Parish's yampah

Moist-meadow flowers, l. to r.: corn lily, sidalcea, Bigelow sneezeweed

Wildflowers, dry meadow: orange agoseris, clustered broomrape, naked broomrape, tower butterweed, elegant cat's ear, Brewer's cinquefoil, Drummond's cinquefoil, fivefinger cinquefoil, sticky cinquefoil, collinsia, grand collomia, western blue flax, firecracker flower, green gentian, goldenrod, alpine knotweed, Davis' knotweed, Nuttall's linanthus, elegant lupine, spotted mountain bells, tansy mustard, Sierra onion, Copeland's owl clover, cobwebby paintbrush, frosty paintbrush, spreading phlox, pussypaws, sheep sorrel, woolly sunflower, yarrow

Dry-meadow flowers, l. to r.: paintbrush, spreading phlox, pussypaws

The meadows are the flower-fancier's mecca. Peak season in the Marbles for the pilgrimage is usually mid-July to mid-August, with variations that depend on the duration of the winter snowpack and the dryness of the summer. Moist and dry flora can often be found in the same meadow, particularly in canyon bottoms, where the moist flora congregate closer to the center of the drainage and the dry flora occupy the better-drained locations near the meadow edges. On a smaller scale, the physiographic influence of small depressions and rises —with their respective emphases on snowpack retention and solar insolation—can create a crazy quilt of moist and dry flora.

Within the dry-meadow community, there is a plant community that appears to be closely tied to soil derived from granitic rock. This association is most commonly found in some of the high meadows in the region of the Wooley Creek pluton in the Ukonom district and the English Peak pluton in the Salmon River district. The shallow, gravelly, easily eroded soil—which the Forest Service labels "DG," for "decomposed granite"—supports a sparse growth of pussypaws, Davis' knotweed, spreading phlox, elegant cat's ear, Copeland's owl clover, cobwebby paintbrush, elegant lupine and Nuttall's linanthus.

There appears to be an unfortunate relationship between meadows and the eutrophication of the lakes they border. Eutrophication is a process in which the nutritional balance in a body of water is upset by an increase in nutrients, resulting in the accelerated growth of lake-bottom vegetation. Areas of extensive meadows are prime summer wet range for cattle, and a neighboring lake makes an attractive camp for horsepackers, for it amply meets their stock's foraging needs. However, when rain and snowmelt wash the elements of horse and cattle dung into the lake, it does more than contaminate the water for human drinking purposes: the nutrients of the feces are a potent fertilizer. Big and Little Elk Lakes and Paradise Lake are all meadow-bordered lakes at which the lake-bottom vegetation is so intense that it discourages all lakeplay but fishing.

While the meadows may be known for their flowers, they also are inhabited by a few characteristic woody species. Incense-cedar is a constituent of the mixed-conifer forest, but it truly comes into its own in and around meadow areas, where it enjoys the lack of competition. The lodgepole pine is rarely found in the Marbles except along the perimeters of meadows above 5300 feet. The quaking aspen, too, finds room here for its vegetatively reproducing colonies to roam. Rarely starting from their minute and fragile seeds, quaking aspens effectively "clone" themselves by sending up new trees from a single, sprawling root system. And finally, the bilberry, a relative of the huckleberry with a tiny, edible, late-season berry, grows extensively in the boggier spaces of upper-elevation meadows.

6. Mountain Chaparral

Shrubs: tobacco brush, greenleaf manzanita, huckleberry oak, Sadler oak, bitter cherry, chokecherry, serviceberry, twinberry, ocean spray, mountain ash, Sierra chinquapin, Nuttall's willow, pinemat manzanita, mock orange, Oregon white oak and canyon live oak (both in scrub form)

Ferns: cliff brake, lace fern

Wildflowers: spear-leaved agoseris, Gray's catchfly, tongue clarkia, staining collomia, wandering daisy, dogbane, arrowleaf eriogonum, nude eriogonum, sulphur eriogonum, fireweed, Nuttall's gayophytum, blue-headed gilia, scarlet gilia, western hawksbeard, houndstongue hawkweed, mountain jewel flower, Lee's lewisia, Siskiyou lewisia, Washington lily, fern-leaved lomatium, giant-seeded lomatium, purple milkweed, mountain monardella, dwarf monkey flower, purple nightshade, Applegate's paintbrush, hot rock penstemon, pincushion penstemon, Siskiyou penstemon, mountain pride, phacelia, spreading rock cress, pioneer rock cress, ballhead sandwort, Nuttall's sandwort, white schoenolirion, rosy Siskiyou sedum, Sierra sedum

Chaparral flowers, l. to r.: scarlet gilia, Siskiyou lewisia, Washington lily

The determining influence for the occurence of mountain chaparral is physiographic, specifically, the orientation of slope. Montain chaparral occurs for the most part on upper, south-facing slopes, where maximal insolation—exposure to the sun's rays—creates the warm, dry conditions favored by these species. This plant community also favors the steeper slopes, with their better drainage and shallower soil.

Montain chaparral tends to be an upper-elevation phenomenon, generally coincident with the red-fir belt. It is also a major component of the group of plants found on mafic soil. Often it extends upslope to the ridgecrest, where you can witness just how decisive an influence slope orientation really is. While the south slope fosters the sun-loving chaparral species, just a few yards across the crest the moist, cool north slope supports mountain hemlock, red fir, western white pine and weeping spruce.

Although there are many species in the montain chaparral community, the dominants are tobacco brush, bitter cherry, and greenleaf manzanita, with huckleberry, canyon live and Oregon white oaks, and serviceberry as subdominants. The list of wildflowers for the montain chaparral community also includes many species found on rocky outcrops and ridgetops with minimally developed soil levels; environments that hardly support anything more complex than lichens, but will support chaparral once sufficient soil is generated.

7. Alpine Fell-Field

Flora: alpine aster, Eschscholtz' buttercup, shrubby cinquefoil, Howell's draba, alpine everlasting, brittle fern, slender hawkweed, mountain heather, bog kalmia, luetkea, milkvetch, alpine paintbrush, partridge foot, western pasqueflower, narrow-petaled sedum, mountain sorrel, arctic wormwood

There are no true alpine ecosystems in the Marble Mountains, but there are a few small pockets whose flora provide a reasonable facsimile of an alpine fell-field. The Uncles Creek Trail along the north face of English Peak, the Garden Gulch Trail above Dollar Meadows, and the Boulder Peak area are a few.

Cross-Community Plant Groupings

The following four plant groupings, largely floral, cut across the boundaries of the plant communities thus far identified. The streamside grouping can be found not only along forested streams and gullies, but also along brooks and standing water in moist meadows. The herbaceous (nonwoody) forest groupings occur throughout the mixed-conifer and red-fir forests and, to a lesser extent, in the mixed-evergreen and subalpine forests. The distinction between the two groupings is their relationship to sunlight. The shade-tolerant grouping forms the lush forest-floor foliage beneath dense stands of conifers. The plants of the sun-tolerant grouping are generally found in forest openings and along the interface between forest and meadow or forest and chaparral.

Most backpackers familiar with the Sierra Nevada are used to the widespread, upper-elevation distribution of Jeffrey pine. In the Marbles, however, Jeffrey pine is the prime indicator of the ultramafic soil grouping, ranging below 3000 feet but always and only on ultramafic soil. Typically this grouping is sparsely forested, with dense clumps of chaparral species scattered about the reddish-brown soil. Along the borders of ultramafic bodies, however, the members of this grouping may be simply additions to a more dominant plant community. This situation may be seen along the first few miles of the Shackleford Creek Trail, where the influence of the great ultramafic bulk of the Red Mountain massif to the north has added Jeffrey pine, western white pine and huckleberry oak to a few stretches of the mixed-conifer forest that dominates the river bottom.

1. Streamside Grouping

Trees: mountain alder, sitka alder, white alder, cascara sagrada, black cottonwood, American dogwood, Pacific dogwood, bigleaf maple, mountain maple, Scouler's willow, variable willow, western yew

Shrubs: goatsbeard, labrador tea, California spikenard

Ferns: five-finger fern, giant chain fern, common horsetail, common scouring rush

Wildflowers: bishop's cap, mountain boykinia, buttercup, red columbine, cow parsnip, tower delphinium, fireweed, fringe cups, grass-of-Parnassus, male habenaria, rigid hedge-nettle, leopard lily, tiger lily, marsh marigold, chickweed monkey flower, Lewis' monkey flower, primrose monkey flower, seepspring monkey flower, littleleaf montia, monks-hood, swamp onion, rein orchid, brook saxifrage, Merten's saxifrage, rusty saxifrage, Jeffrey's shooting star, spring beauty, western trillium

Streamside flowers, l. to r.: red columbine, tower delphinium, Jeffrey's shooting star

2. Shade-Tolerant Herbaceous Flora

Wildflowers: heartleaf arnica, Sierra arnica, bedstraw, California bluebell, Merten's coral-root, spotted coralroot, wild ginger, Oregon grape, inside-out flower, broadleaf lupine, Pacific mitela, Sierra Nevada pea, woodland phlox, pinedrops, pinesap, rattlesnake plan-tain, western prince's pine, one-sided pyrola, white-vein pyrola, queen's cup, snowplant, false Solomon's seal, wood sorrel, woodland star, starflower, sugarstick, mountain sweet cicely, thimbleberry, trail plant, twinflower, twisted stalk, vanilla leaf, American vetch, Macloskey's violet, wood violet

Shade-tolerant flowers, l. to r.: Merten's coralroot, woodland phlox, pinedrops
Shade-tolerant flowers, l. to r.: western prince's pine, queen's cup, twinflower

3. Sun-Tolerant Herbaceous Flora

Wildflowers: Cascade aster, blue-eyed Mary, boschniakia, Bell's catchfly, pearly everlasting, threadstem fireweed, white hawkweed, heuchera, common madia, frosty paintbrush, parrot beak, woodland penstemon, Siskiyou penstemon, mountain spiraea, Jessica stickseed, mountain valerian

4. Ultramafic Soil Grouping

Trees: Jeffrey pine, western white pine, incense-cedar
Shrubs: pinemat and greenleaf manzanita, huckleberry oak, serviceberry

Klamath Mountains Endemics

In addition to the weeping spruce and the shrubs Sadler oak and Hupa gooseberry, endemic *varieties* of the following herbaceous species have been found in the Marbles: buttercup, elegant cat's ear, sticky cinquefoil, clover, collinsia, collomia, daisy, draba, heuchera, lewisia, broadleaf lupine, monkshood, spreading rock cress, saxifrage, sedum, woolly sunflower, tauschia, western trillium.

ZOOLOGY

There was a time when elk, grizzly bear and bighorn sheep roamed the Marbles. Fisher, marten and wolverine, rare in the wilderness now, were once evident enough to have lakes named after them. Beaver, coyote and mountain lion have all been diminished by the fur trade or bounty hunters. Yet black bear and black-tailed deer still abound to delight the big-game fancier, and the Marbles host a forestful of little critters. Those birds, bats and beasties that you might see, hear or inadvertently feed during a wilderness visit are listed here in the ecosystem in which they are most likely to be found. A few of the more evident species are described in greater detail.

1. Low-Elevation Forest (Mixed-Evergreen Forest)

Birds: black-capped chickadee, common crow, red-shafted flicker, black-headed grosbeak, ruffed grouse, Cooper hawk, red-tailed hawk, scrub jay, purple martin, horned owl, screech owl, spotted owl, yellow-bellied sapsucker, song sparrow, Swainson's thrush, solitary vireo, warbling vireo, downy woodpecker, Lewis woodpecker

Mammals: big brown bat, Brazilian freetail bat, hoary bat, lump-nosed bat, black bear, Columbian black-tailed deer, gray fox, California ground squirrel, deer mouse, pinon mouse, fringed myotis, long-ear myotis, long-legged myotis, Yuma myotis, raccoon, spotted skunk, striped skunk, western gray squirrel, dusky-footed woodrat

Reptiles: southern alligator lizard, western fence lizard, western rattlesnake, western skink, western pond turtle

Amphibians: California red-legged frog, foothill yellow-legged frog, tailed frog, arboreal salamander, black salamander, long-toed salamander

Western rattlesnake: Your most likely rendezvous with the only poisonous snake in the Marbles is along a streamside trail such as the Wooley Creek or North Fork trail. They are by no means limited to such low-elevation haunts, however: the author once came across a rattler at 6000 feet, sunning itself on a rock buttress on a recently constructed section of Pacific Crest Trail north of Etna Summit. The rattlesnake is a literally coldblooded creature, whose body temperature is at the mercy of the ambient (surrounding) temperature. To minimize the temperature changes it will have to undergo during the course of the day, the rattler stays in its burrow until the sun warms the air, remains in the shade of underbrush during the heat of the day, and then finds sun-heated stones on which to pass the cool of the evening. It is when it is biding its time in the underbrush that the rattlesnake is most likely to surprise even the vigilant hiker, for its splotchy, earth-toned coloration is a most effective camouflage.

Fortunately, the rattlesnake has no more desire to meet you than you do it, and its highly developed heat and vibration sensors generally allow it to become aware of you and move out of range long before you would notice it. Should you take it by surprise, it will strike only as a last resort. Even if it does strike, the rattlesnake does not always release its venom. Which may be why the controversy continues on the best method of first aid: the age-old cut-and-suck, with the dangers of inadvertently severing a tendon, or the more recently advocated cold treatment and complete immobilization. The best "treatment," however, is prevention: when you come upon a rattler, give it enough room and time to move away unthreatened. Attempting to kill a rattler is unnecessary.

Ticks: While the mosquitos and the more prevalent (and varied) biting flies are accustomed and accepted afflictions for the back-country traveler, the occurrence of ticks is not so widespread and their bite is not so easily dismissed. For one thing, when a tick latches onto you with its barbed proboscis and starts drilling for blood, it doesn't leave when invited nor simply lift out. The most common old-woodsman's methods for removing a tick are to hold a lighted cigarette close to it or pour mineral oil over it; the tick is supposed to back out gracefully in either case. If you discover the tick soon after it's set its hook, you might grab it as close to your skin as possible and pull it out. However, you run the risk of the tick's proboscis breaking off beneath the skin and resulting in infection from the bacteria carried by the tick (the ticks in the Marbles are not known to carry the virulent Rocky Mountain spotted fever, but a less intense "tick fever"). For this reason, it is also inadvisable to simply swat the little bugger as one would a fly or mosquito. The best defense against ticks is a preventive approach. Most insect repellents are effective against ticks, and they are particularly needed along the edges of clothes. Most important, check your clothes often when walking through tick country.

2. Middle-Elevation Forest (Mixed-Conifer and Red-Fir Forest)

Birds: brown creeper, purple finch, olive-sided flycatcher, western flycatcher, blue grouse, sharp-shinned hawk, Steller jay, pigmy nuthatch, pigmy owl, saw-whet owl, spotted owl, western wood peewee, robin, violet-green swallow, Vaux swift, western tanager, varied thrush, solitary vireo, hermit warbler, Nashville warbler, cedar waxwing, hairy woodpecker, white-headed woodpecker, winter wren

Mammals: hoary bat, big brown bat, silver-haired bat, black bear, Townsend's chipmunk, Columbian black-tailed deer, golden-mantled ground squirrel, mountain beaver, deer mouse, red tree mouse, western red-backed mouse, raccoon, Pacific shrew, Trowbridge shrew, Douglas squirrel, northern flying squirrel, bushy-tailed woodrat

Reptiles: Pacific rubber boa, California mountain kingsnake

Amphibians: ensatina, rough-skinned newt, clouded salamander, Pacific giant salamander

Unlike the rattlesnake and the tick, which are discussed above due to the potential danger they represent, the Steller jay and the Douglas squirrel are benign creatures. Their only offense is to your ears.

Douglas squirrel: You will often see the dusky-haired Douglas squirrel, also known as the chickaree, flitting whippetlike through the heights of a dense conifer forest, playing a nimble game of territorial tag with another squirrel perhaps, or looking for choice cones to bite off and drop to the forest floor so it can harvest and cache the seeds. However, it is most obvious when, sounding like a machine gun in heat, it clings to a tree at a safe distance and berates you for entering his forest.

Steller jay: The raucous cry of this member of the crow family is a familiar note in the forest symphony as it monitors your passage or perhaps drops by your campsite to check your pantry—though it is not so audacious a "camp robber" as its cousin, the gray jay. Colorfully plumed in basic blue with a black hood, its most distinguishing physical characteristic may be the pointed crest on its crown.

3. Upper-Elevation Forest (Red-Fir and Subalpine Forest)

Birds: mountain bluebird, mountain chickadee, red crossbill, bald eagle, Cassin finch, Hammond flycatcher, goshawk, evening grosbeak, calliope hummingbird, golden-crowned kinglet, ruby-crowned kinglet, Clark nutcracker, red-breasted nuthatch, osprey, pine siskin, Townsend solitaire, hermit thrush, Audubon warbler, pileated woodpecker

Mammals: black bear, ermine, little brown myotis, vagrant shrew

Black bear: The black bear (whose coat may be as light as cinnamon brown) is widely distributed through the Marbles—the author has seen bears below 3000 feet on the Garden Gulch, Grider Creek, Wooley Creek and North Fork trails, and their scat (feces) can be seen on trails throughout the wilderness—but you are perhaps most likely to see a bear along the ridgecrests and around the high meadows and lakes.

As a rule, the black bear cares little for making the acquaintance of humans. As soon as one catches our scent or sound—their sight is notoriously poor—the usual response is to turn tail and gallop off. There are two critical exceptions to this likely behavior. One is if you surprise a sow and her cubs. She may send her young up a tree and trundle off to a safe distance herself. If she feels sufficiently threatened, regardless of your intent, she may attack. So if you come across a pair of darling cubs, a low-profile retreat is the wisest move, at least until the sow becomes aware of you from a distance and leaves with her family.

The other situation when a bear may not give ground is when food is involved, especially treats like fig newtons, granola and trail snack mix. If you wake in the middle of the night and find that a bear has taken your food captive, it is better to consider your trip unexpectedly foreshortened rather than attempt to challenge the bear; with bears, possession is 11/10 of the law. To prevent such an unwelcome incident, the bearbagging technique still is effective against the bears of the Marbles, which are not in the same class as those in Yosemite (which can probably give a Boy Scout a lesson in knot-tying). A 40-50 foot length of nylon cord should be sufficient to hang your food in a stuff bag from a nearby tree (preferably not one overhanging your tent), allowing 12 feet clearance from the ground and 6 feet from the tree trunk and the branch the food is hung from (this last is as much for protection from woodrats and assorted little critters, which probably eat more backpacker food without invitation than bears do).

A final suggestion regarding food and bears: before beginning your hike, ask at the ranger station if there is a specific bear problem anywhere along your route. It only takes one good feast to get a bear hooked on regular visits to the campsite where it found its free lunch. In 1978, the campsite at the waist of One Mile Lake in the Ukonom district was repeatedly visited, as was Six Mile Camp on the North Fork Trail in 1979.

4. Meadow

Birds: mourning dove, golden eagle, house finch, marsh hawk, Oregon junco, killdeer, western kingbird, common nighthawk, turkey vulture

Mammals: Columbian black-tailed deer, Botta pocket gopher, broad-handed mole, deer mouse, California meadow mouse, longtail meadow mouse, Oregon meadow mouse, Townsend meadow mouse, western harvest mouse, western jumping mouse

Reptiles: racer, common garter snake, western terrestrial garter snake, sharp-tailed snake

Amphibians: bullfrog, western toad

Oregon junco: Although this slight member of the finch family is generally considered a forest bird, it is most easily sighted when a passerby startles it from its food foray along the ground and it pops out of the grasses to dart with the rest of its flock to the branches of the closest tree. In its swooping flight, it exposes a fork of white in the dark tailfeathers; while perched in a tree, commenting on its state of affairs in a terse, muted chirp, its black, hangman's hood accents the white-and-buff-colored plumage of the rest of its body.

Bovidae: It takes more than a little Latin to make the cattle summering in the Marbles into something special. The fact of the matter is they have been there longer than the recreationist—the high meadows of the wilderness started being used as wet range in the 1880s. It was a widespread, year-round practice in the early days, but has diminished to fewer than 1000 head in the wilderness, now on a seasonal basis from mid-July to mid-October. It is tradition that keeps the ranchers driving their herds to the hills. But economics argues against it and, as the older cattlemen retire and sell out to fresh faces unsteeped in the past, the number of cattle heading to the wilderness each summer dwindles.

Perhaps one day, a summer will go by without any cattle returning to the mountains. At the present, however, you can expect to see them throughout the meadows in the Scott River district, along Big Ridge and the meadows on either side of it in the Oak Knoll and Happy Camp districts, on the western edge of the Haypress Meadows area in the Ukonom district, and in the meadows surrounding Chimney Rock and those of the Right Hand Fork drainage in the Salmon River district.

Columbian black-tailed deer: A much more appealing sight in the meadows, quietly browsing beneath the early morning mists, is the Columbian black-tailed deer, a subspecies of mule deer (mule deer are found east of the Marbles and are more familiar in the Cascades). Like the black bear, deer can be seen throughout the wilderness in nearly all habitats—and with far greater frequency than bears. Also like bears, deer tend to shy away from people—though they are more tolerant and, if one does not take them by surprise, they will often continue their browsing in one's presence. In Marble Valley, the deer are often more than merely tolerant and will take advantage of unattended food just as effectively as any bear, jay or ground squirrel.

If you are awakened by things going bump in the night outside your tent, it is likely to be deer causing all the ruckus, pawing through the bark and leaves and grass where you urinated before going to bed: the minerals and salts we expel in our urine appeal to them. You may also hear a sound—something like a wheezing cough, or a steam engine pulling out of a railway station—that is a call for attention, often used as a warning for flight from doe to fawn.

5. Chaparral

Birds: Lazuli bunting, California quail, mountain quail, fox sparrow, white-crowned sparrow, orange-crowned warbler, Bewick wren, wrentit

Mammals: black bear, bobcat, Sonoma chipmunk, Columbian black-tailed deer, mountain lion, brush mouse, brush rabbit, ringtail, long-tail weasel

Reptiles: sagebrush lizard, gopher snake, western whiptail

California quail: You are ambling leisurely along a scrub-bordered trail and, suddenly, there is an explosion of sound and motion. It is the plump, dappled California quail bursting from the underbrush. If you can get your eyes back in focus quickly enough, you might notice a male's short, black plume rising from the crown and arching forward over the beak. Hens also can often be seen walking hurriedly about, attempting to herd their brood to safety as you approach.

Fish

The early stories of the fishing bounty in northern California lakes and streams are rife with hyperbole—three-foot trout in the Klamath River that leap from the water to graze the alfalfa on the banks; the Salmon River so thick with salmon that one couldn't take a horse across without killing a fish at every step—but these stories do set the tone for the area. Forest Service surveys indicate fishing to be the second most popular recreational activity (next to camping) in the wilderness.

The California Department of Fish and Game maintains an active fisheries program which stocks the high-country lakes with trout. The species used are eastern brook, rainbow and brown trout, primarily the first two. Brown trout are much longer-lived and grow to much greater size; in any but the largest lakes in the wilderness they tend to overwhelm the other species in the competition for food. Eastern brook and rainbow trout have quite different survival dynamics. Eastern brook trout are more apt to reproduce successfully in a lake environment and become a self-sustaining population. Rainbow trout, on the other hand, are more adapted to a stream environment, which is why the streams of the Marbles are mostly populated with rainbows; there will be a few eastern brook trout in the streams, fish that have migrated from the lakes. In order to provide diverse fishing opportunities, the Fish and Game Department focuses on the stocking of rainbow trout, attempting to maintain mixed populations in many lakes and to ensure a predominantly or pure rainbow population in at least one lake in every multilaked basin.

The streams provide more consistent fishing than the lakes, for they remain a fairly constant temperature. The lakes will perhaps be more rewarding in early season—through mid-July—but as they warm and the fly hatch dwindles, the fish tend to live deeper in the lakes and look for other sources of food. The fishing in Wooley Creek is a unique opportunity, since it is the only stream in the wilderness to support both a fall run of king salmon and a summer steelhead population. Such a mix is generally the province of major rivers such as the Klamath and the Salmon.

Bigfoot

As a storm breaks and low clouds cling to the deep-green, forested ridge slopes like bolls of cotton, the mountain-country of the Marbles has the look of a land brimful of myths and legends. The most illustrious of these concerns the outsized, subhuman Bigfoot, or Sasquatch. Firmly straddling the fence between belief and scoffery, the author will say only that there have never been any reported sightings within the wilderness. There have been numerous unverified sightings, none recent, to the west and north of the Klamath River above Happy Camp and Orleans.

Chapter 4

Using This Guide

Within the loop of state and county highways, Marble Mountain Wilderness and environs can be viewed roughly as pie-shaped, with the five ranger districts radiating from the center of the wilderness as misshapen wedges of the pie. The organization of the hikes in this book is by ranger district, starting with the Oak Knoll district in the north and moving counter-clockwise around the circumference of the wilderness-pie. This format not only provides an orderly presentation of the area but it presents the districts in approximately their order of usage, from the scantly visited Oak Knoll district to the well-populated Scott River district. Within the districts, too, the hikes have been arranged in the same fashion, following the trailheads counterclockwise around the wilderness perimeter.

The principal criterion in formulating the hikes in this book was to present a survey of the wilderness, informing the reader of every trailhead and every trail available. Hence, while the trips described here generally follow routes that you might choose for yourself if you had no resource other than a map of the wilderness, there are a few contrivances. For in-stance, in order to avoid repeated descriptions of the first several miles of the North Fork Trail in the Salmon River district, the North Fork Trail hike describes several side trips to the various lakes accessible by first following this trail. And the entire 8.2 miles of the rarely used Portuguese Peak Trail in the Ukonom district are described as a single hike and recom-mended as a daytrip, though few people would ever consider the 16.4 mile roundtrip as a day venture, and even fewer would choose this rigorous, nearly waterless route, which lacks campsites, for their backpacking entry to the wilderness.

Although it will become obvious to you as you read through this book and the extent of the hikes becomes clear, it should be stated explicitly: this is a *trail* guide, and only a guide to trails and trailside attractions. With the exception of a pair of off-trail routes to the top of Kings Castle, there are no cross-country trips described here; dozens of lakes and several secluded valleys receive no mention at all. There are several reasons for this: the unwieldy size and weight of the book if it told all; a feeling of empathy for the locals, for whom much of this wilderness has for so long been theirs alone. The foremost consideration, however, is the author's belief that no guide to an area should be exhaustive, that it should never be more than an introduction. Part of the magic of wilderness is the process of discovery in-herent in every visit there. With this guide limited to the footpaths, much of the Magic of the Marbles is left for you to unveil for yourself.

The Trail Descriptions

At the beginning of each hike, there is a brief list of "vital statistics" that present the hike in a nutshell. The list includes hike distance, low and high elevation points on the trail, a recommended trip duration, the amount of traffic the trail receives, and the difficulty of the hike.

Hike **Distance** is a self-explanatory item. With the exception of the few loop trips, for which mileage represents the total trip distance, all the mileages are one-way figures, from trail head to trail's end or some particular destination. The **High** and **Low Elevations** are also objective figures. Taken by themselves, however, they can be deceiving, for they only represent the high and low points *along* the trail. The high elevation is not necessarily the elevation of your destination, for instance. Nor do these figures tell anything of the gross elevation gain. For example, the Johnson's Hunting Ground-Tickner Creek trails hike in the Happy Camp district begins at 4420 feet, climbs to 6350 feet, then descends to Tickner Creek at 5310 feet before climbing again to the pond near the head of Tickner Hole at 6380 feet.

The **Suited For** category is a recommended time investment for the hike, and tends to be a conservative suggestion, generally allowing a hiking pace of 6 to 9 miles per day. The assumption is that you have come to fully experience the wilderness, not to simply pass through it. So the hike to Little Elk Lake in the Scott River district, for instance, is considered a weeked trip, although the 11.6-mile round trip could be completed in one day by many people, doing so would give you too little time for enjoying the lake. Driving time to reach the general area of the Marbles or to set up a car shuttle for an end-to-end trip is not considered in establishing the suggested trip-time. (As for driving time once you have reached the area, keep in mind that after you have turned off the "loop road," you will always be heading uphill to the trailhead on winding, often unpaved roads, a typically slow and tedious process.) Remember, these are only suggestions. There are camping possibilities

The typical trail climbs from a shady, hushed forest to a sunny, windswept lake.

Bridge Creek Trail   Hancock Lake

along all the day-trip trails, and all the trails into this wilderness offer pleasant settings for destinationless day excursions.

The **Usage** designation for each hike—rare, low, moderate, high, extremely high—is based on the author's analysis of Forest Service data from the years 1975-76. Since wilderness-wide usage has remained relatively constant over the past few years, those data are likely to be fairly representative of the present usage situation. The usage designation will not guarantee, for example, that you will be completely alone in rarely visited Tickner Hole or that you will be lost in the crowd in the highly popular Sky High Valley. They do, however, accurately relate the usage pattern of any one area relative to any other.

The degree of **Difficulty**—easy, moderate, strenuous—is the most subjective of the capsule descriptions. It is based *solely* on the trail gradient—disregarding trail surface, maintenance and the like. The most common label is "moderate," since the most common trail is one that makes its way easily up a valley bottom before a hellacious climb to the lakes at the head of the valley. The first several miles of many of these trails offer a pleasant stroll if you are willing to forego the lakes. There is only one "easy" hike in the book—the Grider Creek Trail in the Oak Knoll district—and it is borderline. The Marbles simply are not "easy" country.

Although trail maintenance is not considered in rating the difficulty of a hike, the extreme range of trail-maintenance levels in the Marbles warrants discussion. During the period that the pack horse reigned over the Marbles, the trails were either scrupulously maintained to accomodate stock travel or were left untended. However, the escalation and diversification of recreational use of the wilderness in the last decade has demanded a more flexible maintenance schedule than the all-or-nothing approach. The Forest Service has adopted a four-level maintenance system, ranging from low-level, custodial care to thorough manicuring of paths providing access to the recreational population centers.

Trails receiving minimal maintenance, but remaining passable, are noted in the introduction to each chapter. But even the well-maintained routes occasionally experience moments of obscurity, which are noted in the trail description. Your first recourse when the tread disappears is to look for tree blazes—the i axed into the bark—or ducks—small clusters or stacks of rocks that are obviously man-made. In the forest, log-cuts—a down log with a section sawed out of it to make way for the trail—are another aid for following a sketchy path. On barren hillsides, e.g., the scantily vegetated high meadows in "decomposed granite," look for water bars—a line of bounders or a small log, 3-5 feet in length, half-buried in the hillside across the intended path of the trail to divert water and lessen erosion.

There are a few sections of trail within the wilderness, all in the Scott River district, which Mother Nature has won back from the Forest Service. These are trails cared for under the Marquis de Sade schedule of trail maintenance and include the following:

Second Valley Trail, between its junction with the Deep Lake Trail and the foot of Boulder Peak near the head of Second Valley;

Red Mountain Trail, between its junctions with the Long High Lake Trail and the Wright Lakes Trail;

Kidder Creek Trail, between Hayes Meadow and its ridgetop junction with the Kidder Lake Trail;

Wooley Creek Trail, between Ananias Camp and its junction with the Big Meadows Trail.

They are represented on the topographic maps accompanying this book by a dashed line, since the author was unable to find a sufficiently consistent tread to warrant mapping the "trail." The dashed line represents the course of the trail on USGS topographic maps. If you are interested in visiting the country traversed by these "trails," it is much more sensible to plan a route cross-country, using map and compass, than to take the trouble of attempting to follow a will-o'-the-wisp tread.

Two final comments on the trail description itself. First, you will find interspersed throughout the text a pair of numbers within parentheses. For instance, where the Wooley Creek Trail crosses Deer Lick Creek, there are the numbers (0.5, 920). The "0.5" is the mileage to Deer Lick Creek from the last point so noted, and the "920" is the elevation in feet at the trail's crossing of Deer Lick Creek.

The last item is a matter of terminology. With hundreds of water courses to mention in the book, the use of any one word quickly grows stale. So you will find trickles, rivulets, flows, brooklets, brooks, creeklets, creeks, streams and rivers all coursing through the text. Similarly, water-cut features and related topographic declivities are referred to as depressions, gullies, gulches, ravines, defiles, loosely depending on the degree of local relief. Finally, a "cutblock" is the Forest Service term for a patch of land logged by clearcutting.

The Maps

Four topographic maps are included with this book, drawn from the USGS 15' quadrangles. Using the base information from the USGS maps, the author has redrawn the trails in greater detail, removed buildings no longer in existence, added permanent and intermittent watercourses and official place names not found on the original USGS maps, and even altered an occasional contour line to more accurately represent the lay of the land. Hence these are the most precise and up-to-date 15' topographic maps available. It should be noted that the author made few changes in the natural and manmade features outside the wilderness which don't affect your travel in the Marbles or your use of this book. (Note: In the process of updating its 1955 topographic maps, the USGS has begun issuing 7½' quadrangles based on field work during the last 10 years. There are presently 7½' quadrangles available to the public for the southern portion of the wilderness, previously covered by the *Forks of Salmon* and *Sawyers Bar* 15' quadrangles. These 7½' quadrangles continue to omit watercourses whose drainages do not show sufficient local relief to appear on the aerial photographs, and trails shown on these maps are only approximations of the real routes. With 80-foot contour intervals, the 7½' quadrangles for the southern portion of the wilderness are no more detailed than the 15' quadrangles, only easier to read. The yet-to-be-released 7½' quadrangles for the northern half of the wilderness, however, use 40-foot contour intervals.)

While USGS maps attempt to record everything the aerial cameras have seen, there is one particular feature this book's maps make no effort to show in absolute detail: roads. Logging roads in the national forests multiply like rabbits and their life span is often no greater. Rather than attempt to make comprehensive additions to the 1955 USGS maps, the author has added only those roads which you will use to get to the trailheads; junctions with other new roads (that existed in 1978-9) are indicated but those roads are not drawn in full. Do not expect the roads on these maps to appear as crisp and detailed as the trails, for their routes have simply been taken from more recent government maps rather than surveyed with the same attention as the trails were.

There is one drawback to topographic maps: the way we tend to use them. We give the map little attention until we need to locate ourselves, and by then we no longer have a readily identifiable frame of reference to locate our position on the map. As mentioned above in the discussion of trail maintenance, even the well marked treads can pose route-finding problems. The Marble Mountain Wilderness is a "thinking person's" wilderness. The author was forever meeting people blithely heading up the trail, completely unaware that they had passed their desired trail junction a mile back down the trail. Consult your map often; be aware of the changes in the terrain around you. By making route-finding an on-going process, you become that much more involved with your surroundings, that much closer to the wilderness and the wilderness experience.

There is an additional rule of thumb for route-finding: take any manmade sign with a grain of salt. The greatest offender of accuracy is perhaps the wilderness-boundary sign, particularly the old metal signs, which fail to reflect more recent changes in the boundary. Wilderness boundaries are very hazy creations; even the gray boundary line on the topographic map is labeled "approximate." The few original metal mile tags remaining on trailside trees fail to indicate the generally increased mileage resulting from trail rerouting. The same goes for mileages indicated on older trailhead signs. The Forest Service is omitting mileages on its more recently implaced trailhead signs, acknowledging that a trail is nearly as much process as product. Even the very presence of signs is not to be depended on, for they are continually the victims of vandalism or natural disasters (read: bears). One Forest Service recreational officer commented, only half in jest, that signs get replaced only if the district ranger gets lost following the trail. Another officer is considering phasing out the signs at secondary trail junctions as a means of encouraging wilderness travelers to attend more closely to their path.

The Trail Guide's Golden Qualifier

There is one last remark that must be made regarding the use of this trail guide: we create our own reality. The author had high-precision instruments for mapping the trails of the Marbles, but they were read through his eyes and interpreted in his words. This book, these maps, should be considered as no more than a *guide* to the Marbles; they are not the gospel. The paths you choose, the ease with which you follow them, and, ultimately, your entire wilderness experience, lie in your hands.

Hike and Lake Charts

The two following charts briefly outline the pertinent data on the 27 hikes and 52 lakes discussed in this book. The descriptors on the hike chart were all explained earlier, but there are several items in need of clarification on the lake chart.

The hike number, of course, identifies the hike in which the lake is described. In the case of a lake that is mentioned in more than one hike, such as Ukonom Lake in the Happy Camp district, the hike number refers to the hike in which the lake is portrayed in greatest detail. In most cases, the "Miles from the closest trailhead" figure is the mileage to the lake in the hike in which it is described. In those instances where it is a shorter distance to the lake from some other trailhead, that trailhead is mentioned in parentheses. For instance, in the

Hike Chart

Name	Number	Grid location of trailhead	Distance (in miles)
OAK KNOLL DISTRICT			
Tyler Meadows Trail	1	ScB, B-2	4.2, one-way
Grider Creek Trail	2	UL, A-1	7.4, one-way
HAPPY CAMP DISTRICT			
Bear Creek Trail	3	UL, D-3	6.1, one-way
Elk Creek-Rainy Valley Creek Trails	4	UL, D-2	10.5, one-way
Elk Creek-Granite Creek Trails	5	UL, D-2	9.4, one-way to Blue Granite Lk
			9.8, one-way to Green Granite Lk
Johnson's Hunting Ground-Tickner Hole	6	UL, C-3	6.6, one-way
UKONOM DISTRICT			
Haypress Meadows Trails	7	FS, B-1 and C-1; UL, B-5	1.7-4.7, one-way
Haypress-McCash Trails Loop	8	FS, B-1	11.6, loop
Onemile and Cuddihy Lakes	9	FS, B-1	9.1, one-way to Onemile Lk
			9.9, one-way to Cuddihy Lks
Cedar Flat-Pleasant Lake	10	FS, C-1	9.7, one-way to Pleasant Lk
Wooley Creek Trail	11	FS, B-3	10.2, one-way to Fowler Cabin
Portuguese Peak Trail	12	FS, C-3	8.2, one-way
SALMON RIVER DISTRICT			
Crapo Trail	13	FS, C-5	9.4, one-way
Garden Gulch Trail	14	SaB, B-4	11.6, one-way to Clear Lake
Little North Fork Trail, to English Peak	15	SaB, B-4	13.2, one-way
North Fork Trail, to English Peak	16	SaB, D-3	15.8, one-way
North Fork-Bug Gulch-Shelly Meadows Trails Loop	17	SaB, D-3	33.5, loop
SCOTT RIVER DISTRICT			
Kidder Creek-Kidder Lake Trails	18	ScB, E-5	3.5, one-way to Kidder Lake
Shackleford Creek-Campbell Lake Trails Loop	19	ScB, D-4	11.1, loop
Deep Lake-Wright Lakes Trails	20	ScB, D-3	4.7, one-way to Lower Wright Lk
			5.2, one-way to Upper Wright Lk
Little Elk Lake	21	ScB, C-4	5.8, one-way
Red Rock Valley-Marble Valley Loop	22	ScB, C-4	13.7, loop
Sky High Valley	23	ScB, C-4	5.8, one-way
Rye Patch Trail, to Paradise Lake	24	ScB, B-3	2.1, one-way
Kelsey Creek Trail, to Paradise Lake	25	ScB, C-3	7.6, one-way
CREST TRAILS			
Salmon Mountains Crest Trail	26	UL, B-5 ScB, D-4	31.7, one-way
Pacific Crest Trail	27	ScB, E-3 UL, A-1	49.4, one-way

Ukonom district, the lakes along the Haypress Trail described in the Onemile and Cuddihy Lakes Hike are 0.6 mile closer to the Let 'er Buck trailhead than to that hike's Camp 4 trailhead.

The acreage and depth figures are taken from the California Fish and Game Department's pamphlet "Anglers' Guide to the Marble Mountains." There are some lakes for which there is no acreage and depth information because they are too small or shallow to have ever been stocked, or because stocked populations have often suffered winterkill and the stocking practice was discontinued.

The three basic species of trout found in the Marbles were discussed in the natural history chapter. They are represented in the chart by the following abbreviations: EB—eastern brook, R—rainbow, B—brown. There are two distinct listings of the trout that may be found

Hike Chart (Continued)

Suited for	Usage	Difficulty	Lakes	Side trips
day trip	rare	strenuous	yes	Grider Valley, Turk Lake-Packers Valley
day trip	low	easy	no	——
over night	low	strenuous	yes	Kings Castle
2-3 days	low to moderate	moderate	yes	Marble Gap
2-3 days	low to moderate	moderate	yes	Ukonom Lake, Cuddihy Lakes
day trip	rare	strenuous	yes	Ukonom Lake
day trip	rare to extremely high	moderate	no	——
over night	rare to extremely high	moderate	no	——
2-3 days	high	moderate	yes	Secret Lake, Ukonom Lake
2-3 days	low to moderate	moderate	yes	Medicine Mountain, Onemile and Cuddihy Lakes
2-3 days	moderate	moderate	no	Bridge Creek, farther up Wooley Creek
day trip	rare	strenuous	no	——
day trip	rare	strenuous	no	——
3-4 days	rare to low	strenuous	yes	Clear Lake
3-4 days	moderate	strenuous	yes	Devils Canyon, Smith Cabin, Hamilton Camp-Clear Lake, Pine Lake, Uncles Creek Trail
3-4 days	high	moderate	yes	Lake of the Island, Abbott Lake, Horse Range Lake, Hancock Lake
4-6 days	low to moderate	strenuous	yes	Horse Range Lake, Hell Hole Ridge-Lakes Katherine and Ethel, Big Meadows-Wild Lake, Cabin Gulch, Shelly Meadows
day trip	moderate	moderate	yes	——
over night	extremely high	moderate	yes	Calf-Long High lakes
day trip	extremely high	strenuous	yes	Deep Lake, Boulder Peak, Red Mountain trailhead option
over night	high	moderate	yes	Deep Lake
over night	high to extremely high	moderate	yes	Marble Gap
over night	extremely high	moderate	yes	Marble Valley loop
day trip	high	strenuous	yes	Kings Castle
over night	low to moderate	moderate	yes	Turk Lake
4-6 days	moderate to high	moderate	yes	Ananias Camp, Marble Rim
5-7 days	high	moderate	yes	optional trailheads: Shelly Fork in south,

Lake Chart

Name	District	Grid location	Hike No.	Miles from closest trailhead
Abbott Lake	Salmon R.	SaB, B-2	16	12.6
Bear Lake	Happy Camp	ScB, A-3	3	6.1
Big Elk Lake	Scott R.	ScB, A-5	26	7.3 (Canyon Creek)
Blue Granite Lake	Happy Camp	UL, D-4	5	9.4
Bug Lake	Salmon R.	SaB, C-1	17	6.6 (Shelly Fork)
Burney Lake	Happy Camp	UL, E-4	26	12.2 (Let 'er Buck)
Cabin Gulch	Salmon R.	SaB, C-1	17	7.1 (Shelly Fork)
Calf Lake	Scott R.	ScB, D-4	19	5.0
Campbell Lake	Scott R.	ScB, C-5	19	5.2
Clear Lake	Salmon R.	FS, E-3	14	11.6
Cliff Lake	Scott R.	ScB, C-5	19	6.1
Cuddihy Lakes	Ukonom	UL, D-5	9	9.3 (Let 'er Buck)
Deep Lake	Scott R.	ScB, C-4	21	6.3 (Deep Lake Tr, Hike 20)
Diamond Lake	Salmon R.	SaB, A-2	16	14.5
English Lake	Salmon R.	SaB, A-2	16	13.4
Lake Ethel	Salmon R.	SaB, A-1	17	15.2
Fisher Lake	Scott R.	SaB, C-1	27	5.2 (Shelly Fork)
Frying Pan Lake	Scott R.	ScB, B-4	23	6.1
Gate Lake	Scott R.	ScB, B-4	23	5.1
Gold Granite Lake	Happy Camp	UL, D-4	5	9.9
Green Granite Lake	Happy Camp	UL, D-4	5	9.8
Hancock Lake	Salmon R.	SaB, A-2	16	15.2
Horse Range Lake	Salmon R.	SaB, A-2	16	14.1
Lake Katherine	Salmon R.	SaB, A-1	17	15.9
Kidder Lake	Scott R.	ScB, C-5	18	3.5
Lake of the Island	Salmon R.	SaB, B-2	16	11.7
Little Elk Lake	Scott R.	ScB, C-4	21	5.8
Log Lake	Scott R.	ScB, C-5	19	2.9
Long High Lake	Scott R.	ScB, D-4	19	5.3
Marten Lake	Scott R.	SaB, C-1	27	5.5 (Shelly Fork)
Meteor Lake	Ukonom	UL, D-5	9	6.8 (Let 'er Buck)
Monument Lake	Ukonom	UL, D-5	9	5.8 (Let 'er Buck)
Mud Lake	Salmon R.	SaB, A-4	14	4.8
Onemile Lake	Ukonom	UL, D-5	9	8.5 (Let 'er Buck)
Paradise Lake	Scott R.	ScB, A-3	24	2.1
Pine Lake	Salmon R.	SaB, A-2	15	12.4
Pleasant Lake	Ukonom	UL, D-5	10	9.7
Rainy Lake	Happy Camp	ScB, A-4	4	10.5
Secret Lake	Ukonom	UL, C-5	9	10.4 (Let 'er Buck)
Shadow Lake	Scott R.	ScB, B-5	22	6.4
Lower Sky High Lake	Scott R.	ScB, B-5	23	5.8
Upper Sky High Lake	Scott R.	ScB, B-5	23	6.0
Spirit Lake	Scott R.	UL, E-4	26	10.5 (Canyon Creek)
Summit Lake	Scott R.	ScB, C-5	19	5.0
Turk Lake	Scott R.	ScB, A-3	1	4.1 (Rye Patch)
Ukonom Lake	Happy Camp	UL, C-4	5	8.1 (Johnson's Hunting Ground)
Wild Lake	Salmon R.	SaB, B-1	17	15.3
Lower Wright Lake	Scott R.	ScB, D-4	20	3.1 (Red Mountain)
Upper Wright Lake	Scott R.	ScB, D-4	20	2.5 (Red Mountain)

Lake Chart (Continued)

Min. distance of campsite from lakeshore	Acreage	Depth	Elevation	Trout		Usage
No restriction	8	20'	5660'	EB		low
100'	2	8'	5980'	EB		low
200'	4.5	10'	5970'	EB, R	(R)	moderate
100'	12	28'	5270'	EB	(R)	moderate
No restriction	—	—	6070'	—		low
100'	15	25'	5650'	EB		low
No restriction	—	—	6060'	—		rare
100'	3	30'	6970'	EB		high
200'	33	30'	5770'	EB, R, B	(R)	extremely high
200'	6.5	62'	5800'	EB, R, B	(R)	low
200'	52	175'	6110'	EB, R, B	(R)	extremely high
100'	#1 3.5	18'	5660'	EB		high
	#2 1	5'	5660'	EB		
	#3 7	20'	5700'	EB		
	#4 2.5	20'	5700'	R		
200'	16	68'	6340'	EB, R, B	(EB)	extremely high
No restriction	0.5	—	6770'	—		high
200'	6.5	28'	5810'	EB		high
100'	9	22'	5700'	EB		low
No restriction	1	15'	6170'	EB, R	(EB)	low
200'	—	—	5820'	—		extremely high
No restriction	0.5	12'	5560'	EB, R	(R)	high
No restriction	2	14'	5570'	EB, R	(EB)	moderate
No restriction	4	11'	5570'	EB, R	(EB)	moderate
100'	44	56'	6340'	EB, R, B		extremely high
200'	3.5	8'	5970'	EB		low
100'	5	13'	5740'	EB, R	(EB)	rare
200'	2	15'	5890'	R		moderate
No restriction	13	25'	5640'	EB, R	(EB)	moderate
200'	6	5'	5400'	R, B		high
200'	1	15'	5370'	EB	(R)	high
No restriction	1.5	6'	7150'	EB		high
No restriction	0.8	10'	6340'	EB, R		low
100'	3.5	11'	5710'	R		high
100'	3	13'	5860'	EB, R	(R)	high
No restriction	—	—	6020'	—		rare
200'	22	32'	5750'	EB, R	(R)	high
200'	5	15'	6120'	EB		high
100'	3.5	20'	6230'	EB, R	(EB)	moderate
No restriction	9	37'	5580'	EB	(EB, B)	moderate
100'	5.5	18'	5370'	EB		moderate
200'	8.5	43'	5270'	EB, R	(R)	low
No restriction	2.5	14'	6460'	EB		moderate
200'	12.5	56'	5780'	EB, R, B	(R)	extremely high
200'	4	38'	5780'	EB, R	(R)	extremely high
100'	3.5	41'	5940'	EB		moderate
100'	5	15'	6030'	EB		extremely high
200'	—	—	5820'	—		moderate
100'	67	68'	6050'	EB, R	(R)	high
100'	3.5	24'	5880'	EB, R	(R)	low
200'	26	90'	6910'	EB, R, B	(R)	extremely high
200'	6.5	50'	7400'	EB		extremely high

in a given lake. Those listed on the left side of the column outside the parentheses are mentioned in the "Anglers' Guide to the Marble Mountains," last revised in 1971. The source for the species listed within the parentheses is the Fish and Game Department's stocking data for the years 1975-79, and they are listed only where they differ from those in the older Anglers' Guide.

The topographic maps with this book have a grid overlay to aid you in locating points of interest. The hike and lake charts identify the grid location of trailhead and lake, respectively. The first set of initials identifies the topographic map: FS—Forks of Salmon, SaB—Sawyers Bar, ScB—Scott Bar, UL—Ukonom Lake. The letter-dash-number, such as D-5, refers to the grid coordinates.

Chapter 5

Oak Knoll District

Introduction: The Oak Knoll district amounts to only a narrow wedge of the wilderness pie of the Marble Mountains. There are only two trails under the district's jurisdiction. However, these two trails, one of which is the Marbles' northernmost leg of the Pacific Crest Trail, offer ready access to the wilderness riches of the northern Marble Mountains.

Access: Following State Highway 96 and the Klamath River 45 miles from Interstate 5 brings you to the verdant farmlands of Seiad Valley and the tiny community of the same name; coming from the west, Seiad Valley is 19 miles east of Happy Camp. For wilderness permits, the Oak Knoll Ranger Station is located on Highway 96, 23 miles west of I-5. A more immediate source of permits and information is the Forest Service fire station in Seiad Valley. It is manned year-round; however, rangers may not be there to help you, particularly during peak fire season.

From State Highway 96, access to the trailheads begins with County Road SIS 8D001. East of the Seiad Store in Seiad Valley 1.5 miles, the SIS 8D001 turnoff is not identified by name or number but by a Forest Service destination sign for *Walker Creek, Grider Creek, China Peak*. If you are coming from the east, keep a sharp eye on your odometer, since this turn can be easily missed; it is 3.7 miles past the O'Neil Creek Campground. If you find yourself crossing a highway bridge to the north side of the Klamath River, you have gone about 1/3 mile too far.

There are Forest Service campgrounds on Highway 96 a few miles to either side of Seiad Valley. If you prefer pre- or post-trip accommodations closer to the trail, then use undeveloped campsites at the trailheads at both ends of the Grider Creek Trail, or the rocky parking area at the Tyler Meadows trailhead, which will serve in a pinch if you have brought water.

The Trails: Although represented by only two trails, the offerings of the Oak Knoll district are remarkably diverse. The Tyler Meadows Trail is a ridge-runner's route. Starting high and staying high, it sweeps along the crest of the Marble Mountain range, with enticing views out over the Coast Ranges and the northern Marbles country. The Grider Creek Trail, on the other hand, climbs gently along a rollicking, rainbow-trout-filled creek through a vast, sheltering forest, and begins low enough to provide virtually year-round hiking opportunities.

Neither trail suffers from overuse, for the Klamath River is minimally populated and visitors attracted to this area tend to be automobile-oriented, with fishing needs admirably satisfied by the ample Klamath. Also, lakes, which are prime attractions for wilderness travelers, are absent from both trails. The Tyler Meadows Trail may be the least used trail in the entire wilderness, experiencing little traffic other than the trail-maintenance crew's annual visit. The growing popularity of the Pacific Crest Trail is bringing more traffic to Grider Creek, particularly during late July, when the end-to-enders come "roaring" through on their way to Canada.

The Oak Knoll district does not manage any summer range allocations. However, that serenade of the mountain meadow—the cowbell chorus—can occasionally be heard along the Tyler Meadows Trail above Grider Valley, and Packers Valley is likely to be under bovine rule from early July through mid-October.

The trails of the Oak Knoll district are not a glamorous lot. However, if you are looking for a day's excursion all by yourself, you can't do better than to head for one of these trails of the northern Marbles.

Metamorphic-rock outcrop

Glossy leaves of toabcco brush

Hike 1   Tyler Meadows Trail

Distance: 4.2 miles, one way
Low elevation: 5550'
High elevation: 6790'
Suited for: day trip
Usage: rare along ridgecrest trail; moderate in the Turk Lake/Packers Valley area
Difficulty: strenuous

Directions to trailhead: From Highway 96 head south on paved SIS 8D001 and continue straight ahead on FS 46N64 after 35 yards, where SIS 8D001 turns west toward the Grider Creek trailhead. Road 46N64 becomes an all weather road in about 3 miles, after which there are three road junctions that can cause some confusion due to inadequate markings: at 6.3 miles (from Highway 96) turn sharply left (south); at 13.2 miles continue straight as FS 45N81 comes in on your right; and at 14.0 miles FS 46N65 comes in on your left. At 15.1 miles, you arrive at a junction with FS 45N77, signed for *Faulkenstein Camp* and forking to the right. Follow 45N77 for 5.5 miles, passing several tributary roads forking to the right, to its end at the signed trailhead. If you are planning an early-summer hike, you might want to check with the Forest Service in Oak Knoll or Seiad Valley on the status of 45N77, for the slope above the road is quite unstable and the road can become clogged with rockfall during the spring melt. Since the only water along the trail is a tiny spring after 1.5 miles, you might want to fill your water bottle before reaching the trailhead.

Trail description: Leaving the parking area at the edge of a broad network of clear-cut patches, you begin a moderate descent along the ridgeline of the Marble Mountains range, walking through a mixed-conifer forest of largely white firs and Douglas-firs. After bottoming out in a small saddle (0.4, 5550), the trail turns south and begins an extremely steep climb, soon forsaking the ridgecrest to curve into a lushly gardened opening on the western slope. The climb eases somewhat as you tread metavolcanic clinkers through bitter cherry and scrubby Oregon white oak.

Rounding a slight spur amid scattered red firs and curlleaf mountain mahoganies (0.5, 5950), the hiker bends southeast and continues steeply up the open slope. Some of the metamorphic outcrops seen here present intriguing geologic artwork: a fine cross-hatching of white lines the joints and fissures, likely a carbonate produced in the chemical reaction of water and the rock's minerals. Past another slight bulge in the hillside, you leave the land of manzanita, sage-brush, monardella and eriogonum, and enter a cool, moist, grassy depression (0.6, 6350). The depression's orientation and its enclosed nature cause its winter snowpack to last much later than snowpacks in the surrounding areas, and this condition is reflected by its floral wealth. A tiny spring, bubbling up immediately above the trail as you enter the grassy stretch, is not only extraordinarily refreshing but is the only water along the entire trail. As you contour through the depression, you might notice an occasional small outcrop of low-grade marble buried in the foliage, harbingers of the vast marble body a few miles to the south.

Beyond the depression, the trail makes a gradual descent to a long, open saddle (0.6, 6290). Across the Kelsey Creek valley, Red Mountain rises in the southeast, with Boulder Peak at its apex, and Mt. Shasta in the distance. After traversing the long, narrow saddle, the trail ascends steeply through greenleaf manzanita and tobacco brush, then a few short switchbacks aid the climb to a rock-ribbed ridgecrest. The varihued outcrops are a melange of metavolcanics and metasediments.

The steep ascent is momentarily interrupted by a precipitous notch in the knife-edge ridge, then continues to a viewpoint just south of the summit of Peak 6853 (0.7, 6780). Here the views out over the northern Marbles country are unexcelled. Prominences on the horizon include Kings Castle at 210°, Peak 7636 (which lies just north of Gem and Jewel lakes in the Cliff-Campbell-Summit lakes area) at 155°, Boulder Peak at 130° and Mt. Shasta at 105°.

After you briefly cross to the east side of the ridge, a couple of switchbacks assist a plummeting drop along manzanita-clad slopes. Then the descent eases dramatically as it returns to a patchy red-fir forest. The tread may be ill-defined in places, but tree blazes should see you through to a four-way trail junction in a broad saddle (0.6, 6470).

Upper Grider Valley

The trail to the right is a minimally maintained path, a remnant of the Upper Grider Valley Trail, which drops into the head of Grider Valley and is used primarily by the Oak Knoll trail crew during their annual work trip. Down the path 0.5 mile, just beyond a corn-lily-glutted depression, a small flat above the trail provides an adequate campsite served by a pipe-fed spring. A faint usage trail heads south 40 yards to the campsite just as the brief, steep climb from the depression eases its grade. By midsummer, the cattle grazing Grider Valley will be well below here and you are virtually assured of a solitary stay in this lovely valley.

Big Ridge Cutoff Trail and Turk Lake

The Big Ridge Cutoff Trail, signed for *Packers Valley* and *Turk Lake*, appears well-delineated. However, it has a very low priority on the Scott River district's maintenance schedule and can pose challenging route-finding problems through the maze of cattle paths in Packers Valley. It did receive its triennial maintenance check in 1979 and was reasonably followable when the author mapped it that year. Provided you exercise it before the early July cattle invasion, The Big Ridge Cutoff Trail offers another option for camping privacy.

This gently descending trail makes a long arc to the west-southwest, passing through a few hundred yards of forest before bursting into patchy scrub to begin a short, steep descent into Packers Valley. The tread is occasionally obscure in the grasses of the valley bottom on the approach to heavily flowered, low-flowing Packers Valley creek (0.6, 6260). Even if you are traveling in the months B.C. (Before Cattle), the purity of the water in Packers Valley is highly suspect; one reason, perhaps, why there are no established campsites in evidence.

After climbing out of the willow thickets on the creek's south bank, you reach a trail junction in 0.2 miles. The trail to the west-northwest climbs to a triple junction with the Pacific Crest and Tyler Meadow trails in 0.6 mile. To reach more potable water in Packers Valley, or Turk Lake, follow the trail southeast. After climbing briefly, the trail levels off and soon reaches a heavily willowed, non-cattle-tainted spring. Along the forest edge south of the spring is the best opportunity to continue the practice of no-trace camping in Packers Valley.

Beyond the spring a moderate descent begins, which then levels off to round the east-trending spur of Peak 6923. Then the trail descends steeply through scrub, quaking-aspen thickets, and meadow to the east shore of extremely shallow Turk Lake (1.2, 5820). A spur trail up to the Pacific Crest Trail begins its very steep, 0.7-mile climb by heading north-northwest from a fir signed *Turk Lake*. The 0.6-mile extension of the Big Ridge Cutoff Trail, down to the Kelsey Creek Trail, begins its initially obscure route by heading east-northeast from the campsite 35 yards beyond the signed fir.

The Tyler Meadows Trail continues straight ahead from the four-way trail junction, climbing steeply southwest through trailside sidalcea, aster, paintbrush and angelica, and out onto a semi-open slope. The tread is overgrown in places but is well-ducked and tree-blazed. Contouring west, one passes beneath a knoll of ultramafic rock, indicated as much by the smattering of Jeffrey pine as by the rock color. Your recently passed four-way trail junction marks the northern border of an extensive ultra-mafic body that stretches from Kelsey Creek in the east to Bear Creek in the west and includes the mountain mass of Red Rock, west of Bear Lake.

Continuing its traverse above the head of Packers Valley, the rollercoaster trail passes through a final, colorful burst of high-meadow flora and up to a cluttered signpost marking a junction with the Pacific Crest Trail (0.8, 6790). Whereas the Crest Trail is a well-maintained track, the signed trail dropping east into Packers Valley begins sketchily and requires a steady eye to follow without blunder.

Hike 2

Grider Creek Trail

Distance: 7.4 miles, one way
Low elevation: 1700'
High elevation: 3200'
Suited for: day trip
Usage: low
Difficulty: easy

Directions to trailhead: Thirty-five yards after SIS 8D001 leaves Highway 96, it branches west, following the direction of a Grider Creek destination sign. After 2.4 miles on SIS 8D001, fork left onto all-weather FS 46N66, taking it 1.5 miles to a bridge over Grider Creek, then 0.9 mile farther to an obscurely marked spur road on the left. This leaves 46N66 at a gully where the main road hairpins to the right. Follow the spur ¼ mile down to where it effectively dead-ends at an ample parking space and small car-camping area on the west bank of Grider Creek. The Forest Service has plans to develop this trailhead in the near future, creating a more extensive camping area and corrals for packstock. Just short of the creek, a trail sign directs the hiker toward a footbridge upstream, and the road dives into the creek as a designated ford for horsepackers. The horse ford and hiker trail reunite at a more specifically signed trailhead on the creek's east bank.

Trail description: Beyond the east-bank trailhead sign, you walk a few paces upstream along the abandoned continuation of the dirt road to an obvious trail. This starts switchbacking east-northeast, making a brief, moderate climb above the creek. Then, after bending back to an upstream heading, it begins a gently rolling ascent of Grider Creek canyon. At this point, the riotous vegetative variety of the mixed-evergreen plant community reflects the low-elevation, open-flatland influence of Seiad Valley. The cool, moist pocket found at hop-across No Name Creek (0.6, 1840) is in marked contrast to its more arid surroundings.

Beyond No Name Creek the trail gradually abandons its semilevel nature in the canyon bottom and begins a gentle-to-moderate climb of nearly ½ mile, up onto the wall above the creek. Shortly after leveling off

from this climb, it descends briefly, dipping into a gully with several outcrops of granitic rock. These light-colored outcrops belong to the Slinkard Peak pluton, an intrusive body that underlies Seiad Valley and environs.

The trail meanders lazily through a continuous procession of gullies, rampant with hazelnut and big leaf and vine maples. Despite the numerous gullies, you must go a mile past No Name Creek before you can find one containing water, and even that creeklet will be dry by late season. This trail was completely reconstructed in the early 1970s. The old route stayed down at creekside, criss-crossing the stream a dozen times or more; in fact, several of the log crossings remain and are visible from time to time. As you look down at the dancing riffles and inviting pools, you may regret that the relocation ever took place.

After a gentle climb of ½ mile, the trail dips to a flat on the banks of Grider Creek (2.0, 2100). It is but a momentary creekside rendezvous, though, for the trail immediately begins to climb in stages above the creek and soon leaves it far below again. The gentle, multigullied climb eventually levels off as a few obscure outcrops of metasedimentary rock, including marble, begin to appear. It then descends slightly to swerve into the side canyon of lively Bark Shanty Creek (0.9, 2240) before resuming its easy ascent to a footbridge over Grider Creek (0.4, 2330).

Now on the west bank, continue the up-canyon route through the vibrant greenery of the fecund canyon bottom. The trail curls down to the edge of a large flat in an elbow of a meander in the creek, then quickly climbs above the creek to resume its gently rolling route southward. The creek has cut sharply into the metamorphic bedrock in places, and the trail comes to chasm's edge to look down on a series of dashing cascades shortly before descending to another footbridge over Grider Creek (1.6, 2640). If you have chosen to make this hike into more than just a day trip, you might want to take advantage of a cozy little campsite tucked into the creekside foliage, 30 yards above the bridge on the east bank. Although the creek shows no more than shallow riffles near the bridge, pools for swimming and fishing can be found both up and down the creek.

From here, the trail climbs moderately to steeply for nearly ¼ mile, then eases into a rolling descent for a short distance before beginning another moderate climb. Just after passing above a sharp bend in the creek where it rounds a steep point on the opposite bank, you'll notice some massive, light-colored cliff faces across from you. Continuing up the trail a few moments allows you to examine this rock type more closely as you come alongside a sizable, overhanging, moss-encrusted outcrop. This mottled, light-gray metasediment appears to be related to the great body of marble farther to the south, exposed in the Marble Rim and Marble Valley areas.

Just past the outcrop, two switchbacks gain some needed elevation before grading into a gentle climb around a small spur ridge and into a large patch of ultramafic rock. If the brilliant red soil is not enough for you to recognize the change in bedrock types, the drastic change in the vegetation should be: the Douglas-fir-dominated forest with substantial understory gives way in just a few yards to a sparsely forested slope of Jeffrey pines and incense-cedars, with patches of huckleberry oaks and serviceberries and an occasional yew tree growing in the otherwise barren soil. This is a narrow band of ultramafic rock that intersects the trail, and the passage through this unique association is shortlived, for the trail soon drops to a final footbridge over Grider Creek (1.1, 2890), enlivened here by a lovely minigorge, waterfall and engaging pool. If you wish to extend your waterplay in this area beyond the limitations of a day trip, stay at a small, creekside campsite, hidden away below the trail, some 75 yards above the bridge crossing. As the trail turns west some 90 yards above the bridge, you leave delightful Grider Creek behind to head up Cliff Valley. The trail climbs sporadically through open, forest-border shrubbery of chinquapin, greenleaf manzanita, thimbleberry and alder. After crossing a muted creeklet, the trail climbs more steeply away from Cliff Valley's creek and into the forest before reaching the dirt road at the upper trailhead (0.8, 3200).

Grider Creek, at uppermost bridge

If you wish to set up a car shuttle for an end-to-end hike of the Grider Creek Trail, or if you would rather hike on its less populated southern end, the upper trailhead can be reached by continuing on FS 46N66 another 5.0 miles beyond the lower trailhead turnoff to a four-way, unsigned intersection. Turn left (southeast) on FS 46N77, the Grider Ridge Road, and follow it 9.4 miles to a triple fork. You want the left fork, signed for *Cliff Valley Creek*. The dirt road, which is beginning to wash out in places, heads downhill 3.3 miles to the signed Pacific Crest Trail trailhead of the Grider Creek Trail on the left. Seventy yards beyond the trailhead, where the road bottoms out, there is a creekside car-camp/parking area.

Chapter 6

Happy Camp District

Introduction: Tucked into the northwest corner of the wilderness and draining the high-country arc created by the joining of the Salmon and Marble mountains' crests, the Elk Creek watershed hosts all but one segment of the four trails in the Happy Camp district. With thickly forested, valley-bottom trails climbing various fingers of the watershed to subalpine, glacier-basin lakes, this area provides an inviting setting for serene walks in the forest solitude. Yet all the trails here also provide ready access to ridgecrest panoramas that will delight the eye.

Access: The small logging community of Happy Camp lies on State Highway 96, 64 miles from Interstate 5 at the Klamath River and 130 miles from the coast highway near Arcata. The Happy Camp Ranger Station is located on the south side of Highway 96 in the middle of the roadside business district. One-third mile downriver from the ranger station is signed Elk Creek Road (SIS 7C001 and FS 16N05). This road, paved for its first 7.5 miles, starts south across a bridge over the Klamath River, then turns west downriver for ½ mile before forking left to follow Elk Creek south to all the trailheads in this section.

Sulphur Springs Campground, 13.3 miles up Elk Creek Road, is the only developed camping facility in the immediate vicinity of the trailheads, although there are undeveloped campsites at the Norcross trailhead for the Elk Creek Trail and the Snowshoe Creek trailhead for the Bear Creek Trail. From the south end of the campground parking area, a stairway and a gravel drive lead down to a foot bridge across Elk Creek. The small, attractive campground, found above the opposite bank, has six semi-isolated, rarely filled campsites. In addition to a spacious swimming hole beneath the campground's access bridge, this area features the only hot spring in the Marbles. From the campground sign above the west end of the bridge, follow a path 100 yards downstream to where a short trail winds down the raised bank to a mildly aromatic spring—Sulphur Springs—in a rock-walled pool. The effervescent waters maintain a constant temperature of 85°F and offer an appealing conclusion to a long back-country hike on a crisp autumn day.

The Trails: Because Happy Camp is small and is far from the major northern California highways, the trails in this district receive only low-to-moderate use; indeed, the Johnson Hunting Ground/Tickner Hole Trail is only rarely used. The entry-point data for 1975-76 showed that only 5% of the permits issued were for trailheads in the Happy Camp district. Only Ukonom Lake, which receives much of its traffic from the Ukonom district in the southwest sector of the wilderness, is an area of high use. In addition to the greater potential for wilderness solitude, this section's trails offer a pleasing diversity of landscapes and experiences.

Two of the four trails, the Granite Creek and Rainy Valley trails, are both gentle-to-moderate-climbing valley walks that lead to subalpine lakes perched in glacier-gouged basins at the foot of the Salmon Mountains' crest. The intial few miles along Elk Creek and the lower parts of Granite and Rainy Valley creeks lend themselves nicely to simple dayhikes, and there are several creekside camping spots along these parts that allow for brief overnight trips.

A third trail, the Bear Creek Trail, with two possible trailheads, is similar to the two trails above, for like them it is a creekside route to a lake at the head of a valley. However, it is a far more rigorous exercise with some inordinately steep sections, particularly near the wilderness boundary. Whereas this district's three other trails lie primarily or entirely within the extensive granitic region of the Wooley Creek pluton, Bear Lake lies between the light-grey marble ridge north of Kings Castle and the vibrant hues of ultramafic Red Rock. And while the crest of the Salmon Mountains is easily accessible to the hikers on the other three trails, it doesn't quite achieve the royal perspective that the short, strenuous cross-country jaunt from Bear Lake to the top of Kings Castle affords. To top it off, the dayhiker in good condition can start from the Snowshoe Creek trailhead and enjoy the wide range of pleasures of the Bear Creek Trail in a 7.2-mile round trip to Bear Lake.

The Johnson's Hunting Ground-Tickner Hole hike is this section's offering for the recluse. Despite the wide-angle overview of the Coast Ranges and intriguing perspectives of Black Mountain and the Granite lakes basin from the route along Titus Ridge, this roller-coaster of a trail with its limited water sources is generally shunned by wilderness travelers. The route-finding difficulties in Tickner Hole and its lack of good-sized lakes probably explain why the tranquil ponds near the head of Tickner Creek are largely unvisited. Hence few wilderness travelers view the sizable scattering of weeping spruces, which are fairly rare trees found only in the Klamath Mountains.

With the exception of the Johnson Hunting Ground/Tickner Hole Trail, these are well-maintained trails and generally easy to follow, though some of the permanently unsigned trail junctions can be a bit obscure. Only the Johnson Hunting Ground/Tickner Hole Trail, especially in Tickner Hole, requires considerable attention to trail markings, and areas of particular difficulty are noted in the trail description.

Although the Happy Camp district does not manage any summer-range allocations, the Scott River district's Big Ridge allocation extends down into Bear Valley, and you may run into some cattle along the upper reaches of the Bear Creek Trail.

A final scheduling note: should you be in the Happy Camp area over the Labor Day weekend, you might want to join in the festivities of Bigfoot Days, an annual community event featuring a salmon feed, dances, parade, and various games, performances, contests and exhibits.

Hike 3   Bear Creek Trail

Distance: 6.1 miles, one way
Low elevation: 2400'
High elevation: 6000'
Suited for: overnight
Usage: low
Difficulty: strenuous

Directions to trailhead: Follow Elk Creek Road 14.7 miles to its end at a parking area. Trailhead camping is available at a small creekside site below the southwest corner of the parking lot, some 60 yards along the Norcross spur to the Elk Creek Trail.

If time is of the essence or if you wish to minimize your dalliance along Bear Creek, you can omit the first 2.5 miles of the trail by turning off Elk Creek Road after 12.4 miles and following all-weather road 15N06 for 6 miles to an obscure, un-signed trailhead on your left, 60 yards short of the bridge over Bear Creek. There is an unappealing roadside campsite opposite this trailhead. [Note: 3.3 miles along road 15N06 is an unsigned fork. Although the left fork is a continuation of the road you are on and the right fork appears to be little more than a turnout, you want the right fork, which quickly drops out of view.]

Trail description: From the lower trail-head the trail ducks into the brush be-yond the parking-area clearing and climbs steeply east-northeast for 0.2 mile through mixed-evergreen forest. Then the trail gradient eases and you briefly contour well above Bear Creek before resuming the ascent. A bend north in the path brings you to creekside again at a madly crashing waterfall (0.8, 2720). On a hot midsummer's day, the pool at the bottom of the fall would be inviting indeed, but the steep, crumbly rock and loose turf bordering the fall make the pool nearly inaccessible.

From the waterfall, continue climbing moderately with only limited access to the creek, crossing a gully with early season water and then, 0.2 mile later, hopping across the permanent flow of Buckhorn Creek (0.5, 2980). Beyond Buckhorn Creek climb steeply northeast into a small gully before beginning to head east-southeast above gradually arcing Bear Creek. The climbing becomes moderate with occasional steep sections until a brief, extremely steep and somewhat slick scramble up a gully brings you to Road 15N06 (0.9, 3520). Starting east-southeast along the road, you cross thickly vegetated Snowshoe Creek in ¼ mile and, 110 yards beyond the creek, as the road curves left, come to the Snow-shoe Creek trailhead and the unsigned resumption of the Bear Creek Trail (0.3, 3580), heading steeply uphill on your left.

Since there is an ample 3.6 miles in which to climb the remaining 2400 vertical feet to Bear Lake, the extraordinary steep-ness of the trail as it leaves the road is a bit galling. In the first mile, it climbs 1200 feet.

With all your energies bent on hauling yourself up this torturous incline, you can easily miss the changes going on around you. Shortly after leaving the road, for instance, the trail passes beyond the border of the Wooley Creek pluton and into a region of metavolcanic rock. And with the speedy rise in elevation comes a fairly rapid transition from a mixed-evergreen to a mixed-conifer forest.

As the forest opens, you bend north-east around a spur ridge. A few minutes later, you may pass a corroded metal *wilderness boundary* sign nailed to a tree to the right of the trail (0.8, 4580). This is a prime example of why you should never locate your position by equating trailside wilderness-boundary signs with the boundary lines on your topographic map: the "approximate boundary" line between sections 19 and 20 on your map was crossed over 0.4 mile down the trail.

The gradient eases noticeably to be-come merely steep as the trail arcs east-northeast, and momentarily levels for a seasonally goldenrod-bordered dip back into a usually dry gully. Curving into an-other gully sometimes choked with the bright magenta spikes of fireweed, you cross a semipermanent creeklet. Just ¼ mile farther, you reach a permanent brook (1.0, 5150) amid pearly everlasting and the down-turned, crownlike blossoms of crimson columbine. There is an intimate little camp-site on your right just past this creek.

After a brief, extremely steep climb from the creek, the trail ascends gently through a richly textured fir forest into a brushy opening, an outrider of the mead-ows of Bear Valley. Wading through waist-high flora that would leave one quite soggy on a dew-soaked morning, you step across a couple of intermittent streams and several seeps just as the craggy ridgetop of Red Rock comes into view above its fir-coated northeast slope.

The flora becomes more varied and wildly colored where you enter the mead-ow proper. After briefly passing through a patchy wooded stretch, the trail enters a long, linear meadow, grassy and sparsely flowered, redolent of cattle. Three hun-dred yards into the meadow, it passes through a large, mountain-maple-bordered grove of incense-cedars (0.9, 5450), formerly the site of the Bear Valley cabin.

Leaving the grove, a very sketchy trail angles east-southeast 65 yards toward the upper edge of the meadow; a duck marks the trail's entry into a patchy forest of primarily incense-cedars and alders. However, a large Jeffrey pine and a small western white pine, both liberally dropping cones, give evidence that the ultramafic rock which colors Red Rock across the valley is also contributing to the soil beneath your feet. The rocky, overgrown trail climbs quite steeply through another stretch of meadow and into an open grove of Jeffrey and western white pines and incense-cedars, then levels out just north of a slight knob to edge briefly along the southwest border of a small meadow to a trail junction (0.7, 5980), signed for Bear Lake.

Taking the right fork, south-southeast, you curl around the east side of the knob and pass a lovely campsite on your right as you descend to the northwest edge of Bear Lake (0.2, 5980).

Red Rock above Bear Lake

A usage trail crosses the sluggish outlet creek to a roomy campsite beneath several red firs, 30 yards beyond the creek. There are a couple of small sleeping niches on the lip of the lake bowl along its south shore. Typical of the moraine-dammed, glacier-scoured lakes in this wilderness Bear Lake presents its best swimming and fishing up against the bouldery headwall. From here also one gets a splendid view of the gnarled surface of Red Rock rising to the west.

Kings Castle

From the trail junction at 5980 feet, the left fork heads initially north toward a blazed western white pine, then steeply up a rocky, red staircase of a trail, climbing 600 feet in 2/3 mile to a saddle junction with the Pacific Crest Trail. From here one can head ½ mile east down to shallow, marginally attractive Turk Lake, or 1.6 miles south to often crowded Paradise Lake, with its splendid view of the marble pillbox of Kings Castle.

Better than a view of Kings Castle is the view *from* Kings Castle. Allow 4 to 5 hours round-trip time from Bear Lake. The usage trail crossing the outlet creek of Bear Lake was once an established trail to Kings Castle, but it has been abandoned to the cattle who call the head of Bear Valley their own from early July to mid-October. It is therefore advisable to be well-versed in the use of map and compass before attempting this side trip. By heading south from Bear Lake, through the "notch" of the meadow, one will eventually reach the head of the valley (you want to stay on the west side of the valley, where the ground tends to offer drier footing). A vaguely visible trail remnant can be seen angling south up the ridge through the dense brush, but a bit of bushwhacking southwest up the foot of the headwall is needed in order to intersect it. This north-facing headwall supports a snowpatch well into the summer, which may be a consideration. If you miss the trail, you'll have a continual bushwhack south to the ridgecrest saddle, from which Kings Castle is a 1/3-mile climb east-southeast across alpine flora and lichened rock. The resulting view of the world is the sort to make one cry "author, author."

Ridge north of Kings Castle, from cross-country route

Hike 4   Elk Creek—Rainy Valley Creek Trails

Distance: 10.5 miles, one way
Low elevation: 2200′
High elevation: 5400′
Suited for: 2-3 day trip
Usage: moderate at Rainy Lake; low in Rainy Valley
Difficulty: moderate
Directions to trailhead: Take Elk Creek Road 13.3 miles to the Sulphur Springs Campground parking area. The unsigned trail begins just opposite the Sulphur Springs Campground sign, 25 yards beyond the west end of the bridge over Elk Creek.

To cut 1.1 miles of creekside hiking from the hike, follow Elk Creek Road another 1.4 miles to its end. The Norcross trailhead is at the southwest corner of the parking area. Although this may save some hiking time in mid-to-late season, the crossing of Elk Creek here can be problematic earlier in the year, since it is a split-log bridge that washes away every winter and needs annual replacing. If you are planning an early summer trip, check at the ranger station in Happy Camp to see if this crossing is negotiable.

Trail description: Follow the southwest bank of Elk Creek up a very gentle grade, passing a junction with the Lick Creek Trail in 70 yards, then rock-hopping the narrow channel of Lick Creek itself (0.1, 2220), and passing several well-established usage trails heading off to favored swimming holes. At 0.4 mile, a particularly obvious side trail leads 150 yards to a sandy, creekside campsite. Soon Johnson Creek (0.6, 2310) is crossed, usually on boulders, though the log crossing 30 yards upstream may be necessary in early season. Somewhat above Elk Creek now, continue this delightful forest stroll up to a junction with the Norcross Tie Trail (0.8, 2470), which serves as access to the Elk Creek Trail from the parking area at the end of Elk Creek Road.

Norcross Tie Trail

The Norcross Tie Trail leaves the southwest corner of the parking area, dropping to the bank of Bear Creek just above its confluence with Elk Creek. You head downstream about 100 yards along the rocky edge of the creekbed, which will be submerged in early season in a normal year, and cross where the Forest Service has constructed its split-log bridge. After crossing the long, shaky bridge over shallow but swift Elk Creek, switchback up its southwest bank, then climb southeast to a junction with the Elk Creek Trail from Sulphur Springs (0.3, 2470).

The gently undulating Elk Creek Trail continues its generally southeast course through a lushly understoried, largely deciduous forest. You cross one trickling intermittent stream, then, 0.4 mile farther, descend slightly to cross a large one on a log (0.6, 2540). Just 35 yards past it, you can take a scramble path down to a roomy, forested campsite near the bank of Elk Creek.

The trail gradient steepens and a pair of switchbacks takes one higher above Elk Creek. After crossing an intermittent stream in a wide, brushy opening, you dip back down toward Elk Creek, the trail bringing you creekside but well above the water. Continuing your walk, descend slightly to a large campsite near a small pool (0.7, 2630). Just beyond the campsite, a split-log crossing brings you to Elk Creek's northeast bank. You need to head downstream a few yards, through the rocks and the pearly everlasting, to locate the trail again. After finding it, climb moderately for ¼ mile, then descend slightly to a long, more open flat.

Resume climbing at a gentle-to-moderate grade, crossing a small, sparkling creek (0.8, 2840), then easing off again to a semilevel route. Only 75 yards beyond a large, wooden, wilderness-boundary sign, you come to a large campsite with split-log benches and a table. Here too is a trail junction (0.4, 2900), the right fork heading south-southeast through the campsite to where a trail sign informs you that its destination is Granite Lakes and Tickner Hole.

Elk Creek

The left fork bears east-southeast up toward Rainy Valley. Taking this route, you climb steeply for a few hundred yards, then the grade gradually eases. Soon you bend east into the narrow defile of Hummingbird Creek (0.4, 3050), deeply cut into the granitic rock. After crossing the creek, you ascend moderately, ducking in and out of several small gullies as you traverse a southwest-facing slope. In these humid, shaded gullies, the lushness and density of the vegetation is in marked contrast with the openness of the exposed hillside.

Just beyond a burbling creek in a wide depression (0.9, 3430), the path steepens again, severely so in some places, climbing for ½ mile, then easing as it begins to bend around a spur ridge near the confluence of Elk and Toms Valley creeks. As you complete the bend, you gently descend into a gully and see Peak 6336 to your right, rising between Elk and Rainy valleys. When you emerge from the gully, you can look back through an open forest of mixed conifers, which allows you views to the west-southwest at Peak 6528, separating Toms and Burney valleys.

As the trail curves east to approach a final crossing of Elk Creek, you pass a two-tent campsite above the trail on the inside of the curve. Inviting as this lovely, forested spot may be, continue another 150 yards to the log-and-boulder creek crossing (1.4, 3920). The campsite on the northwest bank of this rollicking creek, with its several cascades and tiny pools dished out of the granitic bedrock, is a stellar attraction. You may want to fill your water bottles before leaving this delightful spot, for your next water source is 2.5 miles up-canyon.

Across Elk Creek, you switchback up very steeply, then your climb eases considerably as you head up the crest of a spur before turning south-southeast toward Rainy Valley Creek. Heading up Rainy Valley, the trail is a rollercoaster of occasionally moderate grade but with no appreciable overall change of elevation. The forest thickens with Douglas-firs and white firs, and patches of the forest floor are carpeted in the lustrous deep greens of the low-lying twinflower.

After a bit of moderate climbing, the trail resumes its rolling course, eventually nearing the edge of a shrubby meadow (2.1, 4480). Through the airy foliage of incense-cedars along the forest border, you can see domineering Elk Peak rising in the southwest. Staying within the forest, you first climb moderately, crossing a seep, then level off for a while before entering a long curve to a hop-across brook. About 270 yards beyond the crossing, you reach a junction with the Marble Gap Trail (0.6, 4680), which offers splendid vistas along its climb to the gap. If you are not watching for this junction, you can miss the narrow, somewhat overgrown side trail, for it disappears east into the underbrush as the trail to Rainy Lake curves south-southwest down toward Rainy Valley Creek.

You remain beneath the forest cover as you descend 160 yards to an easy hop across lushly gardened Rainy Valley Creek, passing a small creekside campsite 35 yards short of the crossing. The metavolcanic boulders snugged up under the foliage indicate you've passed out of the region of the Wooley Creek pluton.

Climbing steeply through huckleberries on the creek's west bank, you head south, then southwest, up the lake fork of Rainy Valley Creek. As you move from the mixed-conifer zone into the red-fir zone, Douglas-fir is replaced by red fir and mountain hemlock. Then as you approach the wetter head of the north-facing valley, the forest begins to be pocketed with brush and wildflowers. Finally, as the trail levels off, the open areas and their flora become more extensive. Behind you, to the east-northeast, the marbled mass of Black Mountain cuts into the horizon. In brush, you cross a closely spaced pair of slight creeklets, then climb along the west bank of Rainy Valley Creek, soon moving away from it to reach a trail intersection (1.1, 5360).

To the left, a slight usage trail heads east-southeast into a grove of red firs and meanders gradually to the northwest shore of Rainy Lake near its outlet creek. To the right, a narrow trail drops west-northwest into a gully, then climbs very steeply—about 600 vertical feet in ½ mile—up to a ridgetop junction with the Salmon Mountains Crest Trail. You could then follow a nearly level trail westward 1.1 miles to Spirit Lake.

To reach Rainy Lake, your best bet is to continue straight ahead, following the border of the firs along the edge of a meadow glutted with mountain ash and oak scrub. In 75 yards the path passes through a finger of the red-fir growth under which it appears more horses than people have camped. About 100 yards beyond this massive camping area is another campsite, pungent with horse dung. Rainy Lake lies 40 yards farther on through the brush.

Snug up against a precipitous headwall, Rainy Lake lies in a charming setting. However, you'll have to look farther than the shallow marsh of its easily accessible west shore if you are to find the pleasurable swimming or fishing offered by its moderate depth.

Black Mountain, from Marble Gap Trail

Marble Gap Trail

This trail stairts east from its junction with the Rainy Valley Trail. The forest closes about you, and the lush understory even more so, particularly the thick growths of trail plant, whose sticky seeds cling in abundance to socks, pants, and leg hair. The climb, moderate at first, eventually eases and the forest gradually opens to admit clumps of Sadler oaks, mountain maples, and willows.

Shortly after hopping across a brush-glutted brook, the trail passes through a quaking-aspen community, then curves northeast at the edge of a meadow (0.8, 5010). After getting a leisurely eyeful of the northwest face of Marble Mountain, rising precipitously above the head of the valley, you begin the arduous climb to the crest that separates Elk and Rainy valleys. The climb through quaking aspens, bitter cherries and varied wildflowers is interrupted momentarily as the trail drops steeply to recross the willow-lined brook. Then, curving into a neighboring gulch, you take what little shade is offered by the few shimmering black cottonwoods as you struggle up the scrub-gauntlet trail.

Curving northwest, climb out of the gully and up through mixed forest, scrub, and meadow. A small spring along the left of the trail is the last source of water this side of Marble Valley. After attaining the crest of a spur, briefly ascend along its crest, then bend roughly north to make a rolling traverse along the scrub-garden slope, which gives you views across Rainy Valley to where Elk Peak rears its ruddy head in the west-southwest. A final ¼ mile of stiff climbing brings one up to the crest at a trail junction (1.3, 6300).

Here, the breathtaking view of Black Mountain's awesome northwest escarpment is perhaps the most striking scene in all the Marbles. As for the trail signs, they indicate a narrow tread descending into Elk Valley. This is the same trail that is signed near Big Rock on the Pacific Crest Trail, yet it doesn't appear on any of the Forest Service or USGS maps dating back to 1955, not even as a primitive trail.

To reach Marble Gap, climb south-southeast through a ridgecrest rock garden, level off briefly as the trail leaves the crest for the west slopes, then climb steeply up to and around the point of the spur. Heading initially eastward now, you find chunks of marble cropping up in the trailside garden, then pass among a scattered growth of rare foxtail pines as the trail describes a long arc up to the saddle of Marble Gap (0.9, 6830). The view from Marble Gap is of the degree of magnificence one comes with time to expect from the high points in the Marbles. A description in greater detail of what can be seen from the Gap is included at the end of the Red Rock Valley-Marble Valley Loop, Hike 22.

Hike 5   Elk Creek—Granite Creek Trails

Distance: 9.4 miles to Blue Granite Lake, one way

9.8 miles to Gold and Green Granite Lakes, one way

Low elevation: 2200'

High elevation: 5590'

Suited for: 2-3 day trips

Usage: low along Granite Creek, but moderate at the lakes

Difficulty: moderate

Directions to trailhead: Follow Elk Creek Road 13.3 miles to the trailhead at Sulphur Springs Campground, or 14.7 miles to the trailhead at road's end (see Hike 4 trailhead directions for details).

Trail description: The first 3.9 miles follow the Elk Creek Trail along the southwest side of Elk Creek, crossing Lick Creek at 0.1 mile and Johnson Creek at 0.7 mile. At 1.4 miles, the 0.3-mile Norcross Tie Trail comes in from the northwest as you continue a generally gentle climb upstream. Cross Elk Creek near a roomy campsite at 2.7 miles, then resume climbing along the creek's east bank until you reach the junction of the Rainy Valley and Granite Creek trails, just inside the wilderness boundary at 3.9 miles (for detailed trail description, see Hike 4).

Taking the right fork at the trail junction, pass through a campsite known as Hummingbird Camp, and drop quickly to a bouldery crossing of Elk Creek. After one look at the beautiful pool above the crossing, you may feel no compulsion to journey farther. Moving south on the narrow flat between Elk and Granite creeks, you soon come to an unstable small-log crossing of Granite Creek (0.2, 2930).

With the last of the creek crossings behind you for a while, climb steeply above and away from rollicking Granite Creek, hiking through open, mixed-conifer forest. After 0.4 mile, the climb eases as the trail contours above the confluence of Granite and Burney Valley creeks. It then climbs in fits and starts, crossing a dribbling intermittent stream, then climbing steeply again. You round into the side canyon of Tickner Creek and, after passing a comfortable, one-

party campsite on the left, descend 70 yards to a boulder-hop of Tickner Creek (1.3, 3480). Happily splashing among the granitic boulders, Tickner Creek offers several small cascades and bathtub pools for your midsummer enjoyment. The trail switchbacks steeply 100 yards up from the souh bank to arrive at a junction with the Tickner Creek Trail.

Tickner Creek Trail

If your destination is actually Tickner Hole or Ukonom Lake and you have taken the Elk Creek and Granite Creek trails simply to avoid the steep, waterless climbing of the Johnson Hunting Ground Trail, then take the right fork here, signed for Tickner Hole and starting northwest. This trail climbs steeply above Tickner Creek through abundant huckleberries and thimbleberries, then switchbacks up to the ridgecrest between Tickner and Granite creeks to climb even more steeply. Having gained nearly 1200 vertical feet in little more than a mile, the gradient eases and one glides through a cool, quiet forest of Douglas-firs and white firs. A vigorous ¼-mile climb returns one to the muted burbling of Tickner Creek (1.6, 5110). Another 0.3 mile of moderate-to-steep climbing levels off at the junction with the Johnson Hunting Ground Trail (0.3, 5310). For a description of the trail into Tickner Hole, see Hike 6.

From the junction with the Tickner Creek Trail, switchback south and continue climbing steeply through the dense underbrush. The trail gradient eases briefly in an open stand of Douglas-firs, then becomes moderate. Granite Creek has cut itself too deeply into the bedrock to be accessible from the trail, yet you are near enough to it to be serenaded by its dashing song and to notice its border of deciduous trees along the break in the conifer canopy. Several small switchbacks bring you closer to the creek, then whisk you away to cross a rivulet amid a scattering of Pacific yews. Curving around a slight swell in the terrain, recross the rivulet, then cross two springs, about 0.2 mile apart.

Beyond the last spring, the path soon approaches a metal bridge whose portal is guarded by a clump of yews on the right (1.7, 4400). Here, by an early-season stream, you'll find a pleasant campsite known as Bridge Camp, situated 20 yards south of the bridge.

Beyond Bridge Camp, a short, moderate climb reaches a vigorous stream (0.3, 4570), from which you begin a gentle stroll up-valley over rolling terrain. After passing into a heavily brushed and flowered opening, the trail skips across three tiny but lasting springs in quick succession, then returns to the forest. Just short of a meadow deeply yellowed with goldenrods and Bigelow sneezeweeds, you come to a frequently used campsite with benches and firepit, perched near a branch of Granite Creek (0.7, 4720).

The trail switchbacks west-northwest to skirt the camp's fragile meadow, climbing briefly above it. Then you level off, stepping over a trio of seeping springs in a small brush patch, and begin a moderate climb through the forest. You pass another spring within the forest before arriving at a junction with the Blue Granite Lake Trail (0.6, 5020). The forest floor in this area is thickly vegetated and the trail junction is often overgrown. In particular, hikers coming *from* Blue Granite Lake or from Green or Gold Granite Lakes might conceivably miss this trail confluence.

Blue Granite Lake

To reach Blue Granite Lake, head south-southeast along the left fork. Walking along an alder-clogged branch of Granite Creek, you pass an overgrown campsite on the right 75 yards from the junction. After crossing this first fork of the creek, the path passes through many huckleberries and quickly comes to a crossing of a second fork. Now climbing south on a moderate-to-steep grade, the trail crosses the outlet gully of the tarn that lies just west of Blue Granite Lake, just before a final, extremely steep climb onto a bench (0.5, 5370). Here, lodgepole pines have suddenly come to dominate the patchy forest while huckleberry oaks and greenleaf manzanitas grow among the granitic outcrops.

As you curl east-southeast, the tarn can just be seen to the south-southwest. Although there are several apparent usage trails to the tarn, none is thoroughly established, and the shallow, brush-shored, pond-lily-blanketed pool offers little attraction. After momentarily winding along the bench, you descend very steeply to several campsites in a large wooded flat on Blue Granite Lake's shallow, grassy, southwest shore, just short of its inlet creek (0.4, 5270). The lake's beautiful setting beneath Peak 6864 and its fairly deep waters can be better enjoyed from the northeast shore, but the campsite there is well inside the 100-foot camping prohibition and should be left alone.

If your destination is to the other Granite Lakes, climb steeply southwest on the right fork from the Blue Granite Lake trail junction, switchbacking several times through the fecund, mixed-conifer forest to arrive at a clearly signed junction with the Green Granite Lake Trail (0.6, 5310). Heading south-southwest on this trail into a grassy breach in the forest cover, you soon come to a pipe-aided spring at the border of a large

Blue Granite Lake

incense-cedar grove, within which lies Granite Meadows campsite. At one time, this area received so much use that the Forest Service put in a pit toilet, located within a wishing-well-style housing, 55 yards southeast of a massive granitic boulder. Just 65 yards beyond the spring and back into the meadows, you pass another campsite, on your left.

Walking on through the meadow, you curve down to a quick creek crossing, then climb with increasing steepness through the lovage and huckleberry-dominated understory to the crest of a ridgelet. After easing its grade for a moment, the trail resumes its steep course until it levels off amid the suddenly lodgepole-pine-dominated forest. The semilevel trail now descends to a slight depression, and here you'll find a small, grassy campsite 25 yards off to your right. You may wonder why anyone has chosen to camp there but, as you walk up out of the depression to the morainal lip of Green Granite Lake's cramped north-northeast shore (0.7, 5570), you will see that the grassy flat is certainly the most "legal" if not also the most pleasant site.

Green and Gold Granite Lakes are small, relatively shallow lakes whose attraction

Green Granite Lake

lies in their abundant supply of trout and in the comparative solitude available at these less "flashy" lakes. If you follow the occasionally tree-blazed usage trail along Green's east shore and over to the north tip of lily-fringed Gold, you will find the large granitic outcrop there to provide far and away the best swimming and diving perch to be found at any of the Granite Lakes.

Ukonom Lake

For wilderness travelers approaching the Marbles from Interstate 5, the Granite Creek Trail provides the most convenient access to the considerable charms of Ukonom Lake and the Cuddihy Lakes. To reach these lakes, switchback north from the junction with the Green Granite Lake Trail, 9.1 miles from the trailhead. You soon cross a little spring bordered with pearly everlasting, wild ginger and Siberian candyflower, the last species having pleasantly edible leaves. Three more switchbacks aid the moderate-to-steep ascent and bring you out onto open slopes, clothed in bitter cherry and aromatic tobacco brush, and affording you a crowning view of the south and east as the glacier-sculpted Granite Lakes basin, split by Peak 6864, opens up below. Still climbing steadily, you re-enter a much sparser forest than the one you left, skip through a tiny gully with a spring, and come to a bustling creek (0.8, 5770).

Past the creek, curve away through lodgepole-pine-dominated forest. The lodgepole disappears as the trail bends back towards the creek, which now flows through a brush-filled meadow. Next, the trail switchbacks up across a small spur with a grassy, flowery meadow on your left. Winding from side to side up the spur, you can notice the distinct differences in vegetation on the opposing slopes: the northwest-facing slope is forested, albeit sparsely, while the southeast-facing slope is largely scrub. After a final series of wiggles, the trail arrives at a multisigned junction with the Ukonom-Cuddihy Lakes Trail (0.8, 6150). Ukonom Lake lies 2.1 miles to the northwest, Cuddihy Lakes an equal distance to the southeast.

If exploring the largest lake in the Marble Mountains Wilderness is your goal, turn northwest and begin switchbacking steeply up the rocky trail above the head of Granite

Creek's west cirque. Monardella and erio-gonums, all lovers of rocky, well-drained soils, now join the trailside garden. The trail then levels off to traverse above a pond-lily-choked tarn. Soon the tip of Mt. Shasta is just visible on the eastern horizon, poking over the north shoulder of Peak 6864 as you switchback briefly down to a sluggish creeklet on the south edge of a grassy mead-ow (0.5, 6320).

After skirting this tarn-dotted, dogleg meadow, the trail climbs sporadically into a forest of predominantly red fir. The pale green carpet growing in the gravelly, open areas is the low-lying elegant lupine, whose mat of silver-green, finely-haired, whorled leaves contributes to its overall color more than do its racemes of purple flowers. Less than 100 yards after the ascent becomes a descent, you meet the Tickner Creek Trail, coming in from the east-southeast (0.6, 6520).

From the junction, your descent into the glacier-scoured Ukonom Lake basin steepens considerably. The ameboid sprawl of the lake soon comes into view as you come out into open slopes of granitic outcrops. Gently now, the trail descends northwest then heads toward a linear, grassy meadow that stretch-es from the lake's northeast tip toward the gently sloping knob of Peak 6540. After angling into the meadow, you switchback in-to the woods and down to a faint trail junc-tion (0.9, 6090). The faint trail is traceable only by the series of ducks heading south. This is the One Mile-Ukonom Lakes Trail, a route more easily negotiated if begun at One Mile Lake (for a description of this trail, see Hike 9).

From the trail junction turn north-north-west and descend to the meadow's edge, then curve along a stand of firs and hem-locks to the lake shore (0.1, 6090). At 67 acres, Ukonom Lake has the largest surface area of any lake in the Marbles, due in large part to the man-made dam at its western tip, which aids and abets the terminal glacial moraine that created the lake. The dam, now deteriorating, was built in the late 1800s to divert water for use in a hydraulic-mine operation at the Bunker Hill Mine, near the Klamath River, 7 miles to the northwest.

The meadow along the northeast shore serves as pasture for the numerous horsemen who patronize this high-use lake, and spa-cious, well-developed campsites are just in-side the trees on either side of the meadow. Far better campsites, more private and esthetic, are found beneath red firs and lodgepole pines just in from the rocky penin-sula that juts out from the east shore. This rocky projection is perhaps the best place for swimming and fishing, though the water also deepens immediately from the rock-walled northwest shore.

Cuddihy Lakes

If you are more intrigued by the glacier-jigsawed Cuddihy Lakes basin, then take the left fork from the junction with the Granite Creek Trail, 10.7 miles from the Elk Creek trailhead. Begin south by snaking among the several bulges in the headwall of Granite Creek's basin. The trail follows the general arc of the headwall to the southeast, de-scending briefly along one spur to curl around a placid, huckleberry-bordered lily-pad pond (0.7, 5970). After descending gently along the pond's outlet creek, you cross it 0.2 mile beyond the pond, then be-gin to climb steeply, with the help of several short switchbacks, toward a saddle in the ridge between the Granite Lakes and Cuddi-hy Lakes. The climb eases momentarily to cross a dry gully that offers a snowpack in early season and sloppy footing in mid season, then pushes steeply on to the saddle (0.6, 6190).

Leaving the north-slope forest behind, you descend steeply south-southwest 275 yards through the dense shrubbery to a junction with the Haypress Trail. This trail to the Cuddihy Lakes, and the lakes them-selves are described in greater depth in Hike 9. For now, let it suffice that you turn northeast and descend 250 steep yards to the Cuddihy Lakes Trail (0.3, 5980).

For a trail to such a high-usage lake basin, the Cuddihy spur is often obscure to the point of being misleading. As long as you take the less obvious right fork at the barely apparent meadow junction, found in 0.2 mile, you can negotiate the gently descend-ing, remaining 0.3 mile by simply head-ing south. One last word of advice: the Cud-dihy Lakes basin is an area of such over-whelming enchantment that a simple day-hike or overnight jaunt cannot hope to do it justice.

Hike 6

Johnson's Hunting Ground—
Tickner Hole

Distance: 6.6 miles, one way
Low elevation: 4420'
High elevation: 6730'
Suited for: day trip
Usage: rare
Difficulty: strenuous

Directions to trailhead: Follow Elk Creek Road 11.1 miles, then, just before crossing a bridge to the east side of Elk Creek, take a right fork signed for *Johnson Hunting Ground*. Proceed on this all-weather road 0.6 mile to another right fork, signed for *Johnson Hunting Ground* and *Ukonom Lake*, which you follow 6 miles to a saddle. As the road switchbacks through the saddle to the east side of the ridge, you'll find your signed trailhead 40 yards southeast along a side road, just before an earth dam that marks the terminus of the Lick Creek Trail. Start hiking with full water bottles, since the first 3 trail miles are waterless.

Trail description: Switchbacking up the crest of Titus Ridge segment at an extraordinarily steep rate, the trail wastes no time

in introducing you to its essential character. After 0.6 mile, the mixed-conifer forest opens up as the ascent eases slightly amid mountain chaparral, then closes back in again. Above an isolated pair of short switchbacks, you climb steeply, then extremely steeply, first in a luscious patch of thimbleberries dotted with lavender spikes of fireweed, then into a sparsely vegetated forest. About ¼ mile beyond the thimbleberry patch, the trail breaks out onto an open slope (1.4, 5840), affording you expansive views west over the Coast Ranges.

Beyond this brief open traverse, a gently undulating descent through a white- and red-fir forest brings you out through a clump of knobcone pines onto a broad slope, densely scrub-covered. The gravelly texture of the soil and the occasional granitic boulders are evidence that you've crossed over into the area underlain by the Wooley Creek pluton and have left metamorphic rocks behind.

Traversing above the Independence Creek watershed, you climb past some evidence of former mine work—a rusty "phone box" and

Granite Lakes basin, from Johnson's Hunting Ground Trail

Black Mountain

wood planks (0.5, 5800)—then briefly pass through a fir grove. Next you climb steeply through knobcone-pine-bordered brush to reach the ridgetop with abundant tanbark-oak scrub and shrubby mountain mahogany.

As the trail crosses just over to the north side of the ridgecrest and climbs quite steeply for a short while, you can look northwest and see Preston Peak, in the High Siskiyous. When the climb levels out and you pass below a couple of small knobs, you might contrast the north-slope forest of red fir, western white pine and mountain hemlock with the knobcone-pine-dotted scrub of the south slope.

Curving from east to south, one passes just beneath a "summit" amid scattered clumps of scarlet gilia, whose red-orange, tubular blossoms put on a brilliant, though short-lived, show. As you begin to descend, ducks mark the sometimes indistinct trail as it passes through pinemat manzanita and sprawling mats of Davis' knotweed. Your route across the seldom traveled stretches of trailless soil is also marked by occasional earthen water bars.

Route finding becomes easier as the path descends steeply into full forest and curves southeast above a small gully, though it still requires some attention. After weaving over and between some rocky swells in the terrain, you turn east and pass a campsite, on your right (south), which is just short of a grassy, willow-thicketed meadow with a spring (1.1, 6000).

Past the campsite, turn south to climb steeply up the huckleberry-lined trail skirting this narrow meadow. Then several switchbacks aid a forested ascent to the crest of the northeast-trending spur of Peak 6463. Continuing your climb southwest now on a broad path cut into the dense cover of tobacco brush and manzanita, you quickly top out (0.5, 6350) just southeast of Peak 6463's broad summit. The ground cover opens here and the trail becomes difficult to follow as it curves south-southwest over this high point in the trail and begins to descend. A blazed tree, 40 yards into the descent, marks the route, and soon another broad swath cut into the dense scrub clearly indicates the trail.

As you descend steeply south, you'll see Black Mountain's precipitous west escarpment standing majestically in the east-southeast. In the opposite direction, on an exceptionally clear day, you might make out a slight V of the Pacific Ocean, which fills a Coast Range notch to the west-southwest. You follow the crest of Peak 6463's southern spur as it bends to the south-southeast. Gradually, the forest returns and thickens as you drop to a saddle (0.6, 5690), from which the abandoned Independence Valley Trail once descended west.

From the saddle, you momentarily climb south up the crest, then ease over to its east slope to descend extremely steeply on a narrow, unstable trail. The grade eases as you near the valley bottom of Tickner Creek, finally leveling out at the junction with the Tickner Creek Trail (0.7, 5310). Hikers who wanted the path of least resistance to Tickner Hole and therefore followed the Elk Creek/Granite Creek/Tickner Creek trails from Sulphur Springs, arrive here from the north-northeast after 7.1 miles along their route.

Starting south-southeast from the trail junction, you immediately step across the burbling thread of Tickner Creek and bend south through a magnificent wildflower garden. Just 120 yards past the creek crossing, as you follow your trail along the east edge of the meadow, you'll meet a side trail that leads right, passing through an opening in the alders, 10 yards to a creekside campsite under mountain hemlocks. Having just descended through a mixed-conifer forest, you are now traveling through a well-established forest inversion due to cold-air drainage in the Tickner Creek valley, for the forest through which you now walk includes mountain hemlock, red fir and western white pine, all from the normally higher red-fir belt.

After a 250-yard walk beyond the campsite spur trail, you angle across the meadow on a very faint, steep tread, first heading west-southwest, then bending southwest.

Your path is marked by ducks but, by midsummer, they are often obscured in the tall grasses; you might want to use your compass, if only for security. Continue climbing steeply west-southwest along a finger of the meadow before turning into the woods for 50 yards to an isolated, linear patch of scrub, along whose southeast border you climb 140 yards before returning to the woods above the meadow. After gently descending, you reach the first of several marshy tarns that dot Tickner Hole (0.6, 5660).

Staying within the open forest of lodgepoles, western white pines and incensecedars, you skirt the west edge of the tarn's meadow, making your way through a standup feast of huckleberries in late summer. After stepping over a tiger-lily-bordered creeklet that vanishes by midsummer, you begin climbing south up a hillock. This ascent is across predominantly granitic outcrops, which make route-finding tedious at times. Watch carefully for trailside ducks.

Next you move briefly west along the north edge of another hillock, then turn south and struggle up an extremely steep path to its top, where you'll find several weeping spruces among the sparse covering of predominantly lodgepole pines. After a

A Tickner Hole tarn

momentary descent, resume a steep ascent on your often rocky, sometimes boggy, occasionally poorly marked trail, finally arriving at a deeply eroded creeklet at the edge of a multifingered meadow (1.1, 6280).

The trail becomes extremely obscure as you follow partly hidden ducks, first south up a narrow strip of grass, then southwest above a willow thicket for a few paces, and finally south again up a slight path through marsh marigolds. Watching closely for ducks, you climb extremely steeply through a gap in the trees to a small, open flat. By walking south across the flat for 50 yards, you'll reach a small, lily-pad tarn (0.1, 6380) with a small sleeping space cleared off near its shore. This is probably the most convenient, if not the most luxurious, camping spot in the Tickner Hole area. Of the numerous ponds in Tickner Hole, two received sufficient use at one time to be given names and therefore be dubbed as lakes. Tickner and Snyder lakes are a devil to get to. Should you be sufficient master of the map and compass to make the effort, however, you are virtually assured of your privacy, even on a Fourth of July weekend.

Ukonom Lake

If you get lonely or need a bit more elbow room in your swimming pool, continue climbing on sketchy tread south-southwest from the open flat near the lily-pad tarn in Tickner Hole. After you work your way up to the diminutive head of the valley (0.1, 6460), stay on the west side of a trailless, grassy strip until you come abreast of a large, white-veined, dark, granitic boulder, near the foot of the headwall. Here the route turns sharply west-northwest, cutting through an opening in the young trees on the perimeter and finding a duck-marked trail climbing into the woods. The trail now is obvious as it winds up a ridiculously steep path to the ridgetop (0.2, 6740).

A west-northwest descent, nearly as steep as the ascent, brings you to a junction with the Ukonom-Cuddihy Lakes Trail (0.2, 6520). Continuing northwest for one mile brings you to the meadowy northeast shore of Ukonom Lake, with large campsites on each forested edge of the meadow, and smaller, more pleasant sites (with better access to swimmable, fishable water) just in from the rocky promontory on its east shore. For a further description of the Ukonom-Cuddihy Lakes Trail and Ukonom Lake, see the side-trips section at the end of Hike 5.

Ukonom Lake. Its better campsites are just in from the rocky peninsula that juts out from the east shore.

Chapter 7

Ukonom District

Introduction: To distinguish the Ukonom district from its mates, one might look to its past rather than at its topography or natural attractions, for, more than any other area in the Marbles, the land of the Ukonom district was Indian country. Indeed, Sugarloaf Mountain, the wedge-shaped monolith that towers above the village of Somes Bar, was held by the Karok Indians to be the Center of the Earth. Tribal shamans had prophesied that when the waters of the Klamath River ate the last of Sugarloaf Mountain, the world would come to an end. Medicine Mountain, which cleaves the courses of Bridge and Wooley creeks, was considered a power mountain, to which the shaman would go to commune with the gods and seek strength for his people. The Jump Dance and the Deerskin Dance, ceremonies to re-create and regenerate the world, were held at various spots along this district's south-flowing section of the Klamath River.

Actually, it's not entirely accurate to refer to the presence of the Karok in the past tense. Karok people still live up and down the river, and they still perform the Jump Dance and the Deerskin Dance each spring and fall, respectively, in their traditional locations. And elder tribesmen still make pilgrimages to the various power mountains in the area. But their influence has waned, particularly in dealing with the Federal government, which built the Ukonom Ranger Station on the site of a former Karok village. An even graver insult was building a lookout tower on Medicine Mountain, which the Forest Service finally removed in 1979.

It could be said that a white man connected with the Ukonom district had the greatest influence on the area and, in fact, on the entire wilderness. In 1925, the Wooley Camp Association, a small group of private citizens which included Herbert Hoover and Stanford University president Ray Lyman Wilbur, purchased the parcel of land several miles up Wooley Creek that is still known as Wooley Camp. Hoover was an avid fisherman, and he made several trips up Wooley Creek and in to Onemile Lake. After he assumed the Presidency in 1929, he appointed Wilbur as his Secretary of the Interior, and together they were in part responsible for the decision to establish a Marble Mountain Primitive Area in 1931.

As for the attractions of the Ukonom district, its lakes are some of the most inviting in the wilderness, the district emphasizing quality rather than quantity. The Bridge Creek canyon, particularly in the area of Cedar Flat, offers a peerless facsimile of the forest primeval, not to mention access to Medicine Mountain and its staircase to the heavens. Furthermore, the Forest Service touts Wooley Creek as being "one of the clearest streams in California," and it is the only tributary of the Klamath and Salmon rivers within the Marbles to support both a spring run of king salmon and a population of summer steelhead. Finally, since the Ukonom district is relatively distant from the regional population centers, it is not heavily used—although the Haypress Trail gets enough traffic at times to almost warrant underpass-overpass construction at some of its lake-trail junctions.

Access: The Ukonom district is located in the southwest sector of the wilderness and hence is more convenient to the coast and an approach from Eureka. It is little more than 80 miles from State Highway 299's junction with US 101 near Arcata to the junction of State Highway 96 and Forest Highway 93 at Somes Bar. It is ¼ mile farther north on Highway 96 to the Somes Bar business district—the general store—and another ¼ mile beyond that to the Ukonom Ranger Station, on the east side of the highway.

The ranger station maintains fairly conventional hours for obtaining wilderness permits and information: 8 a.m. to 6 p.m. seven days a week during the summer, and 8 a.m. to 4:30 p.m. weekdays during the remainder of the year. The Ti Bar guard station, several miles north of Somes Bar and just up FS 13N11, is also a possible summer-season resource for permits. However it is not always "manned," and is convenient only to those coming from the north who intend to take a shortcut up FS 13N11 to the Haypress Meadows trailheads.

There are several possible routes for getting from Highway 96 to the trailheads clustered around the western projection of the wilderness that contains Haypress Meadows. To simplify matters, however, all the "directions to trailhead" begin with FS 15N17, which leaves Forest Highway 93 0.1 mile east of State Highway 96. This is not only the best-maintained road to these trailheads, but also well-signed; every road junction that could possibly cause confusion is marked with destination and, usually, road number sign. The Wooley Creek and Portuguese Peak trailheads are farther east and are fully described in their respective hike descriptions.

There are presently two possibilities for pre-hike camping near the trailheads. Camp 3, located 9.8 miles up FS 15N17, stretches for a couple of hundred yards along both sides of the road. Water is hidden in a small creek in the brush east of the road. The Oak Bottom Campground, more convenient to the Wooley Creek and Portuguese Peak trailheads, is 2.3 miles east from Highway 96 on Forest Highway 93. The Forest Service expects to begin construction of its Sugar Pine trailhead and camping area, on the wilderness' west border north of Stanshaw Meadows, sometime in 1980. Don't expect it to be open for public use before 1981.

The Trails: The Haypress Meadows area, filling the western "peninsula" of the wilderness, probably has more meadowlands per square inch of map than any other part of the wilderness. For, unlike the more common valley-bottom and valley-head meadows, whose borders are delimited by the extreme local relief, the meadows of the Haypress area are relatively unbounded, oozing across the landscape like some great floral ameba. Whether you come in April or October, there will be some species, and more likely some dozen species, of wildflowers to delight your eye and camera.

An area as special as this might be expected to be laced with trails, and it is—though it was the utility of the meadows, and not their beauty, that brought the early settlers up from all directions. There still remains one small summer-range allotment, west of Haypress Meadows. Only a few years ago, there were five distinct trailheads for Haypress Meadows. Three of them, and their respective trails, are described in the Haypress Meadows Trails, Hike 7: Ten Bear Trail, from the northwest, and Haypress and Let 'er Buck trails from the south.

A fourth, the Stanshaw Meadows Trail from the west, was still in service in 1979. However, this trail stands to be relocated, in conjunction with the creation of the Sugar Pine trailhead, and the existing tread will be abandoned.

The Haypress Trail is the Ukonom district's main trail. According to the 1975-76 usage figures, well over 80% of the visitors to the Ukonom district passed through Haypress Meadows. Of these, over 75% came in via Camp 4, the trailhead for the Haypress Trail. Consequently, it is well-maintained and easily followed. The Ten Bear and Let 'er Buck trails don't receive nearly as much attention from trail crews or backpackers. Some of their meadow crossings are worthy of the Everglades; nearly all of them require a compass since the trail description can do no more than give the compass bearing that will reunite you with established trail. Another reason the Haypress Trail is the major thoroughfare is that it represents the quickest route between two points: the trailheads and the lakes. With the exception of Pleasant Lake, all the district's lakes that are accessible by trail are most directly reached by the Haypress Trail. With the additional exception of Secret Lake, all these lakes receive high use.

That may be why God created Wooley and Bridge creeks, as a resource for quietude. If you look at a topographic map of the entire wilderness, Wooley Creek looks like the soft underbelly. No rugged mountains, no glacier-gouged cirques with lake basins. Just streams and trees—no big deal. Yet the farther up Wooley Creek you travel, the closer you come to what is the most extensive wilderness area in the Marbles: the upper Wooley Creek drainage. This is Wilderness. As in wild. As in untamed. As in untrammeled and untouched. This is where the wildlife go when they want to "get away from it all."

Even where there are trails along these creeks, they are neglected (again, by trail crews and backpackers alike). This is because you can't "see anything" on them, as in "wow, what a view from here!" The Cedar Flat-Pleasant Lake hike is for those who want to be weaned gradually from high-country hypnosis. You can bury yourself in "visionless" forest, yet still be within a couple hours' walk of the summit of Medicine Mountain and the subalpine beauty of Pleasant Lake.

The Wooley Creek Trail is nothing but creek trail. It seems like you'll see more poison oak and rattlesnakes than anything else. And first-class swimming holes and good-eatin' trout. Up to now, the trail has received only moderate use, and then rarely beyond Fowler Cabin, near the wilderness boundary. Once across the North Fork of Wooley Creek, the trail is managed by the Scott River district as a primitive trail, an example of that district's famed low-impact-maintenance program. You need a machete as one of your Ten Essentials. The usage of Wooley Creek is likely to increase, however. In 1979, the trail above the North Fork was opened up another 3 miles to connect with the Big Meadows Trail of the Salmon River district. David Atwood, recreation resource officer for the Ukonom district, is promoting a packstock loop that will climb up the Wooley and Big Meadows trails, then swing through the Salmon River district past English Peak and Crapo Meadows, and exit the wilderness on the Portuguese Peak Trail. It is a rigorous, wonderfully varied route.

The Portuguese Peak Trail is rarely used because, despite its remarkable vistas, it takes much work with too little water. It is indeed a strenuous route, and there is no water for nearly 7½ miles. If that weren't enough to keep people away, the ridge along which the trail runs served as the fire line during the vast 1977 Hog Fire—your surroundings are conspicuously toasted in places. What price are you willing to pay for solitude? Yet, if Atwood's loop becomes popular, not even here will you be assured of isolation.

Hike 7:   Haypress Meadows Trails

Let 'er Buck Trail

Distance: 1.7 miles, one way
Low elevation: 4440'
High elevation: 4910'
Suited for: day trip
Usage: low
Difficulty: moderate

Directions to trailhead: Take FS 15N17 for 12.4 miles to FS 13N04, forking right. Follow 13N04 for 1.8 miles to a junction, turn left on 13N04A, and follow it 0.9 mile to its end at the trailhead.

Trail description: After a brief, extremely steep climb through a cutblock, the trail climbs sporadically along a broad ridge through a mixed-conifer forest. After ¾ mile the climb tops out in a forested saddle. You descend steeply to an isolated wing of Haypress Meadows, then, after climbing easily up along erosion channels of a meadow finger, pass through a slight, forested saddle and descend gently into Let 'er Buck Meadow.

After passing through a scattering of lodgepole pines that border the meadow, you cross a single brook at the meadow's edge, then shortly cross a series of trickles that overrun the trail within a thicket of alder, cascara and American dogwood. You then hike 130 yards through patchy forest and drop slightly to the meadow edge again. Despite the appearance of a trail continuing along the east border of the meadow, your route mucks across the meadow, heading 280° toward an apparent opening in the forest opposite you. Within the forest again, the trail curls up to a gravelly opening with pussypaws and lupine, then passes through a band of trees into another sector of Haypress Meadows. The tread fades out here, but several paces across the meadow bring you to a junction with the Haypress Trail (1.7, 4730).

Haypress Trail

Distance: 2.3 miles, one way
Low elevation: 4460'

High elevation: 4840'
Suited for: day trip
Usage: extremely high
Difficulty: moderate

Directions to trailhead: Follow FS 15N17 for 13.5 miles to its junction with FS 15N17E, which turns sharply right and is signed for Camp 4. After 1.2 miles on 15N17E, an unsigned left fork goes 40 yards uphill to an insufficient parking area at the Camp 4 trailhead. Despite the name, there is no camp here.

Trail description: After climbing steeply through the brush of a small cutblock and into a mixed-conifer forest, the trail passes the wilderness boundary in ¼ mile and eases its ascent to contour along the southeast slopes of Peak 5282.

Beyond a small, splashing creeklet, you begin a more rolling course along the steep hillside, whose slopes are liberally clothed with thimbleberries and whose depressions occasionally cradle intermittent streams. After dropping through a fir forest to the edge of an isolated patch of Haypress Meadows, bridge a brook and follow a forest-border path to a boulder crossing of Haypress Creek (2.0, 4680). From a large and lovely campsite on the creek's north bank, the hiker then rolls through red firs and mountain hemlocks to an obscurely signed and somewhat vague junction with the Stanshaw Meadows Trail (0.3, 4720).

Ten Bear Trail

Distance: 4.7 miles, one way
Low elevation: 4600'
High elevation: 5240'
Suited for: day trip
Usage: rare
Difficulty: moderate

Directions to trailhead: Follow FS 15N17, past the turnoffs for Let 'er Buck and Camp 4 trailheads, for 19.9 miles. Ten Bear trailhead is located on the right side of the road, opposite a junction with FS 14N01.

Trail description: You climb steeply ¼ mile through luxuriant mixed-conifer forest to a blocked-off logging road. Starting east-southeast, follow the road 135 yards to where ducks mark a trail heading steeply uphill through a cutblock; this "trailhead" is 35 yards after the road has curved through the head of a gully. After winding through the cutblock, you are rewarded with a vast panorama of the Siskiyou Range. The not-so-distant peak directly to the north is Ten Bear Mountain, for which this trail is named. The route traverses roughly east above the cutblock a few moments before arcing south and descending gently into fir forest.

The trail makes an easy descent to a broad saddle, then undulates along the east slope of Peak 5387. It then drops steeply south-southwest into a gully and curves down to the alder-bordered northwest tip of Ti Creek Meadows (1.5, 5020). The tread disappears as you exit from the alders and follow the southwest edge of the meadow. You'll pick up the trail again as it passes through a constriction in the meadow. About 200 yards beyond the constriction, the trail appears to angle south into the knee-high grasses of the meadow. However, you want to head south-southeast across the boggy, bilberry-filled meadow, aiming for the right side of an island of firs near its far edge. Beyond the clump of firs, you aim toward a blazed tree to cross a narrow band of meadow and head up into the forest.

The forest eventually gives way to large, trailless Ross Meadows. Heading southeast, point for the left edge of the alder thicket at the far side of the meadow. As you reach the alders, turn southwest; a faint trail becomes more obvious as it heads into the edge of the forest. The trail soon turns and climbs steeply past Sadler oaks, crosses a flat-topped rise,

then descends steeply to a junction with the abandoned Ti Creek Trail (1.0, 5190).

From the junction, you quickly reach the edge of Albers Meadows and, after descending briefly along a corridor through the alders, turn south-southeast to cross it. Entering the woods at the meadows' south edge, climb momentarily, then descend to a large, sloping campsite, known as Jawbone Camp. About 100 yards beyond the log crossing of Jawbone Camp's sluggish creek, you reach a junction with the Stanshaw Meadows Trail (0.6, 5030).

As you turn east-southeast onto this trail, you might notice the forest of red fir, mountain hemlock and western white pine into which you have descended. It is indicative of the cold-air-sink inversion so common in the Haypress Meadows area. After dropping through thick growths of Sadler oaks and huckleberries, the trail makes two closely spaced crossings of the creek from Jawbone Camp, then begins a gentle descent, which steepens as it approaches the westernmost outpost of Haypress Meadows. After strolling along the meadow's west edge a while, angle across the meadow to boulder-hop the creek once again. The trail follows the creek for several minutes, then eventually bends away to the northeast to make a short climb over a small spur. After descending to follow a faint trail south-southeast across a finger of meadow, you take a log across a meadow-edge brook, then make a short, steep climb to a small saddle and a junction with the McCash Trail (1.3, 4790).

Descending easily southeast from the saddle, you soon come into a meandering meadow and the skimpy log crossing Haypress Creek, beyond which a brief climb into the edge of a red-fir grove brings you to a junction with the Haypress Trail (0.3, 4720).

Ti Creek Meadows

Hike 8: Haypress—McCash Trails Loop

Distance: 11.6 miles, semiloop trip
Low elevation: 4460'
High elevation: 6186'
Suited for: weekend trip
Usage: rare on McCash Trail, high elsewhere
Difficulty: moderate

Directions to trailhead: See Haypress Trail.

Trail description: After an initial steep climb for 1/3 mile, you contour easily below the summit of Peak 5282, following the forested trail to a crossing of Haypress Creek (2.0, 4680). One-third mile beyond this ford, you come to an obscure trail junction on the southeastern border of Haypress Meadows (0.3, 4720). A more detailed description of this trail segment is found on page 68.

At this point a meadow loop begins that will return you to this trail junction in 7.0 miles. The trail description follows a clockwise route around the loop, since in this direction the climb to Peak 6186 is more gradual, and a first-night camp in the Big Meadow-Long Meadow area is more likely to be unvisited than one in more accessible Round Meadow.

Following a brief stretch of the Stanshaw Trail, you fork northeast across a slender band of meadow to a forested campsite. Turning left (west-northwest) just inside the forest border, you descend 65 yards to the inadequate log crossing of Haypress Creek, then head northwest back into the forest. Climbing easily, you soon come to a trail junction in a small saddle (0.3, 4790). The Stanshaw Trail continues straight ahead to trailheads on the western boundary; you take the McCash Trail north-northwest and descend to the edge of another wing of Haypress Meadows. After following the border of the sprawling meadow, the trail makes a brief, moderate climb over a lupine-matted ridgelet to a seldom used campsite in the forest border (0.3, 4810). This is the only established campsite until you reach Round Meadows, 5.0 miles farther.

Shortly beyond the campsite, the trail pops out of the woods. In a curious move, practiced in several locations in the greater Haypress Meadows area, the Forest Service has abandoned a trail that circled around Big Meadows in favor of cutting directly across the boggy swale. Taking aim northwest through a cutout in a fallen log, head toward the brushy edge of a northwest-trending finger of the meadow. Although it is less than 100 yards across, you can expect at least one of the apparently sturdy tussocks of grass to give way beneath you before you reach the other side, so prepare yourself for mucky feet.

Continuing northwest along the meadow's edge, you pick up the tread again just to the right of two large, closely spaced red firs. By now you've probably become aware of the vegetative inversion that cold-air drainage has created in the Haypress Meadows area, but nowhere is it more marked than here. The red-fir belt's red and white firs, mountain hemlocks and lodgepole pines fringe the meadow; yet, not 50 yards up the gently rising slope, the open forest consists of incense-cedars, ponderosa and sugar pines, and Douglas-firs—all constituents of the normally lower-elevation mixed-conifer forest.

Just after the linear meadow bends toward the northeast, you cut through a break in the brush to cross a meadow and a shallow creeklet, then climb briefly north-northwest into the forest. After crossing a slight saddle, you make a quick plunge down to the dashing creeklet of pristine, bilberry-thicketed Long Meadow (0.6, 4860). The most practical route here skirts the nearby southern end of the meadow, crosses the creek where it is easily hopped then heads north to locate the ducked and blazed trail as it enters the forest.

Indistinct at times, the trail undulates through the forest above Long Meadow before arcing around its north end and leaving the Haypress Meadows area behind to begin an extraordinarily steep ascent along a lushly forested gully toward Peak 5886. It is almost too steep for one to enjoy either the singing creeklet of early summer or the sweet fruit of late summer's thimbleberries and huckleberries. The climb eases momentarily as the gully dies out in an open band

Thimbleberry

of mixed scrub, then a final intense burst through the forest brings you up to the ridgecrest (1.5, 5640).

Here you stroll easily past Sadler oak, tobacco brush and pinemat manzanita, but the climbing soon resumes. Ascending in stages toward Peak 5886, you momentarily contour above the head of a gully, finally leveling off on the ridgecrest just east of the peak's summit (0.4, 5850). In another 100 yards the trail reaches granitic boulders at a window through the brush and trees, the perfect spot to rest your weary bones and survey the high relief of the Ukonom Creek drainage. The Salmon Mountains in this area show their granitic constitution with bold outcrops in their forested flanks. The botanical variance between north- and south-facing slopes is evidenced here by the usually low-to-mid-elevation sugar pines just off the crest on its warmer, drier south face and the upper-elevation mountain hemlocks and weeping spruces reaching toward the crest on its north face.

Following the bouldery, scrub-covered ridgecrest, you traverse well above hemmed-in McCash Lake. With increasing elevation, the view opens behind you: north-northwest

down the McCash Fork toward the crest of the Siskiyou Mountains and west across a sea of ridges to the distant Coast Ranges. With increasing steepness the trail ascends to the flat-topped summit of Peak 6186 (1.3, 6186). Leaving the brush behind, the forested descent ends in 250 yards at a junction with the Haypress Trail. If you want some lake play on this trip—or if you aren't paying attention—you'll continue east-northeast past this easily overlooked junction onto Sandy Ridge and in 1.2 miles reach the 0.4-mile spur trail descending to Monument Lake.

To complete the loop back to Haypress Meadows, make an acute right turn and follow the level trail through the forest. You quickly break out into the open to contour above the old, undiscernible Pickle Camp site, hiking through scattered manzanita and Sadler oak. Back in an open stand of red fir, a brief, gentle ascent brings one to a broad saddle (0.4, 6070).

Through tobacco brush and manzanita, dogbane and elegant lupine, the trail de-

Dogbane

scends steeply from the saddle. Some 100 yards after a single switchback, you enter a scrub-coated south slope, and pass a delightful spring splashing out of the foliage above the trail. An obvious sleeping space neighbors the spring. Shortly after reaching forest cover, you come to an unsigned trail junction (0.7, 5580). Here a trail sweeps precipitously 0.1 mile down to an elaborate campsite on the edge of Round Meadow. A luscious creeklet runs through the middle of this moist, exquisitely flowered meadow.

Beyond the Round Meadows Trail, the descent steepens through the increasingly lush forest before finally breaking free of the forest at a trail junction just inside Halfmoon Meadow (0.7, 5070). A sharp left turn onto the trail to the southeast leads down to Cedar Flat and Bridge Creek. Twen-

ty yards down this trail, an obvious path cuts right 75 yards to cross Halfmoon Creek to an open campsite.

From the junction, the Haypress Trail bends west-northwest, immediately crossing Halfmoon Creek on a plank bridge, and a slender finger of Halfmoon Meadow. Climbing briefly into a forest of red and white firs, you reach a shallow saddle, then steeply descend along the crest of a minor ridge. Coming into the lupine-coated upper end of a Haypress Meadows spur, you descend easily past the obscure junction with the Let 'er Buck Trail, then, 80 yards farther, complete the loop at the junction with the Stanshaw Trail (0.8, 4720). Turning west-southwest, you leave Haypress Meadows behind to retrace your initial 2.3 miles to the Camp 4 trailhead.

Hike 9:   Onemile and Cuddihy Lakes

Distance: 9.1 miles, one way to Onemile Lake
9.1 miles, one way to Cuddihy Lake

Low elevation: 4460'

High elevation: 6410'

Suited for: 2-3 days

Usage: high

Difficulty: moderate

Directions to trailhead: Same as on page 68.

Trail description: The Haypress Trail climbs steeply for 1/3 mile, then traverses high above the defile of Haypress Creek. The creek gradually climbs up to meet the relatively level path in an outrider of Haypress Meadows. One-third mile beyond the crossing of Haypress Creek, we reach an ill marked trail junction at the edge of Haypress Meadows (2.3, 4720). This segment of the Haypress Trail is described in greater detail on page 68.

After curving east to cross a narrow band of meadow, we tread its northern edge, quickly passing an obscure junction with the Let 'er Buck Trail, then we climb quickly in-

to a lodgepole-pine-bordered fir forest. The trail weaves, sometimes quite steeply, up the crest of a minor ridge for ½ mile before passing between two small knobs and dropping briefly to a slender finger of Halfmoon Meadow. Immediately after crossing the meadow and vigorous Halfmoon Creek, one reaches a signed junction with the trail to Cedar Flat (0.8, 5070). Just 20 yards down this right fork, a usage trail heads 75 yards into the meadow to a campsite on the far side of Halfmoon Creek.

Taking the left fork, you climb steeply through a thickly greeneried forest to an unsigned junction with the Round Meadow spur trail (0.7, 5580). This 0.1-mile spur drops 100 vertical feet as it curls down to a highly developed campsite on the edge of Round Meadow. With a chilly creeklet running through its midsection, this little-visited, splendidly flowered meadow is a treat.

As you continue the taxing ascent, the forest gradually gives way to south-slope scrub. The regal blossoms of the Washington lily may highlight the path as you work up to the welcome reward offered by a slight

Monument Lake and Medicine Mountain, from Haypress Trail

spring trickling out of the hillside just above the trail (0.4, 5840). If you are heading directly for Onemile or Cuddihy Lakes, stock up on water here, since the ridgecrest trail has no dependable source of water after the snow melts. In another 0.3 mile the trail crosses the lupine- and manzanita-mantled saddle that marks the end of your rigors. The level path passes briefly through an open stand of red firs, then contours through open scrub above the site of abandoned Pickle Camp. Back in the forest, you soon arrive at a junction with the McCash Trail (0.6, 6070), which turns sharply west toward Peak 6186.

After continuing on the level, largely forested trail along inappropriately named Sandy Ridge, you begin a gradual climb, eventually breaking out near the ridgecrest into a gullied, gravelly opening, skimpily flowered with lupine, pussypaws and Cascade aster. After curving up the south slope of a spur ridge, the trail passes a dry, unrecommended campsite on the spur crest just off to the right. The author does recommend that you drop your pack and walk out a few yards beyond the campsite to a rocky point with superb views out

over the upper Bridge Creek canyon. Medicine Mountain, to the southeast, seems almost close enough to touch and, off to the east-northeast, Black and Marble mountains highlight the crest.

A level traverse of the northeast side of the spur brings you out onto a narrow, rocky ridgecrest, along which you soon come to a junction with the Monument Lake spur trail (1.2, 6180). This 0.4-mile trail rapidly descends a wildly flowered slope, passing a large, wooded campsite on the left about midway to the lake's meadowed northwest shore. Of the two large campsites here, the one on the left gives this charming, cirque-cupped lake the most breathing room. The vicinity of the sluggish outlet creek has the least pleasurable swimming and an illegally close campsite, but it has the best crop of huckleberries.

From the Monument Lake Trail junction, you begin a gentle, then moderate, wooded climb toward an east-trending spur. The path contours along its west side, then descends slightly to the narrow ridgecrest. As the crest and trail bend north to northeast, you reach a saddle and a junction with the Meteor Lake Trail (1.0, 6200). This seldom maintained trail loses nearly 500 feet in elevation in its precipitous 0.4-mile drop to the grassy north shore of the lake. A more pleasing campsite, both esthetically and ecologically, is located on the south shore, 0.1 mile beyond the huckleberry-bilberry-bordered outlet creek.

Climbing moderately northeast from the saddle of the trail junction, you can look down at the headwaters of Bridge Creek canyon, on your right, and Secret Valley, on your left. As the trail traverses the south slope of Peak 6523, it levels off and then descends gently to a scrub-covered saddle. Climbing gradually again, you cross an open slope and soon reach a ridgecrest junction with the Bridge Creek Trail, on your right, and a few paces farther, the Secret Lake Trail, on your left (1.4, 6400).

Onemile Lake

To reach Onemile Lake, as popular as it is large, descend on Secret Lake Trail a bone-jarring half mile to a junction with the Ukonom-Onemile Lakes Trail, which heads north from the edge of a small, sloping meadow. You continue straight ahead along the meadow's edge and curve west into the woods, reaching an unmarked trail junction in 85 yards. Although the more obvious trail continues straight ahead, it has long since been abandoned and it soon dies out. Take the path to the left, which meanders through the undergrowth, passing a usage trail in 110 yards that forks left to cross the inlet creek. Curving west on the main trail, you soon approach the first of a string of campsites along the east shore of the lake (0.7, 5760).

The southern half of hourglass-shaped Onemile Lake is a backpacker's and horse-packer's mecca, and hundreds make the pilgrimage here every summer. For relative seclusion, fresh water, and access to the lake's best swimming, found along the south end under the headwall, walk toward the campsites along the southeast shore. The spacious campsite near the waist of the lake is quite popular with horsefolk. Virtually all the campsites are inside the 200-foot no-camping zone, and since you are unable to obey the letter of the law, give heed to its spirit. The northern half of the lake has no

Onemile Lake

established campsites, but you'll enjoy the small rocky island off the west shore near the lake's neck.

Cuddihy Lakes

An equally popular destination for travelers of the Haypress Trail is the marvelously glacier-sculpted basin of the Cuddihy Lakes. To reach these lakes, follow the crest trail beyond the Secret Lake Trail junction on an initially steep descent. The easternmost Cuddihy Lake comes into view below as you begin a gentle climb, and Mt. Shasta can be seen peeking over a distant ridgetop in the east.

The trail levels off as you bend west into a slight north-facing cove, whose lushly vegetated ecosystem is vastly different from the scrub you arc back into as the descent resumes to a junction with the Ukonom-Cuddihy Lakes Trail (0.8, 6080). This trail heads north-northeast back to the crest, then drops to a junction with the Granite Creek Trail in 1.5 miles and, 2.1 miles farther, drops to the shore of Ukonom Lake.

The Haypress Trail continues the steep descent 225 yards to a junction with the Cuddihy Lakes Trail, which drops off to the

Cuddihy Lakes basin

right. This plummeting spur arcs to the east for 0.2 mile to an unsigned trail junction just beyond a massive cairn in the middle of a meadow. If you continue straight ahead 150 yards, you will come to a pipe spring and campsite just inside a patch of woods. This is an often used horsepackers' site, favored for its ample grazing area. To reach the lakes, however, follow the fainter tread forking right, which meanders indistinctly south 1/3 mile to a spacious campsite on the north tip of the northernmost lake (0.7, 5660).

The major campsites in the Cuddihy Lakes basin are located along the north and northwest shore of this first lake. Beyond the first lake, the scant camping opportunities are little more than sleeping niches scratched into the gravelly flats among the billows of bedrock. Regardless of which lake you visit, you'll find that the swimming is superb, with diving rocks, 10 to 20 feet high, in several places. And the setting is divine, for the Cuddihy Lakes basin is an area of splendid and unique glacial craftwork. Although a jorney to the Cuddihy Lakes can be accomplished as an overnight trip, you do yourself an injustice if you don't take at least an extra day to explore this wilderness wonderland.

Secret Lake

One would think that in the name alone, Secret Lake would have enough mystique to attract hordes of wilderness wanderers in search of seclusion. Yet its usage is low, perhaps due to the poorly maintained trail and to the stiff climb over the ridge between Secret Valley and Onemile Lake.

Starting from the log crossing at the waist of Onemile Lake, hike an almost level path near the southwest shore of the lake's northern half. Approaching the island, the path curves west away from the lake and begins a ridiculously steep climb up a sometimes indecipherable trail to the ridgetop (0.4, 6020). Switchbacking down the gravelly, somewhat more visible trail, you descend the ridge's southwest slope through scrub, then meadow, then well-vegetated forest, to a boulder-hop of a sluggish creeklet (0.5, 5640). After crossing a second, more assertive creeklet, the trail turns to descend along its dank, jungled west bank. You cross a third creeklet as you approach the brushy edge of the

Secret Lake

forest-deep trail so welcoming that it is a lovely walk even if you have no intention of going to Ukonom Lake.

This lower trail heads north from its junction with the Secret Lake Trail, soon descending moderately to a broad, gently sloping meadow (0.2, 5780). After skirting the bilberry-bordered brush at the far end of the meadow, you descend gradually into a white-fir-dominated, mixed-conifer forest, then begin a steady, gentle-to-moderate ascent through the scantily understoried woods. The quiet is extraordinary; the only sounds are the muffled rush of Onemile Creek far below and the impatient scolding of an occasional Douglas squirrel.

The trail's gradient steepens in stages before coming out into an opening with views out over Onemile Creek's canyon toward the Coast Ranges (1.3, 6150). Then it drops through a thick growth of gooseberries to a gurgling bit of a stream choked with water-loving flora. The vegetation thins as you climb out of the moist, chilly microclimate of the well-enclosed depression and begin a rollercoastering traverse of multigullied slopes. A switchback-aided burst of extremely steep climbing reaches the high point of the trail, from which you descend, at first moderately and then gently. A final brief climb through a dry-soil garden brings you to the ridgecrest overlooking spacious Ukonom Lake (1.4, 6290).

Bending eastward around the ridge, you pick your way carefully down the winding, rocky trail. The path drops into the forest and meanders gradually down to a lodgepole-pine-bordered flat. Skirting Ukonom Lake's boggy south shore, the trail crosses a pair of creeklets, then follows the border of a small floral flat to round the lake's southeast point. Sandwiched between willow thickets and forest, you begin a short climb of a hillock, then follow the sketchy, duck-marked tread 65 yards to a junction with the Ukonom-Cuddihy Lakes Trail, coming in from the northeast (0.9, 6090).

United, the trails arc 0.1 mile down to a sandy beach on the northeast tip of the lake. Whether you camp overnight or just visit for the day, the best vantage point for enjoying Ukonom Lake is at the rocky peninsula projecting from its east shore. The water deepens right from the rocks and there are a couple of small campsites back in the trees.

broad meadow of Secret Valley, then resume a moderate-to-steep drop through dense huckleberry thickets. When the lake first comes into view through the trees, its emerald waters seem so rich a color as to almost have texture. Two final switchbacks bring you down to the shore near the lake's southeast corner (0.9, 5270).

Secret Lake is a jewel, well-set in forest and cliff. The lake drops off just a breath away from its heavily brushed-in shores to a depth of 43 feet. At the north end, just east of the outlet creek, a small campsite carved out of the Sadler oak and uncommon rhododendron will bring a smile to the face of the most ardent recluse.

Ukonom Lake

From the Haypress-Secret Lake trails junction, most folks headed for Ukonom Lake will stay up on the crest, taking the Ukonom-Cuddihy Lakes Trail above the Granite Lakes basin, despite the fact that the lower trail is somewhat shorter. If you are camped at Onemile Lake, however, the Ukonom-Onemile Lake Trail is a significantly shorter route. And you will find the quiet intimacy of this

Hike 10:   Cedar Flat—Pleasant Lake

Distance: 9.7 miles, one way to Pleasant
Lake

Low elevation: 4440$'$

High elevation: 5960$'$

Suited for: 2-3 days

Usage: low, though moderate at Pleasant
Lake

Difficulty: moderate

Directions to trailhead: Same as on page 68.

Trail description: The first 1.7 miles of this
hike follows the Let 'er Buck Trail, described in Haypress Meadows Trails, Hike 7.
Turning right onto the Haypress Trail from
the Let 'er Buck Trail, you climb up the
meadow and then into the forest along a minor ridge. The steep ascent ends in ½ mile,
and after crossing a small saddle you drop
quickly into Halfmoon Meadow, coming to a
junction with the Halfmoon Meadow Trail
(0.8, 5070), a few paces beyond narrow
Halfmoon Creek.

The Halfmoon Meadow Trail heads southeast, passing in 20 yards a usage path to an
open campsite on the far side of Halfmoon
Creek. As the path very gradually descends
along the perimeter of this vast, crescent-
shaped meadow, you pass two more camping
opportunities. The meadow's floral display
diminishes as you approach the confluence of
two branches of Halfmoon Creek and, bending sharply northeast for 60 yards, cross a
narrow tributary (0.5, 4980) coming from
Round Meadow.

After climbing steeply away from the
creek, the path curves east into the forest on
an easier grade. You travel an undulating
course through the forest until an ambling
descent of ½ mile brings you to a permanent
stream, which dances merrily through the
hushed forest (1.5, 5180). Several yards below the trail, a flat spot has been cleared
out of the foliage on the creek's east bank to
provide a pleasing, intimate campsite.

After climbing moderately to a nearby
saddle, you turn abruptly northeast to begin
the long descent to Bridge Creek. It is a
moderate-to-steep descent at first, passing
through a strip of tobacco brush/bitter
cherry/chinquapin scrub, then returning to

the forest to cross a burbling creek (0.5,
4970).

The moderate descent continues for a
short while beyond the creek, then lessens to
a gentle gradient. As you descend, the influence of the wetter, cooler valley bottom
can be seen in the increasingly copious understory. The descending trail crosses the
strongly flowing creek (0.7, 4780), which
originates in Horse Pocket, then two more
smaller ones in the next 0.4 mile, before
making its way down to a junction with the
Bridge Creek Trail. Turning northeast, you
go a few paces to a boulder-crossed creek in
full song. After another 0.1 mile of easy uphill you reach Cedar Flat (1.1, 4530).

Although the incense-cedars here share
center stage with the Douglas-firs, the prodigious height and diameter of these trees,
although they are not *true* cedars, make the
spot aptly named. Beneath the stately conifers are two spacious tentsites; with the
forest floor plushly carpeted with trail plant,
vanilla leaf and thimbleberry, this spot is a
veritable Eden. A dependable little spring
flows along the north edge of the upper
campsite.

Pleasant Lake

If you are feeling the pull of Pleasant
Lake, head north-northeast across the spring,
immediately passing a junction with the
Medicine Mountain Trail, which climbs 3.1
miles to the summit of Medicine Mountain
and its sterling panorama (see the trail description at the end of this hike). The climb
up Bridge Creek begins gently, then steepens
to a moderate grade through abundant
thimbleberries. This juicy berry is at its best
when it turns deep red, and then it almost
falls into your hand as you pick it.

The trail ascends to a bridged creeklet,
then crosses several seeps and rivulets within
a patch of alder, cascara sagrada and American dogwood. Beyond this brush the ascent
steepens briefly as the trail follows the bend
in the creek to the north-northwest, and
then it resumes its gentle course through
the fir-and-incense-cedar forest. You pass

through a ¼-mile stretch of meadow that is overgrowing the trail then, after a forested interval, walk along the western border of an alder garden up to a boulder-hop of Bridge Creek (1.3, 5060).

Beyond Bridge Creek the trail climbs at first moderately, then steeply. The well-forested path eases its grade as you approach a tributary of Bridge Creek. One-tenth mile beyond the creek, you arrive at a junction with the Pleasant Lake Trail (0.6, 5460). This trail climbs steadily up the northeast edge of a meadow, then curves up to a flat, across which the often faint tread heads toward a small, lily-pad pond (0.3, 5650), the source of the creeklet you last crossed. You circle around the pond and begin a real heart pumper of a climb through a bouldery scrub garden where you must pay close attention to stay on the trail.

After pausing for breath in the broad saddle at the ridgetop (0.3, 5960), switchback down an extraordinarily steep trail through the scrub. Pleasant Lake soon comes into view, a sapphire tightly set in glacier-

View down Bridge Creek canyon

Pleasant Lake

sculpted granite, with Black and Marble mountains rising as a distant backdrop. Take care as you near the lake for the route can become confusing among the erosion channels and outcrops. After a few final twists in the trail you reach a charming lakeside campsite (0.4, 5580), legal only because there is no campsite-distance regulation at Pleasant Lake. You'll find a lovely sleeping space beneath a clump of red firs near the north edge of the lake, and another small site beyond a rocky, brush-clogged scramble along the south shore. The rock slabs along this shore afford the best vantage for swimming or fishing.

Onemile and Cuddihy Lakes

If Pleasant Lake seems too secluded and you have a hankering for company, you're sure to find it at Onemile and Cuddihy Lakes. To get there from the junction with the Pleasant Lake Trail, continue climbing the Bridge Creek Trail at a steep rate, crossing a quiet bit of running water in 110 yards. The trail gradient continues steeply, then moderates as you ascend along the border of the red-fir forest and into a cornucopia of wildflowers.

The ascent steepens again as you near the head of the valley, passing through a band of red firs and into the headwall meadow, sparsely flowered with lupines and pussypaws. Where the trail arcs west-northwest across the headwall, the gradient steepens dramatically as you trudge up to a ridgecrest junction with the Haypress Trail (1.2, 6400). A few paces to the right is a junction with the Secret Lake Trail, descending in 0.7 mile to Onemile Lake. Nearly one mile north on the Haypress Trail, you come to a junction with the Cuddihy Lakes Trail, which descends ½ mile to these remarkable lakes. These trails are both described in Hike 9.

Medicine Mountain Trail

This rarely used trail takes off from the Bridge Creek Trail just north of the spring in Cedar Flat. Heading east across the flat, the path quickly reaches broad Bridge Creek. A boulder-hop or an early-season log crossing will get you to the resumption of the trail 20 yards upstream. Just 90 yards beyond the crossing, as the trail begins to arc southwest, you pass a superb campsite 20 yards on your left, which offers even greater seclusion than those back at the trail junction. Almost immediately the trail crosses a creek bordered by distinctively tassled goatsbeard, then soon begins to climb steeply up the Smith Fork.

You eventually pull yourself up out of the forest onto a scrub-bordered, granite-staircase path (0.9, 5010), alongside the cascading Smith Fork. The climb abruptly ends as you return to the forest and come to an easy crossing of the now tranquil Smith Fork (0.3, 5230). After ambling through a narrow strip of wildflowers, you pass a pleasant creekside campsite, on your left, which is just northwest of Buns Basin. This basin is your last access to trailside water. From the campsite the trail switchbacks and climbs steeply out of the forest to the scrub-clad ridgecrest of Medicine Mountain's northwest spur (0.6, 5570). The unrelenting ascent continues up the crest of this sun-baked ridge, but after 0.4 mile respite is granted from the sun, if not from the climb, as you wind into an open forest of red firs.

The trail eventually climbs out of the forest, curving onto a scrub-coated ridge of deep-red, rocky soil, which appears to be a patch of ultramafic rock in the midst of this vast region of the Wooley Creek pluton. You weave up the crest on an ever increasing grade; the final 0.6 mile gains 700 vertical feet. Switchbacking up through the ocean-spray-dominated scrub, you finally reach the summit of Medicine Mountain (1.3, 6837).

The old junkheap of a lookout was finally removed in 1979, so you now have nothing to stand in your way of soaking up the nonpareil panoramas. The prominences include:

Peak 6864 above Granite Lakes basin—1°
Twin-peaked Red Butte in the Siskiyou
  Mountains—13°
Kings Castle—31°
Elk Peak—35°
Black Mountain—46°
Boulder Peak, capping the Red Mountain
  complex—64°
Mt. Shasta—95°
Glacier-flanked Mt. Thompson in the Trinity
  Alps—158°
Preston Peak in the Siskiyou Mountains—
  327°

Fowler Cabin, along Wooley Creek Trail

Hike 11

Wooley Creek Trail

Distance: 10.2 miles, one way
Low elevation: 650'
High elevation: 1550'
Suited for: 2-3 days
Usage: moderate
Difficulty: moderate

Directions to trailhead: From State Highway 96 follow Forest Highway 93 east for 3.6 miles to an unsigned driveway on the left, the north entrance to the parking area. There is a packstock corral in the middle of this immense, former earth-excavation site; it is best approached from the turnout's south entrance. The trailhead is 60 yards in from the north entrance, next to a Forest Service bulletin board.

Trail Description: Heading generally northwest, the trail climbs gently through a largely deciduous, mixed-evergreen forest. As the trail curves east-southeast and begins climbing steeply, these plants disappear. What remains in quantity, and what you need to be conscious of—if you are susceptible to it—is poison oak. This plant and young canyon live oak dominate the trailside shrubbery. At a thick-trunked manzanita, you come to a temporary end of your rigors at what the Indians called the Golden Elbow (0.7, 1140). Below, the Salmon River sinuously threads its way toward the Klamath. The path, dug sketchily into loose, "decomposed granite" soil on steep slopes, now heads northeast.

The undulating trail crosses two spikenard-filled creeklets before rounding a small point (1.9, 1020), and beginning to descend steeply. Just 60 yards down the trail an obvious path takes off on your right, directly downhill. This indescribably steep path descends to a stretch of rapids on Wooley Creek that, like Odysseus' Sirens, are as dangerous as they are beautiful. You will continue to pass less apparent trails down to the creek as you descend on the main trail, but be patient: the creek will be more accessible once you round the bend ahead in the creek.

Just before the bend, you descend into a small gully, with an intermittent dribble that nurtures the dainty blossoms of seep-spring monkey flower. About 115 yards beyond

Wooley Creek, from Mile 2.8

this seep, another unreasonable path descends to the creek, but 100 yards beyond it is a path that stays primarily on stable bedrock as it winds down to a vast, clear pool in Wooley Creek. Take warning: Wooley Creek is a fast-moving, powerful stream; even its most mellow, tranquil pools have a current, and this particular pool lies just above the bend's rocks and riffles.

If you like this pool and want to enjoy it the next day, then go 0.1 mile farther along the main trail to a lovely campsite on a flat above the creek. The creek may be accessible from here if you have a bit of mountain goat in you. If not, drinking water is most readily available from Deer Lick Creek (0.5, 920), 240 yards farther down the trail. Deer Lick Creek is so-named for the natural mineral lick in the rocks at its mouth.

After crossing this sprawling creek on a log that may be difficult to reach in early season, you climb out of its ravine and come to an obscure path on your right as the trail levels off and bends north-northwest. This path leads 50 yards to the site of a former cabin, marked by its towering stone fireplace and chimney. Firepits indicate that the area is still used as an overnight residence; the lovely pool in Wooley Creek just below the site is a likely reason why.

The trail now climbs steeply ½ mile before nosing into a gully whose slight creek flows beneath the graceful fronds of giant chain ferns. After rollercoastering a while, you cross two more creeklets. Beyond the series of rockbound, splashing falls of the second, there begins a long, usually gradual ascent to a sandy creeklet, half-buried in shrubbery, including the common horsetail fern, with its whorls of bristlelike leaves, and nonbristled, common scouring-rush. Neither fern nor rush, they are related members of the horsetail family, and both are rich in silica, which gives them an abrasiveness that makes them natural potscrubbers. After steeply ascending from the creeklet, you soon wind into the ravine of Gates Creek (2.2, 1390), using a log to cross its forceful flow just above a beautiful series of cascades.

After climbing from Gates Creek and making a semilevel arc to the south side of a spur ridge, the path rounds the point of the spur and steeply descends to a frolicsome creek (0.9, 1310). In early season its boulder-hop is likely to be partly submerged. Shortly after climbing steeply from the creek, you curve around to a trail junction. The right fork is a private trail descending to the cabins and private land of Wooley Camp. The Wooley Creek Trail is the left fork, a gentle, meandering descent. After hiking down the left fork several minutes, you see one of the Wooley Camp cabins below as you bend north and steeply descend into the cool gulch of dancing Wooley Camp creek (0.8, 1230). This you cross on another rockhop, which may be insufficient in early season. Several paces beyond the creek, you step across a diverted "canal" that has been constructed for the use of the cabins.

The trail levels off briefly as it rounds the spur north of the creek, where there is a junction with the very abandoned Camp Three Trail. Beyond the spur you ascend moderately through an increasingly coniferous forest. Soon you curve into the gulch of Haypress Creek and, at the bottom of a brief descent, pass a trail making an acute right

turn southeast; it heads down to the northernmost of the private cabins of Wooley Camp. You climb briefly, then descend in earnest to the bridge over Haypress Creek (0.8, 1260). This creek is quite a torrent by the time it reaches its confluence with Wooley Creek. One look at the chasm it has cut for itself below you makes the need for the bridge readily understandable.

After leaving the bridge, you ascend steeply to the point of the spur north of the creek, then descend gently to a trail junction and trail sign, unrelated to each other. The side trail, making an acute turn south, descends steeply and faintly 0.1 mile to Haypress Creek near its confluence with Wooley Creek; a hazardous boulder-and-log crossing gets one to a roomy campsite on its south bank. The trail sign is for the steeply climbing Black Mountain Trail, which looks just as abandoned as the Camp Three Trail, but has not officially been crossed off the books. There is a triangle of land, encompassing lower Bridge Creek, Black Mountain, and more of Wooley Creek, that is being considered for addition to the wilderness in order to further protect the Wooley Creek watershed. If this addition goes through, the Black Mountain Trail will likely be resurrected.

Beyond the trail junction descend moderately to the gentle gurgling of an intermittent brook, then bend to an unsigned trail junction 30 yards beyond. The Wooley Creek Trail is the left fork. The right fork reaches a small clearing in 25 yards, and a faint tread heading east-southeast from here curls down to a charming site on the bank of Wooley Creek. By following the creek upstream 70 yards—past a couple of shabby campsites—you'll come to a point where you can scramble down the steep bank to get water.

From the campsite fork the main trail climbs and then descends to the hushed glade of a small brook with a shooting cascade. Beyond the brook it descends steeply to a long flat beside Wooley Creek. A lovely, though quite public campsite takes advantage of this uncommon accessibility to the creek. Enjoy it now, for moments later a steep ascent swings away from the creek. After 1/3 mile of climbing, you undulate past two slender, sylvan brooks, then descend with increasing steepness to Bridge

Creek (2.2, 1360). Bridge Creek has every-thing Haypress Creek offered but bigger: the falls are higher, more turbulent and more gorgeous, the pool at their base larger and less accessible. To find a campsite, simply cross the bridge and follow a usage path 50 yards downstream to a spendid site. Its only deficiency is that you might be unable to sleep for the roar of the creek.

If the weather threatens or you wish a few of the amenities of home, continue along the trail 0.2 mile to a faint trail fork. The left fork, the path less traveled, is the continuation of the Wooley Creek Trail; the right fork continues on ahead 120 yards to Fowler Cabin. The cabin has been left un-locked by the Forest Service in an apparent-ly successful attempt to minimize the vandalism it receives. It has a stove, table and benches, and a couple of army cots. There's little room for sleeping inside except on the cots, but there is a large, covered porch. A pit toilet above the far end of the cabin completes the ensemble. A path be-yond the cabin returns to the Wooley Creek Trail in 225 yards, so you don't even have to backtrack if you wish to continue up-canyon.

Wooley Creek Trail

You can continue on. Since the 1979 trail crew opened up the 3 miles of trail between the North Fork and Big Meadows Creek, there are 8.7 more miles of maintained trail along Wooley Creek.

From the vague trail junction 120 yards short of Fowler Cabin, the Wooley Creek Trail climbs above the cabin meadow, stay-ing just inside the forest edge. In 0.1 mile it reaches a junction with the Bridge Creek Trail, which climbs 7.1 miles to Cedar Flat and another 3.1 miles to a junction with the Haypress Trail above Onemile Lake. In another 0.1 mile the usage trail from Fowler Cabin comes in from the southwest as you begin a pleasant, gently rolling, creekside stroll. The undulations gradually smooth in-to a moderate climb, which tops out just be-fore the dip into the narrow, open ravine of Canyon Creek (1.1, 1520).

Beyond the partly submerged boulder-hop of Canyon Creek, the trail resumes a relatively level course, crossing a narrow, burbling flow before descending to a grassy, oak-clump flat that renews your access to

the wide, boulder-strewn bed of Wooley Creek. However, you soon begin climbing away from this creek, the ascent steepening to round a broad spur, then easing as you traverse the high-angle slopes well above Wooley Creek. The rock outcrops along here are not like the light grey, speckled granitic rock you have been trodding since the trail-head. Reason: you passed beyond the Wooley Creek pluton in the area of Canyon Creek and have entered a vast region of metamorphic rock, which stretches all the way up to the headwaters of Wooley Creek.

You soon bend into a broad, deeply cut ravine, whose creek skims along wide sheets of bedrock before tumbling down a series of rock-block falls below the trail crossing (1.2, 1700). After crossing the creek, follow the rock outcrops south-southeast 20 yards downstream to where an earthen trail re-appears to plunge southeast into the forest. Descend steeply here, then taper off as the now rocky trail brings you down to the flat alongside, but still 30-50 feet above, Wooley Creek. Since Fowler Cabin, you have been traveling on little-used, seldom-maintained trail, and as you climb almost imperceptibly along this flat, you might need to keep a sharp eye out for the trail, since a year or two of deadfall and leaves will mask it very effectively in places. As you can see from the precipitous, slide-prone banks along the flat, one good-sized spring flood would remove the trail from sight altogether.

The trail eventually switchbacks into a brief, extremely steep climb, which then eases into the shady glade of dancing Dead Horse Creek (1.0, 1680). Beyond it, a rocky descent returns you to Wooley Creek. You amble along its banks until a couple of hun-dred yards of moderate climbing bring you to the edge of a grassy opening. Following the north edge of the meadow, the sketchy path soon comes to the ancient sign and skull that identifies this area as Bear Skull Camp (0.8, 1780). This sandy, grassy flat, with its scant patches of Oregon white oak, is not a particularly attractive site. It gets most of its use from autumn hunters and, when the need arises, from firefighters who find it an adequate helipad.

Leaving the meadow through a jungle of lupines, you then climb into the forest. The sporadic ascent is momentarily suspended to descend steeply to a boulder-hop of narrow Bear Skull Creek (0.6, 1850). You ascend moderately through clumps of azalea, whose readymade bouquets of orange-streaked, creamy blossoms perfume the path in late spring, then you follow the sharp eastward bend of Wooley Creek at a slight, mossy cascade bordered by clumps of five-finger fern.

You soon cross another mere slip of a stream, sheeting across metamorphic outcrops, then descend gently to a sandy flat. An easy ascent from the flat brings you to a tiny campsite in the middle of the trail. Beyond it, descend past azalea thickets and occasional Washington lilies, then cross a heavily mossed brook on a shaky "log" before continuing down to the banks of powerful North Fork Wooley Creek (1.0, 1910).

A log crosses the North Fork some 80 yards upstream, but it is not a maintained crossing. If it washes away one spring, you'll be left to wade the creek—an imposing task at any time and a hazardous one early in the summer. Once across the creek, climb steeply above its bouldery floodplain, then resume a meandering course above Wooley Creek. Then, 2/3 mile beyond the North Fork, you pass an overgrown campsite on a small flat just to the right of the trail and, after climbing quickly around a small point, come to another tiny flat with a campsite and a slight stone wall, perhaps the remnant of a miner's hut. Just upstream from the stone wall, there is a pool of extraordinary clarity and depth.

From the stone wall climb steeply, then begin a rollercoaster route, which crosses a trickling intermittent stream before descending to a broad, rocky, sparsely treed flat (1.3, 2180). The undulations in the trail ease considerably as you climb very gradually beside the creek. Shortly after a sharp eastward bend in the creek, cross a small creeklet, then, ¼ mile later, pass a small campsite on the immediate left of the trail just before a brief descent to a wading ford of now narrow Wooley Creek (1.6, 2280).

From the creek climb briefly, soon crossing well-shaded Big Meadows Creek on a touchy boulderhop, and quickly reaching a junction with the Big Meadows Trail (0.1, 2300). This trail climbs steeply 4.9 miles to a 0.3-mile spur trail to Wild Lake, then on into Salmon River country. Just below the

trail junction is a sandy, semi-open campsite near the creek, where your privacy is virtually assured.

Bridge Creek Trail

Whether you are creating a Wooley-Creek-to-Haypress-Meadows loop trip, needing to get away from the occasional crowd at Fowler Cabin, out to help the bears harvest the late-summer thimbleberry crop, or simply wanting a forest-deep experience on a little-used trail, the Bridge Creek Trail will admirably satisfy your desires.

From the obscure trail junction 120 yards below Fowler Cabin, follow the left fork 0.1 mile to the junction with the Bridge Creek Trail. Taking the left fork, climb steeply with the help of a switchback to the crest of the ridge between Bridge and Wooley creeks. The path follows this ridgecrest, then slides off along the south slope a while before switchbacking again to the crest and crossing over to the Bridge Creek side of the ridge (0.4, 1770).

On this west slope, climb extremely steeply at first, ascending a trail that requires some caution, since it is often very narrow and unstable, and is covered in places with tractionless madrone leaves. As you climb, the dogbane that flourished and flowered along the rocky, more open trail now becomes just another member of a growing community of shade-tolerant, forest-floor foliage.

You receive respite from the ascent as you pass an extended pole at the beginning of a curve around a spur (1.3, 2670). The trail will pass two more such poles while rounding the spur and descending slightly into a moist gully. The poles were supports for the phone line up to the since removed Medicine Mountain lookout. Since they are outside the present wilderness boundary, they will remain as convenient milestones.

Beyond the richly understoried gully, resume climbing at a moderate grade. Step across a gaily tumbling freshet beneath an azalea bower (0.8, 2940), then, as the hillside's coat of thimbleberries gradually thickens, you pass through a few more seep- and trickle-filled gullies. As you bend northeast toward Yellow Jacket Creek, the ascent steepens. Shortly beyond a wilderness-boundary sign nailed to a sugar pine, descend gently through a proliferation of mountain maples to Yellow Jacket Creek (1.1, 3640). Just above its splendid cascade, use a log to reach the boulder ford, made amid nodding red columbine and clumps of fireweed and goatsbeard.

After climbing steeply to round the spur north of Yellow Jacket Creek, you follow a semilevel trail several minutes before descending steeply to a lushly vegetated gulch cradling a slight, double-channeled creeklet. In the next major gulch you cross a slender, dashing cascade in a small gully (0.9, 3290), then round an intermediate rise to cross a second, less glamorous flow 150 yards beyond the first. As you climb gently beyond the second creeklet, you might notice that the transition from mixed-evergreen to mixed-conifer forest is nearly complete.

The next steep ascent subsides as you descend briefly to cross the boisterous creek of Snowslide Gulch on partly submerged rocks. Climb another ¼ mile, then descend the often mucky trail to the banks of broad, boulder-channeled Bridge Creek (0.9, 3540). In early season this may effectively be trail's end, but by midsummer there is an obvious boulder-hop for the quick of foot. Just upstream may be a log, which is the safest bet until it gets washed away. Take care, however, for mossy rocks and barkless logs pre-sent quite slippery surfaces to wet bootsoles. Before crossing, take a look west-southwest across the stream to where the trail heads into the forest; the path through the rocky floodplain on the creek's west bank is not always discernible.

Having crossed Bridge Creek and negotiated the boulder field, climb 40 yards into the forest and, just before a switchback to the north, pass a spacious and inviting campsite just off the trail on your left. A smaller, sister site is just beyond it. Purebred mixed-conifer forest, with huge Douglas-firs and white firs, shades your steep climb above Bridge Creek amid copious thimbleberries.

A few minutes above the campsites, you cross the stream spilling down from Horse Pocket, and several more flows. Some sluggish trickles hardly dent the earth, others are aggressive cascades that have cut ravines so steep-sided that little vegetation can get a hold on their banks. A nearly continual ascent, sections of it quite taxing, take the hiker up to a junction with the Halfmoon Trail, coming in from the southwest (1.6, 4490). This trail, and the continuation to the north of the Bridge Creek Trail, are both described in Hike 10. Cedar Flat, with its roomy campsites and its junction with the 3.1-mile Medicine Mountain Trail, is 0.1 mile to the northeast.

Part of the panoramic view the hiker gets from atop Portuguese Peak

Hike 12:

Portuguese Peak Trail

Distance: 8.2 miles, one way
Low elevation: 3180′
High elevation: 6460′
Suited for: day trip
Usage: rare
Difficulty: strenuous

Directions to trailhead: From State Highway 96 follow Forest Highway 93 east for 4.2 miles to a junction with FS 12N01, signed for Steinacher Creek. Turn left on 12N01, cross a bridge over the Salmon River near its confluence with Wooley Creek, and follow the partially paved road 7.1 miles to the trailhead at its end. Be sure to fill your water bottles before you reach the trailhead, since this ridgecrest trail is dry for nearly 7½ miles.

Trail description: There are just a few paces of level leisure before a short switchback leg leads up to a ridge. You begin a serious climb up it, occasionally moving along the south slope, and even less occasionally receiving brief respites of gentle or moderate trail gradient. In a few places, the extent of the 1977 Hog Fire can be seen in the blackened trunks of pine and the charred remains of manzanita.

To skirt the wedge-shaped summit of a small, unnamed peaklet, the trail crosses over to the north side of the ridge (1.5, 4490). Immediately, the microclimate changes, and its effect on the vegetation is dramatic. Gone is the forest in transition from mixed-evergreen to mixed-conifer, replaced by a thick stand of white fir and Douglas-fir. Gone are the gravelly openings, with their clumps of manzanita and tobacco brush, replaced by the lush understory typical of a moist, shaded conifer forest. Through windows in the forest, you can look across the Wooley Creek drainage to the Salmon Mountains, and can pick out Medicine Mountain (20°) and Marble Mountain (35°).

Climbing moderately, the trail arcs through a natural amphitheater shaded with Douglas-firs and richly carpeted with trail plant. Beyond the amphitheater the climb steepens and eventually breaks out onto the rocky, upper slopes of Tom Payne Peak. You then have a short pull up to the crest of the peak's north-trending spur (0.7, 5020), from which there is an unlimited view, from north to west. Unfortunately, since nearly

all of what you can see in that 90° arc is nonwilderness, the panorama is marred by a quilting of cutblocks. For a broader perspective, walk a few paces father along the trail to where a path on the right climbs 100 yards to the summit ridge. From the ridge the view is nearly boundless, the highly corrugated ranges of the Klamath Mountains and Coast Ranges sweeping to the horizon. To the south-southeast lie the Trinity Alps and icy-visaged Mt. Thompson. The course of the Salmon River can be seen cutting through the defile to the west. Across Wooley Creek, Merrill Mountain rises in the northwest and Black Mountain stands farther up that ridge at 350°. Medicine Mountain and Marble Mountain are again in view, and now Red Mountain comes into view in the northeast. The trail's namesake, Portuguese Peak (pronounced "Por' ti gee" by the locals), stands a long swooping walk away at 110°.

Back on the trail, descend extremely steeply from the spur and back onto the crest of the main ridge. The tread often fades as you follow the semilevel crest, but you need to keep a sharp eye out even more to catch the acute, switchbacking turn to the northwest, which takes the trail down onto the north slope (0.3, 4850).

After descending steeply for 200 yards, you amble a while through a veritable jungle of thimbleberries, before descending moderately to the ridgecrest at the saddle west of Portuguese Peak (0.8, 4680).

After traversing the saddle, begin the climb to Portuguese Peak, quickly moving onto its north slope. You push through a wildly flowered and overgrown trail, then switchback up to the crest. The rocky trail climbing along the crest and south slope from here is overgrown to the point of invisibility, making for a troublesome, even hazardous, descent on your return trip. Finally moving above the scrub to the rocky upper slopes of the peak, you use a final switchback to reach the crest just below and northwest of the summit (0.9, 5600).

From the crest, the trail switchbacks east and descends gently along the peak's north slope. Thirty yards past the switchback is a path cut through the scrub that allows you to scramble up to the summit and its 280° of views: from neighboring Peak 6443 (70°) counterclockwise to Mt. Thompson (150°).

Curving onto the northeast face, the descending trail steepens considerably, and then it plummets down the east ridge to a saddle (0.3, 5330). As you then descend moderately along the crest, you might notice the great number of knobcone pines spread throughout the charred forest. The knobcone pine is a vegetative Phoenix: since its cones rarely open to distribute its seeds until this very fire-susceptible tree dies, new knobcones rarely rise except from their ashes.

The descent soon bottoms out and the trail begins to climb toward Peak 6443, staying on the northwest slopes until reaching the confluence of the main ridge and a northwest-trending spur (0.9, 5650). Now moving up along southwest-facing slopes, you gradually climb into a forest-enclosed field of gargantuan granitic boulders. They offer fairly imposing evidence that you have left the band of metamorphic rock that stretched between Tom Payne and Portuguese peaks, and have entered the region of the vast English Peak pluton.

After curving above a slender meadow and back up to the crest, you quickly move onto the northwest face of Peak 6443, and soon begin switchbacking south into the old burn. You steeply ascend the maze of switchbacks and switchback shortcuts until the trail reaches a meadow atop the broad summit of Peak 6443 (0.9, 6410). The trail through the meadow is indistinct at best. Head east 115 yards, passing a large, isolated red fir, on your left. There is visible tread just beyond the fir as you begin descending east.

The trail is still obscure at times as it descends through patchy forest and tobacco brush/bitter cherry/pinemat manzanita scrub. Bending southeast, you begin a level traverse along the southwest face of "peak 6560," then descend steeply beside a long thicket of tobacco brush. Returning to the forest, the descent continues gradually through a heavily burned area to an engaging brook (1.1, 6210). Just 60 yards beyond the creek you come to the edge of an incongruous ridgecrest meadow, pocket-sized and filled with the heatherlike bog kalmia. Beyond the meadow, there begins a relatively constant, moderate ascent, staying just west of the crest, to a junction with the Crapo Trail (0.8, 6450), which is described in Hike 13.

Chapter 8

Salmon River District

Introduction: Of the over 380 miles of trail in and into the Marble Mountain Wilderness, about 30 percent lie within the Salmon River district. Yet the area receives little more than 15 percent of the wilderness traffic; only the much smaller Happy Camp district has fewer visitors per trail mile. With the exception of the high-use corridor of the North Fork Trail to English and Hancock lakes, this is an area to which one comes to lose himself.

This is no place for an idle weekend jaunt, particularly if one has a lakeside camp as a goal. The Salmon River district has nearly as many lakes accessible by trail as does the far more popular Scott River district, but the closest lake is more than 11½ trail miles from the nearest road. Although logging is as rampant in these parts as anywhere else in the Marbles, there are no logging roads to conveniently carry one up to the 4500-foot elevation. The wilderness boundary extends father downslope, and all the trails begin at river level, here between 2000 and 3000 feet. You are forced to travel through fecund, mixed-evergreen forests, along purling rivers whose every pool whispers a gentle come-hither, among the lofty spires of a mixed-conifer forest-primeval, before reaching the lake country. One needn't stop at the lakes, though, for all trails lead to English Peak. Once one has experienced the panorama from its 7316-foot summit, all future journeys there will be as much pilgrimage as wilderness venture.

The Salmon River district holds attractions beyond its wilderness boundaries also. The Salmon River was at the focus of the gold fever in the Marbles area, and remains the site of current mining activity. Until a series of fires in the late 1960s destroyed the hotel and some of the other original buildings, the small village of Sawyers Bar was one of the few communities in California to maintain its 19th Century beginnings; it still reflects its origins in pace and style, if not in structure. The fires didn't take everything, though. On the western edge of the community stands the Catholic church of Father Florian, built in 1855.

Access: The relative dearth of traffic in the Salmon River district is not due to any particular difficulties in finding the place. It just takes so bloody long to get there. A mile or two east of Somes Bar on the major thoroughfare along the Salmon River, there is a speed-limit sign reading *five miles per hour*, right after the sign advising motorists of narrow, winding road—for the next 57 miles! Not only is it a narrow, winding, largely unpaved road, it is also a road on which the logging truck is king. Even five miles an hour can seem too fast when one confronts a Peterbuilt slicing off the inside of a blind turn, a trick that is not so much indulgence as necessity on some of these tight corners.

The road along the Salmon River is known as Forest Highway 93 between Somes Bar and Forks of Salmon, and more obscurely as SIS 1C01 and SIS 2E01 between Forks of Salmon and Etna. To simplify matters, it is referred to as the Somes Bar-Etna road in the "directions to trailhead" of each hike. All five trailheads in this district are on or just off this road.

The Salmon River ranger station, in Sawyers Bar, is the primary source of wilderness permits, and weather and trail information. This station keeps longer hours than any of the others: 7 a.m. to 6 p.m. daily during the summer season, and 7 a.m. to 4:30 p.m. weekdays during the rest of the year. The work station in Forks of Salmon is also a year-round source for wilderness permits.

There are opportunities for camping at or near all the trailheads except the new Pacific Crest Trail trailhead at Etna Summit, and a waterless campground, with corrals, is planned for there in the near future. The spacious Idlewild Campground, at the FS 41N37 turn-off to the Mule Bridge trailhead for the North Fork Trail, charges a small fee, but the other national forest campgrounds are free. The Forest Service asks only that, if you camp at the Little North Fork Campground, do not leave your car in its tiny lot while visiting the wilderness. There is a designated parking area nearby, which is ¼ mile from the Little North Fork trailhead and 0.4 mile from the Garden Gulch trailhead.

The Trails: There are three trails that feed into the Chimney Rock area in the southern arm of the wilderness: the Garden Gulch and Crapo trails of the Salmon River district, and the Portuguese Peak Trail of the Ukonom district. These are all seldom traveled routes, primarily because they require exhausting climbs out of the valley of the Salmon River. In addition, there are few lakes in the area, and only Clear Lake has a trail to it. Moreover, Dollar, Crapo and Morehouse meadows are overrun by as much as 250 cattle from late July to mid-October. In 1977 the area's potential as a tourist attraction was blemished even further by the wide-ranging Hog Fire. Stretching from Orleans Mountain in the west to Sawyers Bar in the east, this dry-lightning fire ravaged the north wall of the Salmon River valley, and was particularly intense on the slopes beneath Portuguese Peak and Chimney Rock. Broadcast seeding of grasses and the regenerative powers of mountain chaparral have aided in reclaiming the burned area, but there's no denying the area's charms have been tainted. That is, unless you are attracted by the promise of wilderness seclusion. In that case, there is no more charming spot in the entire district.

The other hikes in this chapter begin by ascending several miles along the North Fork or Little North Fork to the high-country lakes at the heads of these and neighboring drainages. The North Fork and Little North Fork trails lead ultimately to English Peak, which crowns the entire scene. Indeed, a common trip in this area is a North Fork/Little North Fork loop. This 28-mile trip allows the wilderness traveler to sample from the entire spectrum of delights in this region. Although all the constituent parts of the North Fork/Little North Fork loop are discussed within this chapter, such a hike is not specifically described. If you are considering it, then begin your walk from the Mule Bridge trailhead, for the North Fork Trail gives you an easier climb to the high country. Since the Bug Gulch and Shelly Meadows trails receive relatively little use, the North Fork-Bug Gulch-Shelly Meadows trails loop is the hiker's best opportunity to experience high-country lakes and vistas at the same time and place as wilderness isolation.

Over the winter of 1978-79 the Salmon River district drew up a trail-maintenance plan. At the moment, trail maintenance tends to reflect the usage patterns and the main trails are all fairly well-groomed. The following trails have all been assigned a level-2, low-priority ranking and, as they get a bit scruffier in the next few years, there will be an increasing likelihood of finding solitude along them: Devils Canyon and Old Snowslide trails, described in the Little North Fork Trail hike; Lake of the Island and Abbot Lake trails, described in the North Fork Trail hike; and Bug Gulch, Hell Hole Ridge, Ethel-Katherine lakes, Wild Lake and Cabin Gulch trails, described in the North Fork-Bug Gulch-Shelly Meadows trails loop.

Hike 13

Crapo Trail

Distance: 9.4 miles, one way
Low elevation: 1100'
High elevation: 6500'
Suited for: day trip
Usage: rare
Difficulty: strenuous

Directions to trailhead: The Crapo trailhead is 14.0 miles southeast of State Highway 96 on the Somes Bar-Etna road, and 3.5 miles northwest of the Forest Service guard station in Forks of Salmon. The turn-off to the trailhead is at the south end of the highway bridge over the Salmon River, and is generally unsigned. Follow the all-weather road 0.2 mile to a signed wilderness-area parking lot at an undeveloped camping area used as a seasonal loggers' camp. About 230 yards beyond the parking area, follow a left fork 35 yards down to a footbridge over Crapo Creek. The trail description begins at this footbridge.

Trail description: The first order of business is to fill your water bottles, since the first likelihood of water is 6½ miles distant, and the first dependable water is more than one mile beyond it. Across the footbridge, you follow a continuation of the dirt road as it bends past a tarpaper dwelling and assorted shacks of local miners. At the junction with the road to the Wildcat Placer Mine (0.2, 1200), take the steeply climbing left fork.

In the sparsely timbered oak woodland you are traveling through, the yellow star thistle along and in the road, together with poison oak, seem the most prolific vegetation. The shade eventually offered by the roadside addition of ponderosa pine, madrone and Douglas-fir is a welcome relief as your climb stiffens. It is not permanent relief, however, for the open scrub returns and you push on up through dry-habitat flora to a sharp turn at the south spur of Sauerkraut Peak (1.8, 2790). The road first bears northwest, bends east-northeast onto manzanita-covered slopes, then back north-northwest into the forest, where you immediately come to a trail climbing very steeply to the northwest (0.6, 3430). Leaving the road, you head up this largely poison-oak-lined

Along lower Crapo Trail

trail. It is an often rocky trail and is often covered with slippery leaves of oak and madrone; watch your step!

You wind through several depressions in this east slope of Sauerkraut Peak, eventually climbing high enough for an occasional glorious view through a forest window to Mt. Thompson and the Trinity Alps in the south-southeast. Though the recent Hog Fire may have been the most extensive burn in this area, the great numbers of knobcone pines along the trail indicate that it was not an isolated incident. Knobcone pine has an almost symbiotic relationship with fire: it needs the death of the cone-bearing branches to permit the cones to release the seeds, and these trees are more apt to die by the occasional fire sweeping the dry slopes it inhabits than from old age.

The climb is momentarily interrupted when you reach the saddle east of Sauerkraut Peak (1.0, 4360). For the next 5+ miles, the trail follows this ridgecrest, which stands between Crapo and Morehouse creeks. Head east along the saddle, then leave it to climb steeply, first on a north slope, then through a stunning rock garden amid oak scrub on a south slope.

After returning to the crest just west of Peak 5075, the ascent abruptly ends, and you contour through thin forest and thick thimbleberries on the peak's north slope. The trail then crosses over the crest to traverse the southeast slope of the unnamed peak west of Peak 5413. The prodigious growth of waist-high grass here is a result of broadcast seeding after the Hog Fire. It's easier to see the red, cylindrical blossoms of the firecracker flower, bobbing among the grasstops, then it is to see your feet, much less the trail. By keeping a level course north-northeast, you'll eventually reach a visible tread in the saddle west of Peak 5413 (1.4, 4990).

From the saddle, climb steeply into a thimbleberry jungle on the peak's north slope. The ascent eases and even levels off as you begin to follow the hillside's northward bend, then soon resumes as you round a bulge in a slope, curve into a depression, then curl across its top and hike strenuously up to the ridgecrest (1.1, 5830).

The hike is now a stroll through a fir forest, and the path descends easily for a moment before beginning a gentle ascent. A meadow opens up on the left, and you pass a small, trailside campsite just before leaving some trees to skirt the meadow's edge. A slight brook, almost lost in the willows and American dogwoods clogging its course, is the first water since the trailhead, but its permanency is suspect.

Beyond the campsite, the path climbs gradually along the meadow's perimeter, crossing an occasional seep, then beyond the meadow it climbs steeply up the west slopes of Peak 6325. The trail is often obscured by the deadfall of the red-fir/mountain-hemlock forest. This ascent tops out as you pass through a shallow saddle and begin skirting a lodgepole-pine-bordered meadow on the

right. Beyond the meadow, the semilevel trail passes through another saddle, then eventually curls around the north side of a knob to a burbling creeklet (1.6, 6140). There are fire rings on either side of the trail just before the brook, but sleeping would be easier back down the trail 50 yards or so in the bottom area beneath the knob. From the brook, one begins a vigorous climb toward Peak 6483. You round the north side of this knob, then undulate across a series of knolls to a junction with the Portuguese Peak Trail (0.9, 6450).

From this junction the Crapo Trail continues east-northeast on a traverse of the south slopes of Chimney Rock. It climbs briefly, then levels off upon entering Crapo Meadows. The soil is well-drained "decomposed granite" (you entered the region of the English Peak batholith as you passed Peak 5413 some 3½ miles back). The soil supports the customary floral community of such high meadows: frosty eriogonum, spreading phlox, Davis' knotweed and cobwebby paintbrush. It also "supports" a network of severe erosion channels. The loosely compacted soil and the scant plant cover with root systems that insufficiently anchor the soil both work to leave the hillside victim to spring snowmelt and rain.

Crapo Meadows is not merely well-drained, it's largely dry. However, as the path enters the forest at the meadow's east end, you can see a grassy opening downslope that contains a small brook. Your path remains level through the still beauty of the red-fir forest, then you move out again onto gleaming, gravelly slopes. To the south-southeast, the ridges and valleys sweep off to the jagged peaks of the Trinity Alps. A few steps off the trail to the ridgecrest reveals a snow-capped Mt. Shasta in the distant east; to the northeast, across the glacial basin of Dollar Meadows, rise the chunky bodies of Crapo and English peaks. It is a view worth working for.

Shortly after entering the scattered trees beyond this opening, the Crapo Trail comes to an end at a junction with the Garden Gulch Trail (0.8, 6490). For a day or two of lake play to reward your effort, turn northwest onto the Garden Gulch Trail and take it 1.3 miles to a junction with the Steinacher Ridge Trail, then go steeply up-over-and-down 1.9 miles to Clear Lake.

Hike 14

Garden Gulch Trail

Distance: 11.6 miles, one way to Clear Lake
Low elevation: 2020'
High elevation: 6550'
Suited for: 3-4 days
Usage: rare along trail; low at Clear Lake
Difficulty: strenuous

Directions to trailhead: The trailhead is right on the Somes Bar-Etna Road, 10.6 miles northeast of the Forks of Salmon Guard Station and 4.2 miles west of the Salmon River Ranger Station in Sawyers Bar. A wilderness-visitor parking area has been created 0.4 mile east of the trailhead. Since the trailhead and its sign are sufficiently brush-enclosed to be easily missed when coming from the west, the roadside parking lot is your failsafe landmark.

Trail description: From the road you climb steeply on a former jeep road, ascending through the luxuriant greenery of a mixed-evergreen forest. After ½ mile a particularly steep stretch tapers to an apparent junction, whence the old road arcs north toward a small brook, and a footpath climbs west-northwest. Taking the trail, one finds it quickly reverts back to road as it climbs a small rise and heads up a ridge. This stiff ascent takes a brief break to swerve across an earthen bridge above a sluggish creeklet (0.8, 2640). With the rush of Cronan Gulch creek sounding in your ears, you climb briefly beside the muted brook, then curve away from the water to climb onto steep south slopes clad with ponderosa pines and various oaks.

The trail gradually curves to a generally north-northwest heading, staying above Garden Gulch, then it crosses a whispering rivulet submerged in brush and abruptly leaves the rich forest for logged slopes (1.0, 3500). You wind up through the cutblock, switchbacking a couple of times in and around the forest edge just above Garden Gulch creek before coming up to a logging road (0.5, 3890). Much of the next 1¼-mile hike to the wilderness boundary will follow a network of abandoned logging roads. The junctions of road and trail are sometimes vague, and

the trail signs not always placed to best advantage, so the Forest Service has usually placed logs across the roadway to funnel the hiker onto the trail. One can't trust the permanence of such aids, however, so keep a sharp eye out for the junctions.

The road meanders uphill on an easier grade, at one point revealing expansive views over the defile of the Little North Fork Salmon River and a stretch of the North Fork above Ahlgren Ranch. Thirty-five yards after switchbacking southeast onto a less-eroded road, a duck steers you back onto forested trail (0.3, 4060). Now the climb through a mixed-conifer forest is more rigorous. The trail crosses the head of a ravine, then switchbacks across it before coming out at a road again.

After you turn onto the road, the ascent eases. Little-used now, the roadbed is filled with penstemon and also sheep sorrel. You follow the curving road up to a plateau in the ridgecrest between Cronan and Garden gulches, then follow the nearly level crest northwest. Beyond a dip in the road, you curve west onto a trail climbing into the forest (0.9, 4690). Be thankful that you now have the forest-cool to walk through, for the next 1.7 miles to Yellow Jacket Ridge maintains a 20% grade.

The trail switchbacks up between the gulches, crossing in ½ mile a cascading brook tributary to Cronan Gulch. From the brook you can just see the Trinity Alps to the south-southeast, peeking over Smith and Blue ridges. You are well over 5000 feet now, and the giant chinquapins and sugar and ponderosa pines have faded out, to be replaced by red firs, as the mixed-conifer forest undergoes the transition to red-fir forest. Using granitic boulders as stepping-stones, continue switchbacking up the ridge, crossing en route a small flow that usurps the trail as its channel for a while.

The forest begins to open, before you arrive at a sometimes signed junction with a spur trail to Mud Lake (1.2, 6030). The 0.1-mile spur curls down through a very boggy meadow to this very shallow lake, which has been known to disappear completely

Mud Lake lives up to its name

in very dry years. Its big season is in the fall, when hunters think the meadow above the lake a likely prospect for a rewarding hunt.

The forest opens still more as the highly eroded Garden Gulch Trail winds above Mud Lake and its meadow. As one approaches the crest of Yellow Jacket Ridge, the climb traverses nearly barren slopes of "decomposed granite," sparsely covered with pussy paws, lupine and spreading phlox. The Trinity Alps lie fully revealed to the south-southeast as you follow two final switchbacks to a broad saddle atop Yellow Jacket Ridge (0.5, 6500).

After climbing 4500 feet in 5.2 miles, it would be nice to have some easygoing ridge-running for a while. But the Garden Gulch Trail's original purpose (and still probably its main use) was as a cattle-driving trail, for which a priority was placed on providing access to meadowlands. Hence you plummet through the north slope's red firs and moun-

tain hemlocks and enter scrub above the headwaters of Crapo Creek. Only 75 yards after the trail switchbacks southwest and 5 yards past a large red fir, the easily missed trail switchbacks northwest (0.2, 6290). There is an equally faded tread here that continues southwest; this is a usage path to Jim Camp in the next gulch to the west (in the souteast corner of section 8).

You wind down through the scrub and among granitic boulders, doing your best to differentiate between trail and erosion channels. The trail levels off briefly to pass a grassy flat, crisscrossed with cattle and campsite paths, and then resumes a sporadically steep, more easily followed descent. In fact, if the trail seems uncommonly wide in places on the way down to a monkey-flower-dotted creeklet (0.8, 5680), it's because it follows the fire line dug between Yellow Jacket Ridge and Chimney Rock during the Hog Fire.

Beyond the creeklet one descends a few minutes more, then begins climbing again. The full forest gives way to rocky, scrub-lined trail, with vistas southwest down the valley of Crapo Creek. The trail bends through a saddle in the ridgecrest, then descends moderately to a Crapo Creek tributary. After a brief, easy climb over a small rise, you come to the small front lawn of Ahlgren Cabin (0.8, 5670). Before the influx of 250 head of Herefords, usually around the 3rd week of July, you'll share this meadow—and the lively creek just north of the cabin—with only the deer that come to the salt lick next to the corral. A secluded, creekside campsite can be reached by following a 140-yard path steeply downhill from the south edge of the cabin's meadow.

North across the creek, the trail curves across the lower edge of a soggy meadow, then up into a patchy forest and rock garden. Just 0.1 mile beyond the meadow, a left fork quickly peters out among the scrub and deadfall. Take the right fork, which curves up into full forest. You cross another tributary brook (the last dependable water before Clear Lake, 4.4 miles farther), then, past a dribbling intermittent stream, switchback extremely steeply up to the ridgecrest (0.5, 5930).

The first views are to the north, the head of the Little North Fork lying at your feet, and to the north-northeast, where your eyes follow the deep crease of Snowslide Gulch up the massive ridge slope to the twin spires of Crapo (30°) and English (35°) peaks. As you turn west to follow the crestline trail, vistas to the south gradually appear. The trail climbs moderately, occasionally steeply, along the ridgeline, making excursions every now and then on either slope. A brief descent to a saddle reveals Black Mountain (15°) appearing through a saddle in the ridge to the north. Resuming the ascent, you soon come to a junction with the Crapo Trail (0.9, 6490).

Our Garden Gulch Trail descends steeply northwest, starting an arc above Dollar Meadows. After dropping down a rocky, eroded gully on rebuilt trail, one begins a rolling, twisting traverse through a subalpine setting to the first of four seeping springs, then begins a gentle ascent into forest. The trail climbs past the remaining three springs, none of which is particularly usable, then

curves through a short stretch of scrub to the crest of an east-trending spur. A few paces down the other side brings one to a junction with the Steinacher Ridge Trail (1.3, 6230), the route to Clear Lake. You take this trail, which climbs steeply for 1/3 mile to a ridgecrest saddle that has splendid vistas south to the Trinity Alps and east to Mt. Shasta. Below in the northwest, Clear Lake and aptly named Lily Lake are cradled in glacier-sculpted depressions cut in a granitic basin.

From the saddle, descend onto west slopes amid dense scrub and a rock garden of remarkable diversity. You then climb briefly back to the crest, soon to drop onto the east slope for a short contour through a patchy forest. Returning to the ridgecrest again, the trail immediately crosses to the curving southwest slope and into a thickening forest. The forested trail descends gently to a trail junction (1.2, 6420). Here the slight tread contouring north-northwest is the abandoned continuation of the Steinacher Ridge Trail, which once continued on about 1½ miles to Peak 5613. To reach Clear Lake, take the more obvious left fork, which plunges west.

The descent barrels hell-bent through the forest on a trail whose switchback shortcuts are often better established than the trail itself. The gradient eases as it nears the bottom of the hanging cirque containing Clear Lake. Ducks lead you through a bouldery, subalpine garden on a broad bench. You need to watch closely for the point where the route turns west to drop to the lake, for there is no discernible tread and the ducks aren't particularly distinctive. The turn occurs as a meadow begins opening up on the left. After dropping off the bench, you have a winding 0.1-mile descent to a large campsite next to the inlet creek on the lake's east shore (0.7, 5800).

This lakeshore campsite, despite the cow-skulls decorating the fire ring, is perhaps the most attractive site at the lake, but the 200-foot camping restriction makes it illegal. More appropriate sites can be found above the lake's north shore, and by its northwest corner at the edge of the brush. Regardless where you camp, you'll find the chill waters of this deep lake, and the full range of trout species it contains, to be ample reward for your labors.

Hike 15 Little North Fork Trail, to English Peak

Distance: 13.2 miles, one way
Low elevation: 2000'
High elevation: 7316'
Suited for: 3-4 days
Usage: moderate
Difficulty: strenuous

Directions to trailhead: The trailhead for the Little North Fork Trail is marked by a sign at the foot of the driveway of the former Ahlgren Ranch, 11¼ miles northeast of the Forks of Salmon Guard Station and just over 3½ miles west of the Salmon River Ranger Station in Sawyers Bar. The Little North Fork Campground lies 240 yards southwest of the trailhead, and the wilderness parking lot is another 0.1 mile beyond that.

Trail description: One hundred yards north up the rutted driveway you turn west onto a footpath, which soon curves back toward the north, climbing gently into the oak- and pine-dominated forest. The Little North Fork swings in beneath the trail after 1/3 mile but at this point the steep hillside leaves it accessible only to your eyes.

The trail eventually descends easily to a riverside flat with a thickening forest. Here the cool, moist microclimate of the river bottom has filled the forest floor with luxuriant greenery. Your undulating course passes through several gullies, some moist enough to support California spikenards and giant chain ferns, and all trimmed with Pacific dogwood, hazelnut and mock orange. It is a lush and peaceful forest.

The gradient suddenly steepens as a trail reroute climbs briefly away from the river then quickly descends. You curve into Dog Gulch, with its intermittent stream (1.5, 2270) then, just as you bend north to leave the gulch, you pass a short, steep, scramble-path down to the river. In early season follow this path to the interweaving logs that cross the river. The main trail continues another 0.1 mile, past a small campsite to a ford of the river; you'll have to hitch a ride with a horsepacker if you want to keep your feet dry. However, the riverbed has several sandy spots to ease the footing at this ford,

and there is usually a supply of *ad hoc* walking sticks on each bank. In fact, by late season, wading the river here may be less trouble than working your way from the log crossing through the west-bank boulders and scrub back to the trail.

On the west bank now, climb easily on a sandy trail through a cutblock logged in the late '60s. You pass through a brief strip of timber while rounding a bulge, then come out into the logged plain of Specimen Flat. In late summer 1979, after the author had mapped this trail, a short reroute of the trail was bulldozed through the scrub so that hikers would not have to walk on an active road leading to a mining claim up Specimen Creek or muddle through the unsigned road junctions. Where the new trail reaches the mining road (0.7, 2470), head northwest directly across it onto an old, abandoned dirt road.

Ford at Mile 1.6

The dirt road winds gradually up to an unnamed, hop-across creeklet, then quickly to the shallow brook of Titmouse Gulch. Following the river's bend to the north, the road crosses several more seeps and rivulets. Then, as the road reverts back to trail, you briefly come alongside the rushing waters of the Little North Fork before climbing to a dashing freshet embedded in monkey flowers and mountain boykinias.

Sur Cree Creek

After climbing well above the river, the trail descends briefly into the narrow ravine of Sur Cree Creek (0.9, 2810). Sur Cree Creek is a delight: a long, dancing cascade to a small sitz bath, and a larger, shallower pool. Bordered by great clumps of umbrella-like Indian rhubarb and sun-speckled through the delicate canopy of alders, the creek is a scene from a wilderness fantasy.

Beyond the creek descend to another ford of the Little North Fork. A series of logs and boulders crosses the river 30 yards downstream from the trail ford. However, the low-lying boulders are the weak link in the chain and you might find it less bother to simply doff your boots and wade. There are campsites near the ford; the most inviting is 0.1 mile above the ford, on the inside of the river bend 15 yards above the trail.

Following a trail blasted out of the rock walls, you bend with another meander in the river, passing just above a lovely, readily accessible pool, then head up into a steep climb. Two switchbacks and 200 vertical feet later, the trail begins an undulating contour upstream. If the soil seems to have a distinctly nongranitic tint to it, that's because you've just climbed off the English Peak batholith and into a region of metamorphism.

The route follows the river's sharp bend to the west, then makes a short, but horrendously steep, arcing climb back to the north. Recklessly tossing away the hard-won elevation, it descends steeply nearly to stream level, then climbs briefly to a rolling flat. The flat is a good vantage point for viewing the effects of the great floods of the past 15 years. On a regional scale, the 1964 Christmas flood was the worst in memory. However, the Little North Fork was more severely wracked by an early '70s flood that seemed to focus its force on this drainage. Actually, the greatest devastation was a delayed-action effect: the initial flooding swept deadfall into stupendous logjams, damming the river in several places. When the dams burst during a subsequent storm, the flooding that ensued was devastating. The results were the steeply sheared banks we see and the vast floodplain for a river whose customary channel takes up perhaps one tenth of the available riverbed.

From the flat you climb steeply again, passing through two deep-cut gullies, the second a shady, tranquil glade with a gentle brook. The trail then descends and passes a lovely campsite hidden away in the trees on the right just 25 yards short of the log crossing of Uncles Creek (2.5, 3300).

The trail rises quickly from the creek, curving above several campsites on a flat on the descending ridge that separates river from creek. After leveling off, you have several minutes of easy walking before the climbing resumes, then it gives way to a slight descent to the sign at the front door of the "Timber Hotel" (1.3, 3690), a vast camping area beneath old-growth incense-cedars, Douglas-firs and sugar pines. As for

Deer at Timber Hotel

the facilities: 60 yards south-southeast of the large, central fire ring, an unsheltered pit toilet sits among ferns and trilliums; 25 yards west-southwest from the fire pit, a path leads down through boulders to the narrowing river. Beyond the Timber Hotel, you soon pass into the wilderness, then embark on a steeply switchbacking climb away from the river. In this hushed forest the Little North Fork is only a murmur. Soon after the ascent eases, you arrive at a junction with the Old Snowslide Trail (0.5, 4050).

Old Snowslide Trail

The Forest Service maintains two trails up Snowslide Gulch, but the older trail tends to get short shrift. The Old Snowslide Trail is half the distance of the newer route. Looked at a different way, though, one has twice as much distance in which to gain 1630 feet elevation by taking the main Snowslide Trail. The older trail is easily followed, climbing along the east bank of an intermittent stream, then crossing it in the first of two closely space gullies. It then switchbacks up along the ridgecrest east of the gulch, moving off the crest to cross Snowslide Gulch creek and continue up at a lesser grade to a junction with the Snowslide Trail (1.7, 5680).

If you've come to take your ease and enjoy yourself, you'll want to follow the Little North Fork Trail, first dipping into a gully to cross an intermittent stream, then resuming the climb toward Snowslide Gulch. After descending into the extreme defile of the gulch, you negotiate a creek crossing that is often a ford. However, a log bridge may soon be built. Even after it is built, you may want to get your feet wet in the luscious pool that lies at the foot of an "endless" cascade that seems to be spilling from the skies. From the ford, the trail climbs steeply out of the gulch, soon coming to a junction with the Devils Canyon Trail (0.7, 4300).

Devils Canyon Trail

The Devils Canyon Trail is one of those trails built specifically for driving cattle to a summer range. Except for the late-summer bovines, the canyon is yours for the taking. And if the trail seems less than obvious at times, you needn't fret, for this is one of those classic "you don't have to worry about getting lost 'cause you can follow the stream back to civilization" trails.

The trail descends abruptly to the Little North Fork, crosses its boulder-strewn channel, then climbs quickly up to the ridge-line between Devils Canyon and the Little North Fork. The rocky tread along the crest is often sketchy and requires particular attention. After 0.6 mile, where the trail makes a brief upslope turn to the southwest, a duck off to the left marks a slight usage path heading south 100 yards to a series of small pools and falls. In another ½ mile, as the trail seems to disappear amid a surfeit of bracken ferns, look for a crusty, old, whitish incense-cedar, with new growth curving out of its lightning-truncated original trunk. The tree blaze hidden in its wrinkles directs you west and back to semivisible trail.

At 1.4 miles, an ancient, rotting tree sprawled across the trail creates some route-finding difficulties. Beyond it, however, you have free sailing up to and across an alder-choked tributary creeklet and into the upper meadows, where the trail dies a slow death (1.9, 5160). Low-impact camping is the rule here. You are free to wander about the great open spaces beneath Crapo Mountain, search out the giant incense-cedar that Salmon River district personnel claim to be the largest of its species in the world, or simply sit back and listen to the song of the Swainson's thrush curlicue through the still mountain air.

Beyond the Devils Canyon Trail junction, climb sporadically to a very pleasant trailside campsite. A few steps farther, just short of a shallow murmur of a brook, you reach a junction with the Snowslide Trail (0.5, 4540). The Snowslide Trail starts very steeply up beside the brook, then turns east, easing into a moderate-to-steep grade. Up above the microclimate created by the river and the cold-air well of the valley, the pines assert themselves more, and the trail is luxuriantly soft with their needles.

A series of long switchback legs zigzag up the ridgeslope. Although the sound of

Pine Lake

water is everywhere as the trail works its way up the slopes of Snowslide Gulch creek, there's not a drop to drink until you step across a perky little freshet (1.9, 5620). In another 0.1 mile the Old Snowslide Trail comes in from the south-southeast. Beyond the trail junction you crisscross up a spur ridge on an interminable chain of short switchback legs. The forest, largely red and white firs now, starts to thin, affording views out over the eastern Marbles and up the scrub-clad slopes of Snowslide Gulch to the rocky summit of English Peak. From a tobacco-brush patch just beyond the crossing of another small brook (0.7, 6020), you can just see the Trinity Alps (160°) above a ridge which itself culminates in Crapo Mountain, to the south. The trail quickly leaves the scrub to recross the brook, then weaves up through an open forest to a ridgecrest trail junction with the North Fork Trail (0.6, 6420).

Pine Lake Trail

In August 1979 a Sierra Club service trip added an additional trail to this junction: a new Pine Lake Trail. It leaves the saddle and follows the 6400-foot contour line to a junction with the old Pine Lake Trail on the ridgecrest south of the lake, then continues on down the old route. Since most of the traffic to Pine Lake comes via the Little North Fork Trail, the new Pine Lake Trail eliminates the excessive climbing and dropping of the old route and, from this direction, is shorter. The Marble Mountain Wilderness map with this book indicates the new Pine Lake Trail with a dotted line, because it was constructed after the author had concluded his field work. It will open for public use for the 1980 season. The old Pine Lake Trail is also on the map because the Forest Service was not entirely certain it would abandon this route.

As for the object of all these trails, Pine Lake sticks to the basics: sublime subalpine beauty and moderately deep water for unfettered lakeplay, romantic gazing, and trout fishing. Campsites of marginal legality can be found just beyond the seep near the lake's west tip. On the north shore, just east of the sluggish outlet creek, is a roomy and appropriately distanced site.

We take the North Fork trail east-northeast from the new Pine Lake Trail junction, quickly moving off the crest to the east slope, climbing steadily and steeply. As our trail enters a dry meadow, we pass the junction with the former Pine Lake Trail on the left, then descend quickly to a luscious, fenced-off spring before climbing to the Tom Taylor Cabin just beyond (0.4, 6710).

The Tom Taylor Cabin has already found a place in the national register as a historical landmark, for it is one of the few remaining examples of "frontier construction" in Siskiyou County. It was built in the early 1940s to replace the original Tom Taylor Cabin, which had collapsed; only hand tools and local materials (from the immediate area of the cabin) were used. The original cabin was built in the late 1890s by Tom Pey Taylor, a rancher near the mouth of Russian Creek (on the Salmon River North Fork). The old range custom, that a cabin built on open range gave "title" to that land to the cabin owner, was the likely reason for building there. With the creation of the Klamath Forest Preserve in 1905, however, the

Marble Mountains, and the cabin, came under the ownership of the Federal Government. The cabin became a summer home for lookouts on English Peak, backcountry rangers, trail crews, and others. In extreme weather, it can be a shelter for the hiker also, for its enclosed front porch is left unlocked for emergency use. If you do make use of the cabin, be sure to hang your food from the rafters: inside, it is safe from bears, but vulnerable to the resident wood rats. (Horsepackers take note: due to the obviously extreme erosion in these upper meadows, no grazing of packstock is allowed between the Tom Taylor Cabin and the ridge between Crapo and English peaks.)

To continue on to English Peak, climb steeply north-northeast from the cabin, and on through patchy forest to a junction with the English Peak Trail (0.5, 7030), at the edge of the vast, meadowed amphitheater on the southeast slopes of Crapo Peak.

The English Peak Trail contours through the severely eroded meadow, whose Davis' knotweed, spreading phlox, cobwebby paintbrush and pussy paws simply aren't sufficient to anchor the loosely compacted, decomposed granite soil. The path reaches the saddle northwest of English Peak just a few paces to the right of the ridgecrest junction with the Uncles Creek Trail. Turning southeast, follow the English Peak Trail up the ridgecrest to the small look out atop English Peak (0.5, 7316).

The view from the top of English Peak is without peer in this wilderness. It is, quite simply, riveting. The Forest Service has left its firefinder within the lookout available to the inquisitive backcountry visitor. (The lookout, preserved in conjunction with the Tom Taylor Cabin, is no longer used for firewatch or radio communication, but is being developed into a visitor information center.) Using the following list of bearings, and sighting on a few landmarks with which you are already familiar, you'll soon become a practiced hand with this simple, yet effective, instrument.

Black Mountain—2°
Peak 7636—22°
Boulder Peak—27°
Bear Wallow Peak—46°
Mt. Shasta—89°
Etna Mountain—94°

Yellow Dog Peak—95°
Russian Peak—120°
Tanners Peak—132°
Mt. Thompson—162°
Blue Ridge Lookout—170°
Crapo Mountain—186°
Devils Canyon—192°
Salmon Mountain—214°
Chimney Rock—229°
Crapo Peak—290°
Medicine Mountain—320°
Preston Peak—325°

Smith Cabin and Clear Lake

Most travelers on the Little North Fork Trail are headed for the high country eventually, or coming from there. For a solely river-bottom journey, with an accent on solitude, one might continue on past the Snowslide Gulch pathways. Few others do.

The Little North Fork Trail crosses a brook just beyond the Snowslide Trail junction and, on a slightly rising, slightly falling course, it passes several seeps and rivulets of variable permanency, then resumes its gentle ascent to a double-channeled creek. You pick your way across the creek and the trail-channeled runoff on both its sides (trail reconstruction scheduled for 1980-81 should correct this stream's drooling problem), and soon you reach the turnoff to Smith Cabin (1.0, 4850).

The winding path to Smith Cabin is vague at the outset, rocky and overgrown. However, once you surmount the bouldered rise near midway, you should have no trouble reaching the cabin (0.4, 5020). Smith Cabin is so well concealed and seldom visited that not even the Forest Service remembered it when it made up its cabin kill-list in the early '70s. Having been built in the 19-teens, however, and sporting the knife-script boasts of its early tenants as to who were the finest damn cowpokes in the Whole West, it is pretty well assured of a place in the national register as a historical monument. Although this small, windowless shack is not locked, neither it nor its neighboring campsites are exactly class acts. Which is perhaps why folks tend to head east-southeast 200 yards from the cabin to camp in the tranquil, secluded glen by the headwaters of the Little North Fork.

For some high-country time or lake play to complement your river trip, with far less company than in the English Peak area where use is compounded by North Fork Trail travelers, you can continue up the Little North Fork Trail to the ridge above Hamilton Camp. From there, Clear Lake is the local attraction.

There are dues to pay, though. From the junction with the spur trail to Smith Cabin, the Little North Fork Trail climbs better than 750 vertical feet in 0.6 mile. Survey stakes have already been emplaced, however, and by 1981 there should be a somewhat longer and less extreme route in use. It will still be a stiff pull until you reach a bench in a small ridge. The respite here is short-lived, for the trail soon resumes a steep climb up to a crossing of the small creek (0.9, 5800) that was so unrestrained back by the trail junction. The trail lingers beside the brook a few moments, then climbs a brief rise to a tiny, dry, bouldery meadow. Its proximity to the brook has established it as a camping area.

From this opening, you pass through a brief stretch of woods and exit into spacious Hamilton Camp meadow. Easily accessible water may be a problem in late season, though there will almost always be small pools out in the meadow. It's a lovely meadow at sunrise, with its several breakfast-browsing deer and enchanting mists. As for your own breakfast, in late summer you could make enough bilberry pancakes to feed the city of San Francisco.

After contouring along the meadow's north edge, the trail fades into the hillside. Until trail reconstruction establishes something more definite, your best bet may be to simply follow your compass and map west, up to the nearby ridgecrest saddle. It matters little whether you reunite with the tread that reappears in the dry, highly eroded meadow near the top of the headwall, for you will intersect the ridgecrest trail in the saddle (0.6, 6040). Starting east-northeast, the North Fork Trail contours along this ridgecrest and south slopes, coming to a junction with the Snowslide Trail in 2.1 miles. To reach Clear Lake, you turn southwest onto the Garden Gulch Trail.

On this trail you contour along the crest above the upper meadows of Hamilton Camp, then move off onto east slopes to arc

Storm clouds building over Clear Lake

through a richly forested amphitheater. After 1/3 mile a usage path heads south-southeast 55 yards to a frisky little brook at a meadow border. Where the Garden Gulch Trail crosses it shortly thereafter, the brook is no more than a mucky seep. A moderate climb of another ¼ mile brings you to a junction with the Steinacher Ridge Trail (0.6, 6230). The Steinacher Ridge Trail to Clear Lake is described in detail in the last part of Hike 14.

Uncles Creek Trail

Formerly known as the Tanners Peak Trail, this trail originally followed the ridgecrest above the North Fork, from English Peak to Tanner Peak, then descended to the river. The Forest Service is considering opening up the entire trail again, but for the present, it is opened up only as far as the saddle south of Lake of the Island. With the expansive panoramas southward in its last mile, this trail is an easy day trip from Tom Taylor Cabin, for the wilderness buff who resents the potential company at the English Peak lookout and would rather do his/her ogling in private.

Aside from crossing the snow that lingers on English Peak's north face well into July even in years of scant snowfall, this trail is easily followed, despite its low-priority status. Make sure you have plenty of water when you start, since an intermittent trickle at 3.1 miles is the only possibility for readily accessible water. The trail descends hastily across the peak's rocky north face to the ridge extending northeast from it. You continue the descent—moderate-to-steep with occasional stretches of ease—hiking along soon forested southeast slopes to the soggy semimeadow above the head of a tributary to the Left Hand Fork (1.6, 6210).

Here the trail bends to the southeast and starts an easy climb, then steepens as it approaches the south ridge of Peak 7133. Rounding the ridge, you descend briefly onto scrub-draped slopes as views open up south over the Uncles Creek drainage and east off to Mount Shasta. The meandering, undulating trail contours across southeast slopes until it crosses a seasonal dribblet, beyond which it descends gently 0.4 mile to the saddle above Lake of the Island (1.9, 6220).

The trail has not been brushed out beyond the saddle, and the Sadler-oak/greenleaf-manzanita / tobacco-brush / bitter-cherry scrub becomes horrendous at times. A usage trail continues along the saddle for 75 yards or so, created by those people who wanted to get a good look at the lake.

Hike 16 North Fork Trail, to English Peak

Distance: 15.8 miles, one way
Low elevation: 2810'
High elevation: 7316'
Suited for: 3-4 days
Usage: high; lake usage ranging from low to extremely high (Hancock Lake)
Difficulty: moderate

Directions to trailhead: Forest Service 41N37, beginning at the Idlewild Campground, is most easily reached from the east. Starting at the Etna turn-off from State Highway 3, drive 20 miles along the Somes Bar-Etna Road to FS 41N37. Coming from the west, this road junction is 5.9 miles from the ranger station in Sawyers Bar. Once on 41N37, drive 2.3 miles to the small, non-fee camping area at the Mule Bridge trailhead.

Trail description: Across Mule Bridge, you mount the trail above the North Fork's east bank, climbing moderately. The trail soon levels off and begins a gently rolling course through a forest in transition from mixed evergreen to mixed conifer. Unlike the previously described trails in this district, largely dug into the granitic surface of the English Peak pluton, the North Fork Trail begins in a broad region of metavolcanic rock and won't enter the grantic world until it nears English Lake. After 0.7 mile the trail eases into a steady incline that steepens briefly as it approaches Yellow Dog Creek. You cross the broad, bouldery creek (1.0, 3000) amid California spikenard, Indian rhubarb and thimbleberry. Beyond the creek's ravine, the trail gently rises and falls, then rises agin with the aid of two switchbacks.

As the ascent tapers off, the trail crosses a meager seep, then switchbacks south into a descent. After switchbacking north-north-west, you can spot one of the cabins of The Cedars out on the forested flat below you. The trail levels off after it descends to a riverside flat, the remnant of an old floodplain.

In a short while, you reach a Marble Mountain Wilderness sign and a trail register (1.8, 3090). The sign is in line with a 4-mile stretch of southern boundary passing through Yellow Dog Peak, but in fact a 1½-mile strip of non-wilderness parallels the North Fork

upstream in order to exclude the private holdings of the Abbott Ranch from the pristine fellowship of wilderness. Putting legalities aside, you'll find, a few steps beyond the sign, the deep-dish pool at the foot of a rollicking cascade to be a delight, regardless of its status. If you need more elbow room for getting used to the chilly waters, take a few minutes' walk upstream to a short usage path down to a larger pool, whose pellucid, green waters seem even more penetratingly clear than the first. Then, quickly skipping across a minor, Indian rhubarb-shaded rivulet, you amble upstream to a bouldery crossing of alder-bordered Big Creek (0.5, 3130).

About 200 yards past Big Creek, you come alongside a campsite, on your left, and another outstanding pool just beyond it. Swimming in the North Fork is a bit like eating the late-summer huckleberries and thimbleberries in these mountains. Just when you think you've eaten your fill, you notice a plump, juicy berry staring you right in the taste buds and you're right back at it again. Similarly, each pool you come to seems more beautiful and inviting then the one before.

From this last swimming hole, you continue your impreceptibly climbing stroll along the creekside flat. The flat narrows and then disappears altogether as the trail comes out onto the foot of a sunny hillside. Closely following the bends in the river, the trail winds gradually up to the second mule bridge, which crosses a pool-laced minigorge in the North Fork (0.8, 3210). On the west bank now, you can look up-river at bulky Bear Wallow Peak as you briefly descend the rocky trail to a stock gate on the south boundary of the Abbott Ranch. The campsite just beyond is on private land, and hence off limits (as if this trail needed any more campsites).

The next ½ mile traverses the Abbott Ranch, now used for purely recreational purposes by a Scott Valley family. The Abbott Ranch was homesteaded by Keyes Abbott in the 1880s, perhaps even earlier. One of the first to recognize the summer range potential

North Fork's minigorge

of this mountain country, Abbott contracted with Scott Valley ranchers to drive their cattle to their mountain-meadow pastures.

You leave the Abbott Ranch property soon after passing beyond the north edge of the ranch's long, linear meadow. Then, a quickly reached, narrow strip of pleasant, creekside campsites is your first opportunity to camp in the wilderness. Past them you make a short, level hike to Deer Pen Creek (1.0, 3270), whose name originated with Keyes Abbott. He built a deer pen there a salt lick and a trap door, and would set the trap whenever he needed to stock his larder. If there was only a young deer there in the morning, Abbott would let it go, but a choice buck would be killed and dressed out for the table.

From Deer Pen Creek the trail climbs leisurely through patchy forest. It goes through a stock gate and passes two more campsites before arriving at a junction with the Shelly Meadows Trail, cutting through spacious Six Mile Camp (1.1, 3370). If all the North Fork camping areas have been too public for your tastes, take the Shelly Meadows Trail's tightwire boulder crossing over the North Fork to a large, less obvious site

in the crotch of the North Fork/Right Hand Fork confluence.

The North Fork Trail bends westward and soon traverses an open slope, sparsely clad with currants and thimbleberries, just before reaching double-channeled Deadman Gulch creek, whose bubbling nature belies its name. The path then climbs gently along the western-yew-bordered trail to a crossing of the North Fork (0.7, 3460). Even in late season you might find this crossing most easily negotiated by wading, although a boulder-hop for the nimble-footed should surface just upstream by midsummer. The riverbed here offers a graphic example of the river's transport power: the loose granitic boulders were transported during floods from the area of the English Peak pluton, several miles upstream.

On the northeast bank now, you leave a large campsite behind at the crossing and pass another tiny site next to a nice pool 80 yards up-canyon. One-half mile above the crossing, you spy a charming, creekside site below a depression, tucked in an arbor of bigleaf maples and Douglas-firs. With the proliferation of campsites along its banks, the North Fork seems to be evolving toward a wilderness megalopolis. This river is too attractive for its own good.

Shortly after crossing a shallow, rocky creeklet, the trail tops out its climb and descends gently past two more campsites to another boulder crossing of the North Fork (1.3, 3640). In the early season use a partly hidden log downstream, below the bend in the river.

Beyond the crossing, the North Fork Trail begins acting more like a mountain trail than a river trail, climbing with increasing steepness. After rounding a bulge, you cross a precipitous, slide-prone open slope, on which huckleberry is one of the few shrubs managing to gain some purchase. Vistas open up along the trail here: north up Grant Creek's notch to the balding pate of Peak 7721, and straight ahead to the scrub-robed southeast slopes of Peak 6925.

As the climb tapers off, you round a point opposite Snowslide Gulch and descend once again to the banks of the North Fork (1.1, 3950). Surprisingly, there are no campsites. Not surprisingly, there is no assured dry crossing. Ducks lead you west-northwest across a trailless, boulder-field floodplain to where a few leaps among large boulders will get you across the river. The trail climbs away from the river, then switchbacks upstream to ascend steeply to a junction with the Lake of the Island Trail (0.4, 4190).

Lake of the Island

Despite the steep, rocky, overgrown, primitive trail to Lake of the Island, it receives a moderate amount of visitors, for it is the first lake "along" the North Fork Trail. And its use may increase, since the Forest Service intends to brush out the trail.

This trail weaves its way down to a variety of log and boulder crossings of the North Fork, then quickly climbs to a ridgecrest among Sadler oaks, chinquapins and Oregon boxwoods that dominate both the understory and the trail. After a few moments of easy ascent, the serious climbing begins. The shrubbery becomes so overwhelming at times—at least in 1979—that it embowers the trail as you climb to a pooling, intermittent stream (0.9, 4640).

The brush begins to diversify as the forest thins, then opens up to admit patches of moist-meadow flora. As the ascent eases into the region of former alpine glaciation, you cross areas of considerably shallower soil, and the forest gives way to a rock garden.

Just past a quaking-aspen community, the trail fades into a pocket of lush grasses. Ten yards short of the pocket's small firepit, bend southwest and you'll soon pick up the tread again amid wildflowers, bitter cherry and cascara. The ascent escalates dramatically, working up through scrub and sketchy forest to the north shore of Lake of the Island (1.2, 5680).

The origin of the name is obvious, though unremarkable: a small, grassy hummock in the northwest corner of the lake. The picturesque setting of the lake suffers from no such understatement: deep-set in a high-walled glacial bowl, its footwaters are richly trimmed in huckleberries, western yews and assorted shrubbery.

Beyond the trail junction, the ascent soon eases and then curls past a campsite off to the left, with bench and bearbagging bar, before reaching aptly named Boulder Creek

Lake of the Island

(0.3, 4250). Fifty yards farther, you cross the North Fork yet again on rocks or logs. There is a small north-bank campsite, hidden from the trail, 20 yards upstream.

After the crossing you begin a steady, moderate ascent on a Sadler-oak-lined trail. This endemic shrub is as reliable an indicator of the completion of the transition from mixed-evergreen to mixed-conifer forest as the trees themselves. Beyond a powerful spring overrunning the trail, the climb eases and slopes diminish as you enter an open stand of white firs. The low-growing rug of shade-tolerant flora here almost seems manicured. The forest opens even more as the trail passes through one of the uncommon colonies of quaking aspens, with waist-high ferns and flowers. Returning to the forest, the trail soon reaches a final log crossing of the now shallow North Fork (1.1, 4700).

On the northwest bank now, the trail continues to climb easily. In 210 yards you pass a usage trail heading west-northwest, which leads in 200 yards to a packer camp at the site of an old cabin. There's a nice spring

50 yards uphill from the stone fireplace that remains from the cabin. As the North Fork Trail continues up-canyon, a grassy meadow begins to spread through the center of the glacier-broadened valley bottom. You soon reach a meadow-edge junction with the Abbott Lake and Bug Gulch trails (0.5, 4850).

The two large camping areas near the trail junction—one in the trees on your left, just before the junction, and another above the junction at the site of Abbott's Upper Cabin—provide access to Abbott and Horse Range lakes, both little used.

Abbott Lake

The most difficult part of the trail to Abbott Lake may be finding it in the first place. Ignore the various treads you might see faintly curving through the meadow, and simply head south-southeast from the junction toward the river, aiming just to the right of two riverside incense-cedars.

Beyond the skimpy river crossing, you climb steeply along the forested canyon wall. After ½ mile two quick switchbacks carry you through a brief opening, from which you curve south to climb alongside the lake's outlet creek. The path soon leaves the forest permanently behind to wind up through the scrub and a highly varied, granitic rock garden. The trail is overgrown in places, ducked but vague in others. Shortly after the trail levels off on the glacial moraine that dams Abbott Lake, you reach an unsigned fork (1.0, 5630).

The right fork crosses the outlet creek and burrows through the brush to reach the grassy shore at a tiny campsite. The left fork is not only the shortest path—75 yards—to the lake, but it is also unencumbered by brush and leads to an excellent lakeshore campsite beneath firs and western white pines. Here the lake deepens immediately out from its shore, and the rock-cupped splendor of Abbott Lake spreads out before your eyes.

Horse Range Lake

Horse Range Lake is not as readily accessible as Abbott Lake, for it is a 2½-mile trip from the North Fork Trail. Turning west-northwest onto the Bug Gulch Trail, you climb off the valley floor and steeply up-slope. The ascent eases as it passes into scrub near the top of the canyon's ridge. After cresting the ridge, you make a short, gentle ascent through a stand of white firs to a junction with the Horse Range Lake Trail (0.8, 5350).

Turning west, the Horse Range Lake Trail passes through a bracken-fern meadow, then soon returns to open forest, climbing along a creeklet choked with willows and American dogwoods. After 0.6 mile the trail curves up-slope to climb the ridge. The tread through this curve is quite faint; the curve occurs just as the trail appears to level off near the head of the creeklet's gully, with a large, brush-filled meadow opening up ahead.

After curving up to the ridgecrest, the path descends moderately along its south slope. An interesting process is occuring here. Beneath the trees, you can see dead manzanita and scrub skeletons. A red-fir forest has come up the north face of the ridge and is spilling over onto the south side, creating sufficient shade to kill off some south-slope scrub and give conifer seedlings the protection they need to survive.

You soon leave the forest behind to continue the descent through the more customary chaparral residents of a south slope. As you gradually curve into the glacier-carved side canyon containing Horse Range Lake, you get an impressive view across the North Fork's canyon. The descent ends in meadow adjoining the lake's outlet creek (1.3, 5670), then your trail immediately begins an extremely steep climb up a small draw. The gradient lessens somewhat after you step across its creeklet and enter a magnificently flowered meadow. It is difficult to spare enough attention for route-finding in the face of the extraordinary diversity of the flora. And up-valley there is an interesting geologic contrast, since the saddle at the head of the valley marks the contact between the light granitic rock of the English Peak pluton to the south and the "earth tone" metasediments to the north. This contact is a line of weakness that streams eroded along, later followed by a series of glaciers that excavated the basin holding today's Horse Range Lake.

The moist-meadow flora give way to drier types as the trail nears the glacial moraine damming the lake, and you quickly descend to a large camping area on the lake's north shore (0.4, 5980). If the north-shore campsites seem too open, cross the boggy meadow above the brushy northwest shore to a tiny site, just in the firs near the west edge of the lake.

From the four-way trail junction the North Fork Trail gently undulates just outside the meadow. If you want to camp near the junction but want a tad more seclusion, keep an eye out for a gargantuan-trunked incense-cedar on your left. A lovely, meadow-edge campsite near a small spring lies 60 yards south of the tree. In 1/3 mile you cross the Horse Range Lake outlet creek, whose flow has gone completely underground by midsummer.

Beyond the "creek crossing" the trail begins to climb steeply from the canyon floor onto the scrub-clad north wall. As you begin to notice the advent of granitic rocks along the trail, you can look across the canyon to where the entire south wall lies within the region of the English Peak pluton. The creation of the glacial ripsaw on that canyon wall may not rival the walls of Yosemite, but it is a magnificent piece of work, both in scale and effect.

The steady ascent tops out momentarily at a blocky spur and passes through a variegated flower show, then winds through a broad depression. You next climb a double-rutted tread that soon reaches another flat-top spur (1.7, 5870), this one with a side trail heading to English Lake. This 300-yard spur trail descends to a spacious lakeside campsite on English Lake's northwest shore.

English Lake

English Lake

Historically, English Lake is a popular area. As early as the turn of the century, Herbert Finley was bringing his tourist packtrips here, perhaps to this very campsite at trail's end (Finley once operated a camp near today's Idlewild Campground). As the first lake on this major, easily traveled trail, English Lake has had high use. Given the large meadow area below Upper English Lake, it has also been a very attractive spot for horsepackers. However, the author has visited this lake in midsummer, at the height of the tourist crush, and found it deserted. And it's no puddle—there's a lot of lake to

go around. All the campsites are on the northwest shore, and a pit toilet has been placed just uphill of the site closest to the outlet (all the campsites are well inside the 200-foot camping regulation; the topography leaves you little choice). Near the northwest corner of the lake, a usage trail heads up into the meadow and beyond to small, shallow Upper English Lake.

From the junction with the English Lake spur trail, the North Fork Trail climbs steeply into forest, then soon switchbacks into a multihued, subalpine rock garden. The ascent steepens even more as you move onto the canyon headwall. The view over English Lake and the canyon of the North Fork almost lets you forget all about the 20% gradient up the granite staircase to the ridgecrest. Then, leaving the crest behind, you descend 0.1 mile to a junction with the Hancock Lake Trail (1.2, 6810). Tiny, frog-serenaded Diamond Lake lies 50 yards south, with a smattering of open to semi-open campsites above its north shore.

Hancock Lake

Hancock Lake is one of the most visited lakes in the wilderness. Its major deterrent is that the north-slope trail to it remains snow-patched late in the summer, and is mucky and steep regardless of snow. A less effective deterrent is that, perhaps due to its great size and depth, it is not an easy lake to fish.

The attractions of this area begin right from the trail junction, as you descend steeply through a forest community that is unique in the Marbles. The Pacific silver fir that shares dominance with the mountain hemlock is found in only one other place in the Marbles (off-trail in the Ukonom Lake area). The stand here and the one on the northeast slopes above Diamond Lake are the southernmost Pacific silver firs in the United States. The most readily distinguishing characteristic of this tree is that it looks like a fir that never grew up: even when mature, the bark remains light grey, with blotches of an even lighter, nearly white color, and the bark surface remains relatively smooth and unseamed.

The trail stays within the forest as it descends along the west edge of a narrow

Hancock Lake

meadow, passing an attractive, wooded campsite in 0.3 mile. You descend an accordian of short switchback legs that finally end at a peninsula on the lake's south shore

Mt. Thompson crowns the Trinity Alps, south of Marble Mountain Wilderness.

Mt. Shasta, to the east, is a landmark seen from many ridgecrest views.

(0.7, 6340). The peninsula offers the most glamorous and least legitimate campsites on the lake. For a more appropriate site, look for an open campsite just east of the inlet creek, well back from the lake.

There are more camping possibilities on the north shore, particularly near the north-west tip of the lake. This area, reached by a ¾-mile-long trail, is a favorite with horse-packers, for they can turn their stock loose in the "box canyon" of Tobacco Lake. This camping area received sufficient use to have a pit toilet installed, hidden on the top of the fledgling ridgecrest beyond the campsite. The disadvantage of the north-shore sites is that they catch the brunt of the winds which rifle down the north slope and across the lake.

From the Hancock Lake Trail junction, the North Fork Trail heads west-southwest into dense forest. Within ½ mile you reach the ridgecrest, and then cross over to the west slope to make an arcing traverse above Toms Lake. Returning to the crest and spec-tacular vistas straight down the North Fork canyon, you resume climbing to a saddle (0.7, 7220) northeast of Crapo Peak. The

reason for the sign *No grazing in drainage* is readily apparent in the numerous severe erosion gullies splitting the high meadows below Crapo Peak. The grazing restriction extends south to the meadow above Tom Taylor Cabin.

Mt. Thompson and the Trinity Alps tickle the sky to the south-southeast, and as the trail heads toward English Peak, Mt. Shasta rises in the east. You soon reach a ridgecrest trail junction. From here the North Fork Trail switchbacks west, reaching the Tom Taylor Cabin in 0.6 mile. For English Peak you stay on the ridgecrest on the English Peak Trail. In 0.1 mile this path passes a saddle junction with the Uncles Creek Trail and, a few paces beyond, reaches a spur of the English Peak Trail coming from the west-northwest. After another 0.3-mile climb you reach the small lookout tower/visitor infor-mation center atop English Peak (0.6, 7316). The panorama revealed from English Peak is glorious. To know more specifically what it is that you are seeing, use the firefinder that the Forest Service left emplaced in the now-retired lookout, and consult the list of land-marks and bearings included in Hike 15, the Little North Fork Trail.

Hike 17   North Fork—Bug Gulch—Shelly
Meadows Trails Loop

Distance: 33.5 miles, semiloop trip
Low elevation: 2810'
High elevation: 6930'
Suited for: 4-6 days
Usage: high on the North Fork Trail; low on
Bug Gulch/Shelly Meadows trails
Difficulty: strenuous
Directions to trailhead: Same as on page 101.

Trail description: The first 11.6 miles of this
hike follow the North Fork Trail to its junction with the Bug Gulch Trail, and they are
described in detail in Hike 16. Following the
Bug Gulch Trail, you climb steeply 0.8 mile
up the north slopes of the North Fork canyon to a junction with the Horse Range
Lake Trail. The 1.7-mile trail to this little-
used lake is fully described in Hike 16.

Just beyond the junction with the Horse
Range Lake Trail, the Bug Gulch Trail
crosses the burbling creeklet of Pierces
Draw, then climbs steeply up a spur and over
to cascading Cold Springs Creek. The junction with the Hell Hole Ridge Trail is 55
yards farther (0.4, 5500).

Lakes Ethel and Katherine

Due to the steepness and remoteness of
the Hell Hole Ridge Trail to Lakes Katherine
and Ethel, these two gems are seldom visited.
Hence, these lakes offer a Thoreauvian ambience that will certainly reward your effort.

The Hell Hole Ridge Trail initially heads
steeply up a shallow depression and onto the
ridge slope. The ascent eases as the trail enters a large, verdant meadow and quickly
crosses a brisk freshet. But it steepens again
as the trail follows an erosion channel up
through a willow thicket, then traverses the
head of the meadow and returns to forest.
Through open forest and pocket meadows
you labor upslope on a trail sometimes vague
due to forest litter and overgrowth. After
following the edge of a last meadow above
the head of Cold Springs Creek, the trail
switchbacks up through a heavily lichened
stand of red firs to the crest of Hell Hole
Ridge (1.3, 6700). Across the defile of
Wooley Creek, Medicine Mountain is prominent in the west-northwest, and Black
Mountain, to the north, is visible through
trees.

A few paces short of a ridgecrest trail
sign, a faint tread can be seen heading southwest, just off the crest. This is the continuation of the Hell Hole Ridge Trail, a 1¼-mile
primitive trail that is not as difficult to
follow as it appears at the outset. It climbs
moderately along the ridgecrest, then descends onto the snow-trapping north face of
Peak 7071. Regaining the ridgecrest, the trail
undulates through a colorful rock garden.
The panorama here is as exciting as it is
extensive: from the Salmon Mountains in
the north past the purling flow of Coast

Deer drinking in Boulder Creek

Range ridges in the west, to the deeply gouged canyon beneath Hancock Lake. The extremely meandering trail climbs along the south face of Peak 6968, then returns to the treeless crest for a while before descending into huckleberries on the northeast slopes above Lake Katherine. The trail soon fades away, first from lack of maintenance, then from lack of construction.

The Ethel-Katherine Lakes Trail leaves the ridgecrest, descending rapidly northeast. On a north-trending spur it crosses a saddle and then contours through a lavish rock garden above the head of Big Meadows. Soon it returns to the crest of this spur, from which you can see Lake Ethel sitting calmly at the foot of its well-sculpted cirque. The trail descends gently along the spur crest, then more steeply as it drops onto the west slope. After a switchback aims you toward the lake, the trail gradient becomes even more absurd, approaching 30° at times, before bottoming out near the lake's north shore (1.1, 5700). Not only are the campsites on the timbered flat here more attractive than those crowded along the north shore, but they also show some regard for the 100-foot camping restriction.

If you wish to enjoy more remote Lake Katherine, pay no heed to the trail indication on the Lake Ethel sign, pointing off into the underbrush across the flat. Instead, follow the path along Lake Ethel's north and west shores to a high-impact campsite, 0.1 mile beyond the low-flowing outlet creek. From the hind end of the campsite, the trail makes a brief, steep climb, then disappears into a meadow. If you are along the meadow's lower edge, you'll pick up a distinct tread in its northwest corner. The path leads north-northwest down a shallow, grassy draw, then quickly turns west-northwest to contour through the forest to the berry-bordered north shore of Lake Katherine (0.7, 5750). Though huckleberries, gooseberries, and twinberries thickly flank the lake, there is enough open space above the outlet creek's west bank for a very pleasant campsite.

The Bug Gulch Trail climbs steadily from the junction with the Hell Hole Ridge Trail, leaving the white-fir stand back at the creekside for a more diversified forest. This creek

Wild Lake

is your last water until you reach a small spill just west of Grants Meadows, 5½ miles ahead. After rounding a spur point, the trail weaves through brushy depressions, rocky outcrops and patchy forest in an arcing climb above the head of Crystal Clear Creek. As it nears the ridgecrest, the trail climbs through a fir forest to a crest saddle and a junction with the Big Meadows Trail (1.4, 6390).

Wild Lake and Big Meadows

The Big Meadows Trail is a seldom traveled path that connects Wooley Creek with the Salmon River high country. That it drops over 4000 feet in 5.7 miles is one large reason for its minimal use. However, there are two attractions—Wild Lake and Big Meadows—which might entice you a short way down this trail.

Turning north onto the open slopes of metasedimentary outcrops and rubble, you draw a bead on Black Mountain in the distance and hurtle down the rocky trail. After a flurry of switchbacks, the trail returns to its northward course, descending through a melange of open forest, rocky terrain and moist gardens to a junction with the Wild Lake Trail (0.8, 5620).

The Wild Lake Trail is a relatively recent addition to the Marbles trail system. Since it was built for purely recreational reasons, it is curious that the Forest Service chose not to follow a 5900-foot contour to the lake. Short of bushwhacking a more sensibly graded route, you have no recourse but to struggle up the trail. Once across a ridge, the climb eases considerably for the short walk to the prominent moraine that is Wild Lake's north shore (0.3, 5890).

Wild Lake may be as far removed from a trailhead as any lake in this wilderness area, but the word is getting out. On one three-day stay there, the author went from a first night of solitude to a last supper with 11 campmates, all of whom were exclaiming, "Gee, I didn't expect to see anyone else here."

Big Meadows can be reached by continuing beyond the Wild Lake trail junction,

Wooley Creek, near Big Meadows Creek

switchbacking down a more benignly graded trail. At the fourth switchback, where the Big Meadows Trail turns north again beneath a blanket of bracken fern (0.5, 5300), a spur trail continues on south-southwest toward Big Meadows. In 225 yards, just as the trail leaves the forest, it follows an eroded route steeply down to a creek. After a brief scramble up from the creek, you quickly come to a couple of small campsites above the west bank at the edge of Big Meadows. Seated at the base of towering, forested walls, this wondrous garden and its soft-spoken creek are enough to kindle the home-steading fires in the heart of the most city bound tourists.

If Big Meadows doesn't deliver the solitude you were expecting, then walk 0.2 mile farther down the Big Meadows Trail, pushing through the bracken-fern jungle to hop-across Wild Lake creek, with a small campsite above its south bank. The remaining steep but evenly graded 4.2 miles down to Wooley Creek have no campsites and little easily reached water. On the other hand, the last mile of trail is well supplied with thimbleberries and red huckleberries, and the sparkling pools and secluded campsites of Wooley Creek await the wanderer of this path "less traveled by."

Having attained the crest of the north wall of the North Fork's canyon, the Bug Gulch Trail more or less remains there. The ascent through a fir-and-pine forest continues until you reach the point of a south-west-trending spur. Leaving the forest here, you can see the Trinity Alps glistening in the south-southeast, and the canyon of the North Fork spilling away below you. After gently climbing through a lovely rock garden, the trail soon returns to the crest in a saddle, which adds vistas over the Wooley Creek drainage. Black Mountain (350°) and Medicine Mountain (290°) are the foremost eminences. The trail then continues its generally south-slope arc above the head of Boulder Creek.

After rounding the southeast spur of Peak 6925, the trail makes a long, moderate-to-steep descent to the saddle west of Peak 6814 (2.0, 6290). Although the climb from this saddle to the southeast spur of Peak 6814 is only 0.3 mile long, it's a 20% grade through shadeless scrub.

From Peak 6814's southeast spur, the verdant swath of Grants Meadows lies seductively in the northeast. With the distant murmur of Grant Creek falls in your ears, you descend the rocky, scrub-bound east slopes. The trail has passed into the freckled granitic rock of the Heather Lake pluton, yet you'll notice a few scattered patches of metasediments, still to be swept away by the whisk broom of time. The descent bottoms out at the gleaming, granitic saddle north-northeast of Peak 6814, with weeping spruce dotting its north-slope forest. Then you climb gradually along the south slopes of Peak 7721. Shortly after easing into a gentle descent, you cross a small trickle that is almost too shallow for use (1.7, 6180). The descent continues to the edge of Grants Meadows (0.4, 6110), through which the trail is about as decipherable as a doctor's handwriting.

The tread disappears in the grass, but you can rediscover it by heading east-northeast. You quickly reach a small, sloping campsite beneath a cluster of firs on your right, beyond which the trail appears to head right down to the creek. However, an obscure path, indicated by an even more obscure trail sign, turns upslope 15 yards past the campsite. This faint tread, heading through a cut in a massive fallen log, is the Bug Gulch Trail.

Beyond the fallen log, the trail becomes a vague, gravelly path steeply climbing past scrub and rock. It is difficult to follow at times even with the help of the numerous ducks. One-quarter mile beyond the campsite-turn, the trail bends east-northeast and quickly dips to a boulder-hop of Grant Creek. Past the crossing you point toward a pair of isolated red firs and continue east-northeast 50 yards up a shallow erosion channel. At the firs the trail becomes obvious again, turning south-southwest.

Grants Meadows is early-season rotation range for the Shelly Meadows allotment, but the heady aroma of cowpies baking in the sun is soon overcome by the sweet smell of tobacco brush as you climb onto scrub-draped slopes. Fill your water bottles at the perky little spring overrunning the trail, 0.3 mile above the red-fir turn. This spring is the only trustworthy water in Grants Meadows, and the last good water until you reach the small spring below Bug Lake.

After the trail bends to the east-southeast, the extremely steep ascent eases and rises gently through an open forest to a saddle just north of Bear Wallow Peak (1.4, 6930). This saddle is this hike's best opportunity to survey the wilderness. Better yet, follow a ridgecrest path 60 yards south to a small pinnacle from which the vistas are truly awesome. Bear Wallow Peak, dead ahead, splits the drainages of the Right Hand Fork to its east and the North Fork to its west. The snowclad peaks of the Trinity Alps dap-

Bear Wallow Peak

Bug Lake, nestled in a mosquito-rich meadow

ple the horizon in the south-southeast. Mt. Shasta in the east crowns the south-curving crest of the Salmon Mountains.

Now you are ready for the horrifically steep trail down to Bug Lake. With a grade of 25%, the next 2/3 mile may be the steepest extended trail challenge the Marbles has to offer. Switchback cuts are rampant and the trail disappears entirely in a small, grassy meadow about midway down. Here, head around the south side of a small hummock by a trickling creek, and the tread will reappear. Using cattle-plagued Bug Lake as a beacon, work your way down to the meadow along the north side of the lake, where the trail vanishes again.

Traversing the meadow along its upper edge, head east-northeast toward a large, blazed red fir, then northeast along a downed tree to where the tread re-establishes itself. A few minutes farther, you pass a

small spring just below the trail. The cattle are apparently happy enough with Bug Lake and its creek, for this spring is unpolluted and delicious.

The steep descent continues down a gravelly trail on alluvium, a remnant of our geologically recent glacial age. The trail poses no further route-finding problems and you can divert your attention to watching the transition from a red-fir forest community to a mixed-conifer forest.

There's an obscure turn in the trail as it arrives at a shallow, puddling spring and a large, lovely campsite beneath towering sugar pines, Douglas-firs, and incense-cedars (1.9, 4810). The trail once crossed the spring and continued straight ahead 110 yards to rampaging Cabin Gulch creek. Too vigorous one spring, the creek washed away the trail on its east bank. Now the trail makes a sharp turn to the south-southeast, a step or two before reaching the spring. The mucky trail winds its way steeply down to a boulder-leap of Cabin Gulch creek and soon reaches a junction with the Cabin Gulch Trail (0.2, 4710).

Cabin Gulch Trail

The Cabin Gulch Trail is a primitive trail that is quite difficult to follow in its upper section. It is hot, rocky and steep. The gulch is filled with cattle near its head, so the water is suspect. There are all sorts of arguments against venturing up this trail, which is probably why it is so rarely used. On the positive side, however, is the magnificent geologic tapestry of the cirque at the head of the gulch; an area of such prodigious scale and subalpine beauty is rarely accessible by trail in the Marbles. And before the mid-July cattle invasion, you will likely have it all to yourself.

The trail looks anything but primitive as it begins the ascent as a broad swath cut through the brush. The climb is interrupted after 2/3 mile by a brief descent nearly to creekside, then resumes its steep course upward. The gradient eases once again, 1/3 mile farther, as it takes advantage of a bit of forest shade. Soon steepening again, the trail crosses an undependable seep spring amid Bigelow sneezeweeds, corn lilies and alders, then continues up to a slight intermittent stream (1.2, 5750).

Cabin Gulch tarn

Out of the forest now, you can gaze up at the imposing headwall, but the trail soon requires all your attention. The tread fades away as the ascent eases into a small, grassy plot. Head north-northwest toward a blazed incense-cedar, then north following ducks. Ignore the reappearance of a tread immediately beyond the incense-cedar, since it is only a cattlepath to a salt lick. Keeping a sharp eye out for ducks, an occasional tree blaze, and a sketchy tread, you climb away from the creek. The trail levels off again as it approaches the head of the gulch, descends briefly to a break in alders to cross a dribbling creeklet, then fades away for good as it enters a rock-pimpled meadow. A westward course soon brings you to the edge of the depression cupping the smaller tarn at the head of Cabin Gulch (0.8, 6070).

Camping is permissible in these upper meadows, with a low-impact ethic the order of the day. In the early '60s, beaver dams built up the depth of the tarns, but they are little more than shallow, snowmelt pools now. One comes to Cabin Gulch for the ambience, not for the fishing.

Beyond the Cabin Gulch Trail junction, the Bug Gulch Trail descends into forest, passing by a large campsite on the right in 100 yards, and through the middle of anoth-

er 0.2 mile beyond that; both campsites are 100-150 brush-bound yards away from and above the creek. Below the second campsite the trail quickly reaches a short spur trail up to the Shelly Meadows Trail. In another 250 yards you reach a junction with the Shelly Meadows Trail (0.4, 4480). Since the early '70s, this trail has been a section of temporary Pacific Crest Trail.

Shelly Meadows Trail to PCT

For a high-country conclusion to this loop trip, you can follow the Shelly Meadows Trail upslope to the ridgecrest junction with the permanent Pacific Crest Trail and follow that trail out to Etna Summit. This high country route is 2.5 miles longer than the riverside route and, of course, requires a lot of climbing—1840 feet, to be exact—at the outset.

The Shelly Meadows Trail heads steeply uphill, shortly meeting with its westward spur, then crossing Harry Hall Gulch creek in ¼ mile. Passing between dense scrub on the outer slope and shady, young forest in the depressions, it meanders steadily up to double-barreled Timothy Gulch creek (1.0, 5070). The trail curves up into scrub, where the dominant tree species seems to be the occasional knobcone pine. After crossing several more seeps and feeder rivulets, the trail arcs through the Timothy Gulch drainage to a spur point (1.0, 5770).

The rush of Shelly Gulch creek rises to your ears as you head up through scrub and then fir forest to an outrider of Shelly Meadows. Just inside the forest again on the uphill side of this linear meadow, you pass a 1/3-mile spur trail heading east to intersect with the Pacific Crest Trail, just above the main Shelly Meadow. The Shelly Meadows Trail crosses another boggy finger of meadow, then heads up through an open stand of red firs to a junction with the Pacific Crest Trail in the ridgecrest saddle above the Shelly Fork (0.7, 6380). The 11.2 miles of Pacific Crest Trail out to Etna Summit is described, in reverse direction, in the beginning of the Pacific Crest Trail, Hike 27.

The low country route turns east-southeast onto the Shelly Meadows Trail, then follows a semilevel course through the thick, mixed-conifer forest. Beyond the narrow cut of Harry Hall Gulch, the trail descends steeply, passing above an attractive, creekside campsite before arriving at a log crossing of Bug Gulch creek (0.3, 4370). Just 40 yards before this crossing, a usage path heads east-southeast to two small campsites near the bank of Timothy Gulch creek. In 1979 there was a Forest Service sign at the log crossing identifying the area as Shelly Gulch. Since you are at the confluence of Bug and Timothy gulches, and Shelly Gulch is considerably farther downstream, pay the sign no mind if it is there.

After a brief climb, the trail gradually descends along the creek's south bank. As the creek swings out toward the mouth of Shelly Gulch, the descent bottoms out and the trail climbs steeply. As Bug Gulch creek bends back to the south below Shelly Gulch, it takes on the more prestigious title of the Right Hand Fork of the Salmon River. As it follows the bend in the creek, the trail eases its ascent and reverts back to a descending course.

The trail soon dips into a monkey-flower-and-fireweed-tinted gully to cross a sturdy little creek. Weaving in and out of nooks and crannies, the trail continues descending steadily. It steepens as it approaches an Indian-rhubarb-canopied intermittent streamlet, and again as it approaches river level near Pointers Gulch. Below the mouth of Pointers Gulch, river and trail bend sharply west-northwest, and your descent eases as the trail passes just above two spacious campsites on riverside flats (1.9, 3780). The Right Hand Fork has gained enough energy and volume by this point to create some rather inviting pools. However, for a swimming hole to make even the river gods drool, continue downtrail 300 yards from the campsites to the gorgious pool just before the river's bend back to the southwest.

Yours is a riverside trail now, descending easily along sandy "pine flats." A brief rise and fall brings you to the pooling cascade of Slide Creek (0.7, 3710), whose severely folded metasedimentary creekbed reflects the tectonic torture to which these mountains have been submitted. Just beyond Slide Creek the trail descends past a long, campsite-laden flat, and into a more moist, lush forest.

A brief climb precedes the descent to the mouth of Bear Wallow Gulch creek, which spills into the adjacent Right Hand Fork (1.1, 3520). There are two more short climbs below Bear Wallow Gulch to lend variety to the final descent to the North Fork. As you approach the confluence of the North Fork and the Right Hand Fork, the flat over which the trail passes broadens, providing enough room for a vast camping area in the nose of land at the confluence. The trail then curls around to the banks of the North Fork, and a boulder crossing that requires a light touch by late season (in early season, it doesn't even exist). After crossing through Six Mile Camp on the south bank of the North Fork, you quickly come to a junction with the North Fork Trail (1.1, 3370). You then retrace your steps 6.2 miles down-canyon to the trailhead at Mule Bridge.

Chapter 9

Scott River District

Introduction: The Scott River district represents the best and worst of the Marble Mountain Wilderness. It is superlative country, with the hushed intimacy of forested creek bottoms, the kaleidoscope of color in its many-flowered meadows, the cool sparkle of its subalpine lakes, and the viewful ridgecrest at the head of its glaciated valleys. It has the high point in the wilderness—Boulder Peak, at 8299 feet—and the deepest lake—Cliff Lake, at 175 feet. It is the most geologically diverse area, with ultramafic Red Mountain, the gleaming, marbled mass of Black and Marble mountains, a gabbro and diorite intrusion along lower Kelsey Creek, scattered, small granitic masses, and a preponderance of varied metasediments and metavolcanics throughout.

However, for the backpacker who believes that seclusion is a basic characteristic of wilderness, the Scott River district is hardly worthy of wilderness classification at all. It is far and away the most popular district, receiving over half of the wilderness' recreational traffic. The Lovers Camp and Shackleford Creek trailheads alone (used for Hikes 19, 21, 22 and 23) serve as the entry point for nearly half the backcountry visitors. With the exception of Haypress Meadows in the Ukonom district and Hancock Lake in the Salmon River district, all the extremely high use areas in the Marbles are in this district. Of all its lakes that can be reached by trail, only Big Elk and Kidder lakes are moderately used.

This area's overuse is not due to the magnificence of its natural features, but rather to its accessibility. The Salmon Mountains crest and virtually all of this district's lakes are within a half-day hike from a trailhead. And the trailheads are all on the east side of the wilderness, closest to the Interstate 5 pipeline from the population centers of southern Oregon and northern California—not to mention the greatest concentration of local population, the Scott Valley area. What's more, though backpackers outnumber horsepackers by an ever increasing margin, the bulk of the horse traffic is in the Scott River district; most of the commercial packers working the wilderness are located in Scott Valley.

Access: With the exception of the Kidder Creek Trail, all the trails described here are reached from the Scott River Road (SIS 7F01), an often winding, narrow road that is the northeast segment of the motorway loop around the wilderness. The most common approach to the Scott River Road is at its junction with State Highway 3, at the south end of Fort Jones, a small valley community. This junction lies 15.4 miles southwest from Interstate 5's Highway 3 exit, on the south edge of Yreka.

Wilderness permits and information are available at the Scott River Ranger Station, at the junction of Highway 3 and the Scott River Road. During summer, wilderness permits may also be available from the guard station at Kelsey Creek, though this is not a dependable resource because the crews are often out in the field. Finally, the Forest Service work center in Callahan (13 miles south from the Etna junction on Highway 3), has a summer office person who dispenses permits on weekends and on some weekdays.

Only on the east side of the wilderness do you run into problems with private lands. The roads to the Kidder Creek, Mill Creek Ponds, Red Mountain and Shackleford Creek trailheads are all on private lands, for the most part owned by International Paper Co. There is no problem in reaching the Shackleford Creek Trail, for due to its popularity the Forest Service purchased an easement on the road to its trailhead. Your ability to reach the other trailheads, however, is a function of logging schedules and economic expediency. The Mill Creek Ponds Trail starts from an abandoned logging road no longer maintained by International Paper. Since conventional autos can't reach the trailhead, this trail has been excluded from this book. The road to the Red Mountain trailhead is serviceable on a year-to-year basis. Although the road to the Kidder Creek trailhead is well-maintained—due to continued logging—it is subject to closure. To protect their equipment from vandalism, the logging company put up a locked gate to prohibit passage at night and on Sundays. Although the hours of closure are generally posted, vandalism of the sign once resulted in several weekend parties leaving the trail on Sunday afternoon only to find themselves "locked in" the wilderness. If you have designs on any of the above trails, then first check with the Forest Service about their accessibility.

As for off-trail camping, there are several Forest Service campgrounds in the Scott Bar area along Scott River Road. Both the Shackleford Creek and Lovers Camp trailheads have developed camping areas, including corrals for packstock. There are additional camping areas along Shackleford Creek, 1.3 miles up FS 43N21, just beyond the bridge over the creek: one camping area is below the road on your right; the other is a couple of hundred yards up road 3A, which turns left off 43N21 shortly after the bridge crossing. This latter area offers the additional treat of a waterfall, diving rocks, and a seemingly bottomless swimming hole.

The Trails: The Scott River district is cradled within the encircling arms of the north-trending Marble Mountains and the southeast-trending segment of the Salmon Mountains. With the exception of the trails winding among the bulges and creases of the Red Mountain complex—a linear, ultramafic spur of the Salmon Mountains—the trails of this district are all relatively short canyon walks through forest and meadow up to one or more lakes nested in the glacier-cut hollows at the heads of the canyons. The only exception is Marble Valley, at the head of Canyon Creek, for water percolates down through its porous bedrock, rather than creating pools. In this valley you'll just have to be content with the brilliant spectacle of the marble outcrops.

The Pacific Crest Trail tightwires along the crest of the Salmon and Marble mountains, and canyon trails descend from it to various trailheads. Using the Crest Trail as a connector, you can mix and match the canyon trails to create a wide range of loop-trip and shuttle-trip possibilities. Most of these trips will require a car shuttle between trailheads, but one exception is the Red Rock Valley-Marble Valley Loop, Hike 22.

The Scott River district utilizes the full array of maintenance levels in establishing its trail-care priorities. Trails of lesser concern include:

Back Meadows Trail	Long High Lake Trail
Big Ridge Cutoff Trail, and associated paths to Turk Lake	Marble Rim Trail
Deep Lake Trail	Red Mountain Trail
Kelsey Creek Trail	Shadow Lake Trail

With the exception of the bulk of the Red Mountain Trail, these routes are not unduly difficult to follow, but they will likely have deadfall obstacles remaining well into the hiking season.

The following trails receive only triennial maintenance at best and, due to the impossibility of competing with the cattle paths for dominance, some of the meadow trails are left completely unimproved. Should you wish to travel along these "trails," consider them to be nonexistent and rely on your map and compass skills:

Kidder Creek Trail above Hayes Meadow
Red Mountain Trail, between its junction with Wright Lakes and Long High Lake trails
Second Valley Trail
Wooley Creek Trail, between Ananias Camp and its junction with the Big Meadows Trail

While route-finding problems created by cattle may vary, their presence does not: they are everywhere. Since this district is near the ranchlands of Scott Valley, after mid-July you can expect bovine company in every good-sized meadow area except Sky High Valley.

Hike 18   Kidder Creek—Kidder Lake Trails

Distance: 3.5 miles, one way to Kidder Lake

Low elevation: 4600'

High elevation: 5890'

Suited for: day trip

Usage: moderate

Difficulty: moderate

Directions to trailhead: From the Scott River Ranger Station at the junction of State Highway 3 and the Scott River Road, take Highway 3 south 4.4 miles to a right turn on to the Greenview-Quartz Valley Road (SIS 6F01). Follow this road 1/3 mile to Main Street in Greenview. Turn left and follow Main Street 0.2 mile to the Kidder Creek road, next to the Greenview Post Office. Turn right on the Kidder Creek road and go 9.9 miles to its end at the trailhead. Where the paving ends, after 3½ miles, this road comes under the jurisdiction of International Paper Co., which provides no signs at the road junctions. At 5.2 miles, take the level left fork rather than the uphill right fork. At 8.4 miles, shun the left fork heading across the creek for the Shelly Fork Trail and take the steeply climbing right fork. Another 1.5 miles straight ahead brings you to the road-end parking area in a former logging landing

area. The unsigned trailhead is at the west end of the parking area; the trail starts up a former skid road.

Trail description: The skid-road trail quickly narrows and enters a dense, mixed-conifer forest, the likes of which would make any logging-company executive drool. Massive examples of sugar and ponderosa pine, Douglas-fir and incense-cedar stud the path as you amble along the semilevel trail. As the trail dips into a small gully at 0.3 mile to cross its softly singing brook, there is an overwhelming tranquility in the hushed cool.

The nearly level trail continues a while; then a brief, brisk rise and fall brings one to the brink of Kidder Creek (0.8, 4620). Curling around a clump of chinquapins, the path climbs briefly above the creek, then drops steeply to its side at a narrow, richly flowered gulch. After another short, stiff rise and fall, you head west along a creekside flat.

Soon passing a wilderness boundary sign, the trail begins a gradual climb. Shortly you traverse a broad band of scrub, then return to the forest again to cross a mossy trickle. Within the forest, the trail climbs easily through several grassy patches and crosses the outlet creek of Buzzard Lake before reaching a junction of the Kidder Creek and Kidder Lake trails (1.4, 4940).

Kidder Creek Trail

The Kidder Creek Trail, along which you have been hiking, turns west-southwest to quickly cross Kidder Creek, then winds 0.3 mile through the forest to the edge of Hayes Meadow. Semiderelict Hayes Cabin stands 65 yards into the meadow, its status as a historical site presently undecided. But the attraction of this side trail is the grassy vastness of this rarely visited meadow, the exceptional stand of towering quaking aspens toward its west end, and the multispired ridgecrest of the Salmon Mountains soaring above the head of Kidder Creek. The Kidder Creek Trail continues on through Hayes Meadow and up 2.2 miles to a ridgecrest reunion with the Kidder Lake Trail in the saddle west of Peak 6554. However, this path is so difficult to follow, that it is best approached as a cross-country route.

The Kidder Lake Trail, heading west-northwest, offers pleasures of a different sort, but you'll have to work for them. The ascent begins easily, but soon stiffens as the trail climbs through a forest in transition from mixed-conifer community to red-fir association. You cross an intermittent creeklet (0.7, 5470), then wind up among a network of rivulets and dry channels, hiking through forest, patches of brush, and moist-habitat wildflowers. After 1/3 mile, the path crosses a pair of healthy brooks and climbs steeply into a rocky opening.

Turning west, you start a climb up out of the rocks and steeply through a predominantly red-fir/mountain-hemlock forest to a grassy flat, besmirched with campers' fire rings. You then have only a short walk on level trail to the sluggish outlet creek of Kidder Lake (0.6, 5890).

Kidder Lake, as well as the various other Kidder features, was named for LeRoy Kidder, an early settler in Scott Valley. At 2 acres, it is an intimate lake, set in a glacier-gouged bowl in the southeast tip of a small granitic body that stretches up toward the ridge above Cliff Lake. It is a sufficiently popular site to be ringed with campsites at nearly every flat spot. Due to the 200-foot

Kidder Lake and Peak 7550

camping regulation, however, only the site to the left of the trail just after you cross the outlet creek is worth considering.

Pacific Crest Trail

In 1978 a new route was constructed from Kidder Lake up to the Pacific Crest Trail. Initially, it follows the old trail from the crossing of the outlet creek, as it climbs above the south shore of the lake. After 200 yards, the new trail section bends south, then quickly switchbacks northeast. You climb moderately along this heading to the edge of the forest, then curl back to the west-southwest and begin a sustained steep ascent through the forest to the ridgecrest saddle west of Peak 6554 (0.7, 6390). The narrow tread of the Kidder Creek Trail heads east down the ridgecrest. The Kidder Lake Trail turns west to wind up through a brilliant ridgecrest rock garden to a junction with the Pacific Crest Trail (0.4, 6600).

Hike 19   Shackleford Creek—Campbell Lake Trails Loop

Distance: 11.1 miles, semiloop trip
Low elevation: 4750'
High elevation: 6170'
Suited for: weekend
Usage: extremely high
Difficulty: moderate

Directions to trailhead: Follow the Scott River Road 7.0 miles west from its junction with State Highway 3 at the Scott River Ranger Station in Fort Jones, to Quartz Valley Road (23 miles on the Scott River Road from its junction with State Highway 96). Turn south on Quartz Valley Road and take it 4.0 miles to FS 43N21 on the right, indicated by a large road sign for the Shackleford and Big Meadows trailheads. Following all-weather road 43N21, with signs for Shackleford Trail at every major junction, you'll come in 6.9 miles to a large camping and main parking area. Another ½ mile up an extremely rocky and pitted extension of the road brings you to the signed trailhead at a small map-and-information shelter.

Trail description: Climbing easily into the mixed-conifer forest, you soon come to a log-and-boulder crossing of dashing Back Meadows Creek. Beyond the creek begins a gently rolling ascent along Shackleford Creek, leading up to a stock gate at the edge of a tiny, grassy meadow (0.5, 4850). After skirting the meadow, the trail levels out through a predominantly white-fir/Douglas-fir forest, and later turns away from the creek momentarily to pass through a meadow bordered with lodgepole pines and incense-cedars. Any summer weekend will find fly fishermen leaving the trail here to work the pools of Shackleford Creek for its sleek rainbow trout.

Returning to the forest, the path climbs briefly to broad and shallow Long High Creek (0.7, 4890), difficult to cross without getting your boots wet, regardless of season. After a 70-yard descent from this creek, you pass a large *Marble Mountain Wilderness* sign. Beyond the sign begins an almost imperceptible ascent through a forest broken by

patches of meadow. Within a particularly large, incense-cedar-bordered meadow, you cross a small but reliable creeklet (1.0, 5000). At the west end of this meadow, beyond a seeping, intermittent creek, the path enters forest and climbs immediately to a fork with an abandoned trail to Campbell Lake. Two small campsites nearby take advantage of the beauty of swiftly cascading Shackleford Creek.

Bending west-northwest from the fork, you begin a steep, switchbacking climb through old-growth forest. Trimmed with thickets of huckleberry oak, the trail winds among several massive ultramafic boulders and a scattering of Jeffrey pines and western white pines—both associated with ultramafic soil—before moderating its grade at an insignificant, trickling creek. The route continues on across a more substantial creek and then, 0.1 mile farther, reaches a junction with the Red Mountain Trail (0.6, 5350). An excursion following this trail and the Long High Lake Trail to Calf and Long High lakes is described at the end of this hike.

Skirting a small, sidalcea-trimmed meadow, one leaves the trail junction to almost immediately come alongside Log Lake. Log Lake's name is well-suited, for a large-scale snow avalanche in the early '60s left its wreckage in and around the small lake. The debris is cosmetically unappealing—hence the two trailside campsites above its west and southwest shores are seldom used except by fishermen familiar with the rainbow trout that lurk beneath the lake's lily pads.

Leaving the lake, the trail arcs across the treeless path of the avalanche, then enters a short strip of forest. Trading the forest for a long, broad, grassy meadow, you follow its northwest border as the trail bends back toward Shakleford Creek. Shortly after coming alongside the creek, you reach a trail fork (0.6, 4370) that begins the actual loop of this hike. The left fork heads for Campbell and Cliff lakes; the right fork leads first to Summit Lake. The trail description here takes the right fork, mainly because it is a more evenly graded climb.

You leave the deep-cut banks of Shackleford Creek to head west-southwest on the right fork through the fading edge of the meadow. A gentle-to-moderate climb begins as the path enters forest, and it occasionally nears the creek to give a view of a foaming waterfall or a series of dashing cascades.

The ascent nearly levels off after you enter a rocky, incense-cedar-bordered meadow (0.8, 5680). Staying high along the sloping meadow's north edge, the trail passes through patches of manzanita and scattered wildflowers as it heads toward the grandly arcing walls of the Salmon Mountains' crest. Entering the forest at the far end of the meadow, you climb steeply for a while, then ease into another open area beneath some towering walls. Shortly thereafter the trail bends down to a crossing (0.4, 5810) of a small tributary to Shackleford Creek. To the trail's right, just before crossing the creek, you might notice a hand-carved log sign buried in the grasses, indicating the start of a primitive trail to Little Elk Lake. This unmaintained, initially gullied trail poses a few sticky, routefinding problems in its first ¼ mile and considerable difficulties once it drops below the headwall on the north side of the ridge. It is also quite physically challenging, and should be considered a shortcut to Little Elk Lake only by strong hikers competent in the use of map and compass.

Beyond the creek crossing, one meanders through the forest on a gently ascending grade, crossing another small creek within the forest. If you follow the creek 75 yards down from the trail, you'll reach a red-fir-sheltered campsite that offers a pleasant alternative to soon reached Summit Lake. Climbing steeply from this creek, the trail soon comes to a junction with the Campbell Lake Trail (0.4, 6020). The right fork climbs, occasionally steeply, one mile to a ridgecrest junction with the Pacific Crest Trail. Even if you have no destination to be reached by using this trail, it is a worthy side trip, since after 0.8 mile you reach the top of a cliff that provides a perfect vantage point for viewing the glacial craftwork in the Shackleford Creek area.

The Campbell Lake Trail quickly climbs to a boulder ford of Summit Lake's outlet creek, just before reaching the lake's northwest shore. Summit Lake receives a great deal of use and, due to the steep-sided bowl it rests in and its modest surface area, 5 acres, there is no place to put all the people without highly impacting the lake. All the campsites are well within the lake's 100-foot no-camping zone. Whether camping or day-hiking here, you'll find pleasure swimming or fishing near the avalanched rocks along its southwest shore.

This hike's loop trail continues past the ford of the outlet creek in a clockwise route along the lake's north and east shores. From the southeast corner of the lake, bend south-southeast along the brief, boggy creek connecting Summit Lake with Summit Meadow Lake. The twin pools of Summit Meadow Lake are more marsh than lake. However, the linear meadow above the east end of the lake has established it as a prime horse-packers' camp.

Beyond the lakes, you climb moderately to the top of a knoll, dip briefly down to a tarn then, amid a seasonal profusion of brilliant scarlet gilia, you start down the rocky trail in a moderate descent of the open slope. After curving through isolated stands of lodgepole pine and clumps of manzanita, you come alongside a narrow brook. Through a red-fir forest adjoining the creek, the trail then begins switchbacking steeply, but eases its descent as it approaches a broad alder thicket along the border of a meadow.

Turning south-southeast at the alders, you cross the creek to climb briefly along a forested rise, then follow the curving meadow border, staying just inside the trees until reaching a campsite near the meadow's southeast corner. Then, after crossing a last finger of grassy meadow, climb steeply into the forest to the top of a knoll, and level off just short of a junction with the Cliff Lake Trail (1.7, 5810).

Cliff Lake

To visit Cliff Lake, turn right at the trail junction and, a few paces along the way, pass a second trail fork. The left fork descends 0.1 mile—past a little red pit toilet—to the shores of Campbell Lake at its inlet creek. Campsites, mostly within Campbell Lake's 200-foot no-camping zone, are located on either side of the creek and along the 0.2-mile extension of this spur trail toward the south end of the lake.

The Cliff Lake Trail descends briefly south-southeast, then begins the meandering, largely moderate climb to Cliff Lake. Vistas open up along the way: north-northeast toward the ocher bulk of Red Mountain and west to the long arc of the Salmon Mountains. A final steep climb brings you up near Cliff Lake's outlet creek, along which you ascend gently, on the lake-impounding moraine, to the north shore of the lake (0.7, 6120). A path on the left drops 25 yards to a shoreside usage trail. However, the main trail continues counterclockwise around the lake for over ½ mile before dwindling to a usage trail that soon terminates near the massive rockfall near the lake's south shore.

Originally called Upper Campbell Lake, aptly named Cliff Lake is a stunning and remarkable area. Being 175 feet deep, it is easily the deepest lake in this wilderness. Although the precipitous cliffs surrounding the lake are an indicator of the severe glaciation in this cirque, the great depth of the lake is not due to natural ingredients alone. In the late 1800s a low dam was built at this lake's outlet to aid the irrigation needs of Quartz Valley ranchers.

The shores of Cliff Lake are littered with campsites, most of which ignore the 200-foot camping limit. There are three major sites along the established west-shore trail, but the only one that gives the lake breathing room is near the south shore, where the usage trail extension comes to an end at the second inlet creek.

The Campbell Lake Trail turns left at the junction with the Cliff Lake Trail and winds its way north, just west of Campbell Lake's campsite-laden west shore. On any given summer weekend, this shore appears beset by urban blight. Beyond the west tip of Campbell Lake, the trail climbs momentarily to a stock gate (0.2, 5770) and an unsigned trail junction just beyond. (Cliff and Campbell lakes receive so much human use during the summer months that the impact of the cattle in the Shackleford range allocation, both on the lake environment and on the enjoyment of the wilderness traveler, would be intolerable. Therefore, cattle are permitted in the lakes area only during the first two weeks of October.)

Cliff Lake and Red Mountain

Campbell Lake and Peak 7636

From the junction you can continue straight ahead on a ½-mile-long trail that curves east to an airy, lakeshore campsite on the far side of the lake's outlet creek. Just before reaching the creek, this path crosses the top of a stone dam, built in 1875, which is still used for irrigation purposes.

The Campbell Lake Trail, however, turns sharply west-northwest at the junction and gently descends through the red-fir forest. In 100 yards you come to another unsigned trail junction, just short of another stock gate. This stock gate closes off a trail that once headed for Campbell Lake's west shore. From this lower trail junction, turn north and begin a steeply switchbacking descent. The descent eases as you reach the valley bottom and leave the forest to cross the first of several broad, shallow channels of Shackleford Creek. By midsummer, most of these channels are dry; but an early season crossing might require some wading, particularly if the sometimes flimsy log crossings wash away in the spring melt. Beyond the creek crossings, the path soon reaches the junction with the Shackleford Creek Trail at which you started the loop (0.8, 5370). Turning

east-northeast, you follow Shackleford Creek back along the initial 3.4 miles of this description to reach the trailhead.

Calf Lake and Long High Lake

If only due to hiker overflow from Cliff, Campbell and Summit lakes, Calf and Long High lakes receive high usage. However, these two small lakes, perched high on the walls of Red Mountain, are more likely to provide the experience of wilderness intimacy that their big sisters below can only promise.

Leaving the Shackleford Creek Trail at its 2.8-mile point, just east of Log Lake, the Red Mountain Trail curves to a crossing of an alder-clogged creek, then begins climbing steeply through a highly variegated forest. The conglomeration of sugar pine, Douglas-fir, incense-cedar, white and red firs, Jeffrey and western white pines together represent an interface between mixed-conifer, red-fir and ultramafic-soil communities.

Beyond a series of short switchbacks, the trail comes up to a dense alder thicket at the lower edge of Dog Wallow meadow. Skirting the alders, you quickly come to a shallow, stepping-stone-crossed creeklet with a ramshackle stock gate, then angle across the narrow meadow and enter the forest near Reynolds Cabin (0.6, 5630). The original Reynolds Cabin, now only a small pile of stone remnants at the forest edge, was built shortly after the turn of the century. The present cabin is of more recent vintage—1954—and is presently under archeological study for consideration as a historical monument.

Beyond the small cabin, an undulating climb through the forest reaches the edge of a final stretch of meadow, bordered with ponderosa pines and incense-cedars. The route then begins a steady, steep climb that lasts almost to the lakes. The ascent through the open, ultramafic-soil forest eventually reaches a junction with the Long High Lake Trail (0.5, 5950). The Red Mountain Trail continues east to contour through the upper-

An open, ultramafic-soil forest

slope meadows of Red Mountain's southeast flank—but only on the map. Due to the fecund meadow vegetation and the maze of annually re-entrenched cattle wanderings, the Forest Service has adopted a policy of benign neglect toward this trail through Back and Big Meadows. You should view it as a bushwhack and chart your own route once the trail disappears into the meadows.

After you turn north onto the Long High Lake Trail the ascent becomes extremely strenuous as it climbs directly up a ridgecrest. There is occasional relief when the trail momentarily drops off the ridgeline, but the grade does not moderate with any consistency until the trail leaves this ridge for good and winds through the patchy scrub and redfir/western-white-pine stands toward the muted call of Long High Lake's outlet creek. The trail is indistinct at times in this area's scruffy meadows. The route curves from north to west up across a final meadow, then becomes very rocky and uncertain near the meadow's upper end. By this time, however, you are only a few paces short of a seasonal brook and the rim of Calf Lake (1.1, 7030).

Cupped in a tight, rocky cirque, Calf Lake is a lovely sight, and a fitting spot to enjoy it is from a roomy campsite above the cove near its southeast corner. Indeed, it is the only spot. A short scramble up the rocks above its south shore brings you to the top of a moraine with views south over the spectacular earthworks of the Salmon Mountains and Shackleford Creek's valley.

Despite its name, the Long High Lake Trail effectively ends at Calf Lake. To reach a sketchy path to Long High Lake, start from the triple-trunked western white pine near where the trail approached the shore of Calf Lake, and head up through the greenery 60 yards at a 15° bearing. Little more than a game trail, this path heads for a break in the moraine enclosing Long High Lake. From the western white pine at which you started, this depression in the moraine lies along a 30° bearing.

Your ¼-mile climb tops out at the lake's brush-choked outlet creek, which you cross on a rickety collection of branches. Long High Lake has encroaching grasses at its northeast end and ankle-deep water at its southwest end. In between, however, the surface of its 6-foot-deep water ripples with eastern brook trout coming to the fly.

Hike 20   Deep Lake—Wrights Lakes Trails

Distance: 4.7 miles, one way to Lower
Wright Lake
5.2 miles, one way to Upper
Wright Lake

Low elevation: 4040'

High elevation: 7400'

Suited for: day trip

Usage: extremely high

Difficulty: strenuous

Directions to trailhead: Leaving the Scott
River Road at its junction with FS 44N45,
14 miles west of State Highway 3 and 16.5
miles south of State Highway 96, follow all-
weather FS 44N45 past the Indian Scotty
Campground entrance to the first road junction on the left, with FS 44N53. Turning
left, follow dirt road 44N53 for 3.0 miles to
where it "dead ends," just after a switchback,
at an overgrown jeep road. The jeep road becomes "trail" after 30 yards.

But for an intermittent stream at 1/3
mile and a poorly established spring at 1 1/3
miles, there is effectively no water along the
trail until it reaches Boulder Creek at 4.1
miles.

Trail description: Shortly after the start of
the hike, the overgrown jeep road appears to
change into a trail, for the Forest Service
constructed earth bars to discourage motorized use along the route's first 2.5 miles.
Until the early '70s this initial portion was a
well-graded logging road. Within a couple of
hundred yards, the ragged trail resumes its
easily followed road form, and begins a
moderate climb westward, ducking into a
creek-bottomed major gully in 1/3 mile. One
advantage of hiking a former road is that
you needn't pay so much attention to your
footing and can relax and enjoy the panoramic views. To the north are the Scott Bar
Mountains and the Marble Mountains beyond, whose northeastern ridge is capped by
Lake Mountain and Tom Martin Peak.

A switchback in the road (0.9, 4390) directs the ascent to the east-southeast, and
nearly ½ mile beyond the turn you cross a
spring that has cut a miniature channel in
the road. As your route approaches the defile of Boulder Creek and bends south from

its north-slope exposure, some mountain ash
and greenleaf manzanita—and great quanti-
ties of aromatic, glossy-leaved tobacco brush
—coat the hillside. Now on the slopes above
Boulder Creek, the road switchbacks to the
north (0.9, 4780) and arcs back onto the
north slope. The climb steepens as it approaches a fork in the road (0.3, 4980). After you take the more trail-like left fork, the
route steepens even more as you curl up the
northeast side of a spur ridge. In ¼ mile the
road comes to a brushy end at the crest of
the spur and ducks then direct you briefly
south, then west, to where an actual trail
heads southwest into the white-fir/Douglas-
fir forest (0.4, 5300).

You climb to and along a narrow ridge at
the extreme rate of 1400 vertical feet per
mile to reach the sun-soaked ridgecrest. As
the trail enters the wilderness, you can look
through windows in the forest west-southwest up Canyon Creek to Marble and Black
mountains. The ascent eases to merely steep
as you leave the crestline to climb along an
open scrub slope. The occasional trail forks
you come to when you return to the open
forest are the result of often used switchback cuts. As you approach a major, northwest-trending gully (0.6, 5990), a right fork
heads 55 yards down to a seeping spring.

From the gully a torturously steep trail
ascends to a narrow, rocky ridgecrest just
south of Peak 6330. Following the crest
south, the path soon curves into the forest
and up to a junction with the Wright Lakes
Trail (0.4, 6440). The Deep Lake Trail continues straight ahead, reaching Deep Lake in
2.8 miles.

Starting south-southeast on the Wright
Lakes Trail, you cross an open flat, then
follow a rollercoaster trail through patchy
forest into the broad valley of Boulder Creek.
The trail gently ascends through scrub, then
makes a brief, steep climb to a boulder-hop
of Boulder Creek (0.7, 6620). The strong
odor of cattle should make you think twice
before casually dipping into this stream; this
water should be purified before drinking.

Beyond the creek, the trail has been relocated to avoid—as much as possible—the

fragile, corn-lily-choked meadow. After climbing steeply east almost to a large red fir, turn south to follow a sometimes obscure, semilevel path across the meadow and its severe erosion channels. Climbing steeply again, you zigzag through a clutch of whitebark pines, then follow a fading trail across the morainal lip of the extensive meadow below Lower Wright Lake. The meanderings of the large summer cattle population eradicate any man-made tread. After you head generally south-southwest 0.2 mile up the often boggy meadow and through a band of willows, you reach the top of the lake-impounding moraine, and Lower Wright Lake is just beyond (0.5, 6910). When you leave this lake to head back down the meadow, take a bearing on the large, centrally located cluster of whitebark pines, with protruding red firs; the trail will be evident within these trees.

Lower Wright Lake is one of the largest and deepest lakes in the wilderness, and it offers a unique feature for fishermen: its brown, rainbow and eastern brook trout,

Lower Wright Lake and Boulder Peak

particularly the latter, have red meat. This rare phenomenon is dependent on the presence of copepods—minute, fresh-water crustaceans—in their diet, and a combination of other, singular conditions in their environment. Another interesting feature is Boulder Peak, which soars 1400 feet above the south shore and provides a most dramatic setting. The only drawback to this lake is that the potential campsites by the northeast shores are quite barren and relatively uninviting. These campsites are found beneath a couple of isolated foxtail pines, which, as uncommon conifers, are attractions in their own right.

Upper Wright Lake

For a somewhat more intimate camping experience at the highest lake in the wilderness, and closer access to the Boulder Peak Trail, take the steeply climbing trail to Upper Wright Lake. The trail may not be apparent as you head east-southeast along the moraine bordering Lower Wright Lake's north end, but you can see where it is cut into the hillside as it begins to climb south above the lake. The switchbacking ascent continues up the hillside dotted with foxtail and whitebark pines before a final switchback turns you southeast toward the morainal lip overlooking Upper Wright Lake (0.5, 7400). Here, a cozy, little campsite is tucked in under the pine on your right. A more inviting campsite is located on a forested rise above the lake's south shore.

Boulder Peak

An added feature of the Wright Lakes is that they are the perfect starting point for a day hike to 8299-foot Boulder Peak, the highest point in the Marble Mountain Wilderness. From the southeast corner of Upper Wright Lake, two or three paths climb southward to the southeast corner of a small meadow, to join in an extremely steep, switchbacking climb to a trail junction at the crest of linear Red Mountain (0.2, 7680). It's not uncommon to find pockets of snow remaining on this trail in August.

The Wright Lakes Trail continues to the east-northeast and descends to Big Meadows. A very faint tread, marked by a duck 10 yards on your right, is the Back Meadows

Trail, which leads you along the ridgeline toward Boulder Peak. As this trail to the south-southwest becomes more evident, you can take time off from your route-finding and enjoy the sweeping views. After your semilevel trail skirts the southeast side of a knoll, it returns to the crest to begin the ascent to Boulder Peak.

Where the gradient steepens, the trail switchbacks fiercely to negotiate the last ¼ mile to the saddle just south of the summit of Boulder Peak (1.1, 8180). The most direct route to the summit leaves the trail, heading north, just before the trail makes the final switchback west-southwest toward the saddle. If you have come all the way to the saddle, don't be deluded by the pile of rusty, lichened rock, a short 100 yards north along the ridge. This is a false summit. After contouring around its east side, scramble up a larger pile of dark, lichened boulders to a massive summit cairn.

As befits the crowning peak of the Marbles, Boulder Peak has a commanding view of the Klamath Mountains country. A grand and glorious panorama encircles you. After first looking down at Lower Wright Lake, lying at the peak's base 1400 feet below, you then gaze east to Mt. Shasta, which soars above the closer, broad, greensward of Scott Valley. Turning south, you see glacier-faced Mt. Thompson, the premier peak in the distant Trinity Alps. In the west Black and Marble mountains bare their gleaming flanks, and in the far north the twin spires of Red Butte cap the Siskiyous near the California-Oregon border.

The most efficient way back to Wright Lake is to backtrack the way you came. To explore new country, however, you can make a loop by scrambling down the precipitous southwest slope of the peak to the head of Second Valley (0.5, 7500). The trail north down this lovely valley is obscure, and the Forest Service "abandoned" it when faced with the impossible task of maintaining a single, distinctive tread among the network of cattle tracks. You might hit stretches of identifiable trail by staying east of the valley's creek, but you should really consider this descent a cross-country walk and therefore pull out your map and compass. The very obscurity of this trail makes an approach to Boulder Peak from Second valley a very difficult undertaking.

By staying on the east side of the valley, you will more easily make the connection with the Deep Lake Trail. You meet this trail at the north end of a large, grassy meadow (1.3, 6700), where the broad, glacier-carved valley pinches in at a terminal moraine and Second Valley Creek meanders into the brush and begins its plunge to Canyon Creek. On this trail, you first descend moderately, but then ascend steeply to round the nose of Boulder Peak's north-trending ridge. You then descend extremely steeply to a junction with the Wright Lakes Trail (0.7,

Upper Wright Lake

Lower Wright Lake, from summit of Boulder Peak

6440). This trail junction can be easily missed since the signs are on the far side of four large red firs guarding the junction, and the acute right turn onto the Wright Lakes Trail is also obscured by these trees. Look for the junction as your steep descent eases off. To complete the loop, you then go 1.2 miles to Lower Wright Lake, and another ½ mile to Upper Wright Lake.

Deep Lake

If the Wright Lakes aren't enough, try sapphirine Deep Lake, which is easily accessible. From the junction with the Wright Lakes Trail, located 3.5 miles from the trailhead, head south on the Deep Lake Trail. This steepening path switchbacks up to the crest of the ridge extending north from Boulder Peak. Then, after steeply descending through the scrub and scattered trees of its west slope, the trail enters a nearly pure stand of Jeffrey pines, indicators of the ultramafic rocks that constitute the Red Mountain massif. After bottoming out amid pines, you climb moderately to hop-across fords of Second Valley Creek's twin branches (0.7, 6700). Your route here is obscure,

for the most obvious path continues into the large, lower meadow of Second Valley. Just as your climb levels off at the north edge of this meadow and the creek comes alongside, turn west, crossing the creek to ascend the morainal ridge that encloses the meadow.

After a brief ascent of the moraine, gently curve to the west-northwest and then make a gradual, generally forested descent to the nose of the ridge between Second Valley and Muse Meadow. As you round the tip of the ridge, greenleaf manzanita ushers you out of the red-fir forest and into a richly toned rock garden. Curlleaf mountain mahogany dots the path as you gradually descend south among the ultramafic boulders and metavolcanic rubble, hiking toward the deep concavity of Muse Meadow, with its creek delineated from a distance by a dark green stripe of willows and alders.

After crossing the brushy, thimbleberry-bordered creek (0.9, 6450), the trail arcs out of Muse Meadow and disappears into a fir-and-hemlock forest. After you bend back to the south, patchy forest accompanies the level stroll to a recessional moraine that encloses the north end of meadows below Deep Lake. Curving west-southwest, the path descends along the moraine, then curves briefly down to a meadow-edge junction with the spur trail to Deep Lake (0.8, 6260). You turn left, then follow the bend in the trail to hike south across the meadow on the often seep-muddied spur trail. You soon reach the shores of Deep Lake (0.4, 6340), picturesquely set into the base of Red Mountain.

Red Mountain Trail
to Wright Lakes

There is a back door into the Wright Lakes that is considerably shorter—only 2.5 miles to Upper Wright Lake—and starts at a point 2400 feet higher than the Deep Lake Trail. It is the Red Mountain Trail, which approaches the Wright Lakes from the east. It is offered as an option rather than as the principal route, for its accessibility is not assured. During the winter of 1977-78, sections of the steeply switchbacking, heavily eroded dirt road to the trailhead were washed out, leaving it passable to little more than 4-wheel drives. That the road was slightly more serviceable in 1979 was due not to any spirit of altruism on the part of International Paper Co., sole owners of the road, but to their decision to facilitate a final spate of logging. The Forest Service makes no effort to keep up-to-date information on its status since this road is not their responsibility.

To reach the trailhead, follow the Scott River Road from Fort Jones 7.0 miles and the Quartz Valley-Greenview road 4.0 miles to FS 43N21, indicated by road signs for the Shackleford and Big Meadows trailheads. After 4.4 miles of following signs for the Shackleford Creek Trail, take a right fork signed for Big Meadows. At another road junction ½ mile later, follow a Big Meadows sign to the west. Following occasional Big Meadows signs at subsequent junctions, you come to a sharp left turn, 5.7 miles after you have turned off FS 43N21; this turn is not obvious and the signs are even less so. If the road conditions have been giving you trouble up to here, you might want to park your car here and walk the remaining 1.3 miles to the trailhead. Anyhow, the road gets so bad that it is not all that much faster to drive it. Just ½ mile beyond the sharp left turn, there is an acute turn to the right; if you are

driving anything larger than a motorcycle, continue straight ahead through a turn-around loop that will get you pointed the right way for the turn and the last 0.8 mile to road's end.

The Red Mountain Trail begins innocently enough, winding quite clearly through forest, then meadow, and reaching a small brook in 1/3 mile, with a wilderness boundary sign bolted to a boulder just beyond. The trail quickly fades, however, and the only obvious path curls to the right to a shady salt lick left for the bovine tenants of Big Meadows. You head west-southwest toward a skull-topped cairn 130 yards beyond the boundary sign. From the cairn, the tread becomes more obvious and leads you up a slight rise to a junction with the Wright Lakes Trail (0.5, 6560). The labyrinthine Red Mountain Trail through Back Meadows continues straight ahead. Turning away from the splendid views east over Scott Valley toward Mt. Shasta, you begin the climb toward Wright Lakes along a line of quaking aspens.

The climb through multiflowered Big Meadows becomes extremely steep, finally easing as you curve to the southwest, crossing two small trickles before entering an open grove of red firs. Shortly you descend into a meadowed depression and, a few paces beyond the hop-across creeklet there, come to a faint trail junction (1.0, 7240). The fainter right fork, heading up the edge of the depression, is an abandoned trail to Wright Lakes, which entailed more climbing and greater distance than the present route along the left fork.

You continue along semilevel trail through meadows and clumps of firs, then begin a generally steep climb. As you climb, the clumps of trees add mountain hemlock, then whitebark pine, and finally the uncommon foxtail pine, while the meadows offer vistas of the glacier-clad Trinity Alps to the south beyond the waves of less distant ridges. The climb moderates as you curve through a small bowl amid curlleaf mountain mahogany, then come to an obscure, unsigned junction with the Back Meadows Trail in a broad ridgecrest saddle (0.8, 7680). From here, the Wright Lakes Trail descends the north slope ¼ mile to the southeast shore of Upper Wright Lake. The less apparent Back Meadows Trail follows ridgecrest ducks toward Boulder Peak.

Hike 21

Little Elk Lake

Distance: 5.8 miles, one way
Low elevation: 4220'
High elevation: 5990'
Suited for: weekend
Usage: high
Difficulty: moderate

Directions to trailhead: Leaving the Scott River Road at its junction with FS 44N45, 14 miles west of State Highway 3 and 16.5 miles south of State Highway 96, follow all-weather FS 44N45 across the bridge over the Scott River and up for 5.5 miles to a switchbacking left turn onto FS 43N45. Just 1¾ miles up FS 43N45 brings you to Lovers Camp's two parking areas, each with a camping area and a trailhead. The lower parking area, with its corral and loading ramp, is Horsepacker Central. Stock and stock trucks are not allowed at the upper parking area, 0.1 mile farther. The trails from both areas meet at a map kiosk within ¼ mile of their respective trailheads. The trail description begins at the upper trailhead.

Note: Both parking areas are graced with a lovely, but *incorrect,* map of the trailhead area. Red Rock Creek Trail does not have a separate trailhead at the lower parking area, but rather this trail forks off the Canyon Creek Trail 0.6 mile beyond the map kiosk.

Trail description: Following a jeep path remaining from recent selective logging, you carve a grand, moderately ascending, then descending, arc to reach a map-and-information kiosk in ¼ mile. Climbing away from it on a trail, you begin a winding, gently rolling walk high above the muffled chatter of Canyon Creek, crossing several seeps and horse-fouled trickles. You pass a *Marble Mountain Wilderness* sign on a short stretch of downhill that ends by a usage path, which descends 30 yards to an alder-lined swimming hole in now nearby Canyon Creek. After another 0.2 mile, the Canyon Creek Trail reaches a well-publicized junction with the Red Rock Valley Trail (0.9, 4300).

Turning south, the Red Rock Valley Trail quickly reaches the creek, curling past a pleasant little campsite on the bank to reach the deep-channeled creek, which you may be able to cross on a log. From this creek your trail heads downstream, then makes a generally moderate climb that uses a few long switchback legs to reach the nose of a broad ridge (0.9, 4800) west of Red Rock Valley.

Red Rock Valley

As you turn this nose on your dusty, red-dirt trail, you can see evidence of a vegetation inversion due to cold air descending to the valley bottom. Note how ponderosa pine and incense-cedar—both lower-elevation species—suddenly appear on this sun-stroked crest while red fir joins the white fir and Douglas-fir in the damp chill of the valley bottom.

Your ascent just off the crest of this broad ridge is briefly interrupted as you traverse through a small, shaded field of Bigelow sneezeweed and arrowhead butterweed to a smaller ridge, which is a glacial moraine. Your trail then resumes a moderate climb, meandering among the great glacier-strewn boulders of ultramafic rock that dot the ridge. Leaving its crest on a gentle descent, you soon reach a hushed creeklet. A log-trough salt lick just beyond the creek stands as a doorman to cattle country for, moments later, the trail heads into the first of Red Rock Valley's slender band of meadows (0.8, 4930).

Beyond this small meadow, the path passes through a short stretch of woods, richly carpeted with moisture-loving flora, then enters the more extensive "cabin" meadow. Making your way up the east side of this meadow, flanked with incense-cedars and black cottonwoods, you pull abreast of Red Rock Cabin, standing derelict at the upper edge of the meadow (0.3, 5000). Whether Red Rock Cabin is a cultural artifact or merely an eyesore was being determined in an archeological study undertaken in 1978.

Beyond the cabin, the trail closely follows a meander of Red Rock Creek, before following a two-lane path steeply up into the woods. Past a stock gate the climb eases, then becomes a gradual descent back to creekside just below an apparent confluence of two creeks and a trail junction (0.6, 5140). The confluence is only apparent because, in fact, the two flows are both parts of Red Rock Creek, rejoining at the north end of an island. At the north tip of the island is the junction of the Red Rock Valley and Little Elk Lake trails. However, hikers headed for Little Elk Lake commonly bypass the island, and the more obvious route crosses directly to the east bank of Red Rock Creek; the official Little Elk Lake Trail meets this path several yards upstream on the east bank. By skirting the island, lake-bound hikers also bypass a pine-and-fir-canopied campsite that is perhaps the most attractive site in Red Rock Valley.

After crossing to the east bank of Red Rock Creek, the Little Elk Lake Trail heads south through a corn-lily meadow before climbing into the woods. The ascent soon steepens, following long switchback legs through a forest of Douglas-fir and white fir up to the ridgecrest (1.2, 5990). When you leave the ridgecrest, the descent is generally moderate, ending with a long curve from south to north-northeast that finally brings you out into a vast meadow, buttered with Bigelow sneezeweed and woolly sunflower. After you hike a short way into the meadow, Little Elk Lake appears, encircled by trees below you on the right. Less than 0.1 mile farther you come to its north shore by its outlet (1.1, 5400).

With Peak 7636 towering beyond its southern end, Little Elk Lake enjoys a picturesque setting. If you want more than good looks, however, you had better be fond of fishing rather than swimming, since the lake is only a chest-deep bowl of primordial ooze derived from the area's metavolcanic

Little Elk Lake and Peak 7636

rock. None of the campsites surrounding the lake heeds the 200-foot camping limit. For a campsite that does, and also provides a modicum of privacy while maintaining contact with the lake, head north 75 yards on a footpath into the meadow. On your right, next to the creek and amid two downed firs, is a pleasant spot. The meadow trail continues another 0.2 mile, terminating within the forest at the locked Burton cabin.

Saddle east of Peak 7636

To stretch your legs a bit during your stay at Little Elk Lake and give your route-finding abilities a challenge, try to follow the continuation of the Deep Lake Trail up to the saddle east of Peak 7636. This saddle rewards you with splendid views over Shackleford Creek and the stunning Cliff and Campbell lakes area. The approximately 1.8 miles of trail, which extends from the path along Little Elk Lake's east shore, is "maintained" by the Forest Service as a primitive trail, that is, they do nothing more than provide minimal erosion controls. There are enough tree blazes and ducks along its unforgivingly steep length to indicate that it was, in fact, a constructed trail at one time.

Deep Lake

To reach Deep Lake, which is 3.7 trail miles from Little Elk Lake, begin by crossing the outlet creek and angling up through the small east-bank meadow into the forest. The moderate, forested climb curls into a gully filled by a magnificent cascade above the trail (0.5, 5700). After a brief, steep climb away from the cascade, you settle into a moderate ascent, topping out after ¾ mile. The trail then descends easily for ¼ mile, bending north-northwest along the slopes of bulbous Peak 6350 before beginning a semilevel walk toward the nose of its ridge. About the time you begin thinking this ridge might extend into Oregon, the trail makes a gently climbing bend to the ridgecrest (1.4, 5890).

After a brief descent from the crest, you start a semilevel traverse of Peak 6350's east slope. On an autumn hike, the clumps of mountain maple provide a fiery punctuation to the forested slopes, and a slide of meta-sedimentary rock midway along the slope offers a rugged exclamation point. Past a moment of gentle descent, you come to the ford of Deep Lake Creek and its two outrider creeklets, all in a broad gully (0.6, 5810). The creek banks are shallow enough that they are easily overrun during spring runoff, making for a soggy crossing of the gully.

Several paces beyond the gully, you pass a junction on the right with the old trail to Deep Lake, abandoned because of the severe impact the traffic was having on the fragile, creekside meadows below the lake. Beyond this junction the climb steepens, eventually switchbacking south-southeast to begin the ascent to the lake. Pulling up out of a fir forest, the path arcs around a large, scrub-coated depression in the hillside, with a rare quaking-aspen community filling the inside of the curve, then climbs up over a recessional moraine left by the glacier that gouged out the head of this valley over 10,000 years ago.

Atop the moraine you turn abruptly northeast and, passing by several curlleaf mountain mahoganies, come to a cairned trail junction (0.8, 6260). The Deep Lake Trail continues on toward the Wright Lakes, heading obscurely uphill on your left but quickly becoming an easily followed path. To reach Deep Lake from the trail junction you curve south, crossing a series of mucky seeps and trickles as the trail gently ascends the broad meadow below the lake. It is thought that the disjointed strings of boulders that stretch across the meadow are the remnants of minor, recessional moraines.

The trail becomes a sketchy tread as you amble through the sagebrush-dotted open meadow to the north shore of Deep Lake (0.4, 6340). Set well into the flank of Red Mountain, aptly monikered Deep Lake has extremely high usage due in part to its exceptional beauty and its high-quality swimming and fishing. The bulk of its campsites are located in the trees along its northwest shore, though none are outside the 200-foot no-camping zone impractical here due to the steep slopes rising almost directly from the shore. The prime real estate is on the peninsula protruding from the lake's southeast shore. There, a central camping area in a bit of a hollow probably attracts hordes of Deep Lake cognoscenti, but it is definitely worth the extra effort to get to.

Hike 22   Red Rock Valley—Marble Valley Loop

Distance: 13.7 miles, loop trip
Low elevation: 4220′
High elevation: 6610′
Suited for: weekend
Usage: high in Red Rock Valley; extremely
   high in Marble Valley and along
   Canyon Creek
Difficulty: moderate
Directions to trailhead: Same as on page 129.

Trail description: An initial, curving ¼ mile
brings you to a map and information kiosk.
Climbing away from it, the trail continues a
semilevel course to a junction with the Red
Rock Valley Trail (0.9, 4300). The trail
quickly reaches Canyon Creek at an awk-
ward log crossing. Beyond, it switchbacks up
a moderate grade to a ridgecrest, traverses
briefly to a tributary spur of the ridge, then
resumes its moderate ascent. Beyond the
crest you have a gentle descent to a creeklet,
which you cross just before reaching the first
of Red Rock Valley's meadows (1.7, 4930).

Amid the summertime cattle, you gently
ascend through the meadows, passing Red
Rock Cabin, before a forested rise and fall
brings you to the bank of Red Rock Creek
at the junction with the Deep Lake Trail
(0.9, 5140). The Deep Lake Trail heads
south-southeast, directly across Red Rock
Creek to its east bank. To continue up Red
Rock Valley, turn south to cross over to an
island with a roomy campsite that is en-
veloped by a grove of firs and pines. This is
far and away the most inviting campsite in
Red Rock Valley. This 3.5-mile section of
trail is more extensively described in the beginning of Hike 21.

Beyond the campsite, you quickly come
to a skimpy stepping-stone crossing of one
of the branches of Red Rock Creek that
creates the island; in early season, you may
have to wade. Beyond the creek the trail
climbs moderately past scattered conifers
and into a vast, sprawling meadow. At times
waistdeep in the lush floral growth, you
make your way up the meadow, the soaring
pinnacle of Peak 7636 rising high across the
valley to the southeast. Where the climb

moderates, a gurgling creeklet flows from a
gathering of trees on the left.

Back into an arm of the meadow, one
passes through a column of black cottonwoods and starts climbing toward a good-
sized hillside community of quaking aspens.
The term "community" is used advisedly
here, since an entire grove of aspens will
often sprout from a wide-ranging, horizontal
root network just below the earth surface.
Since their miniscule seeds are too fragile
to be consistently viable reproductive agents,
the aspen has evolved a vegatative reproductive system that, in essence, clones new trees
from the single, far-reaching parent root.

The climb steepens amid the quaking
aspens, then breaks out into the meadow
again on a deeply rutted trail. As your meadow ascent eases, the route curls down to a
step-across creeklet, follows an indistinct
tread through a field of corn lilies, then up
a moraine. Soon you arrive at a crossing of
Red Rock Creek, found at a rocky break in
its shielding willows (1.5, 5920).

About 100 yards beyond the creek, as the
trail momentarily levels off, you pass a
blocked spur trail on the right, which leads
150 yards south-southeast to a pond at the
head of the valley. Once a tranquil camping
location, the pond is swiftly becoming a
marsh, too fragile and inconvenient for human use, hence the trail is obstructed. There
then ensues a severe climb up the Red Rock
Valley headwall, which crosses a few mucky
and mossy seeps beneath the scattered tress
of the red-fir forest before curving up to a
junction with the Pacific Crest Trail (0.6,
6350). Your route along the Crest Trail
heads west as a gently ascending ridgecrest
stroll to the junction with the Shadow Lake
Trail (0.4, 6470).

Shadow Lake

This 0.4-mile trail takes off steeply uphill,
eventually curling into a dry meadow on
Peak 6817's east slope. The trail is easy to
lose in this opening; 85 yards into the meadow, at a young, double-trunked red fir, cut

Frying Pan Lake and Black Mountain
Shadow Lake

northwest across the hillside and a duck will soon appear to lead you down to the more apparent trail as it re-enters the forest. A rolling traverse through open forest brings you up to the crest of a slight spur, from which you swoop quickly to another ridge-let. Your precipitous drop continues on the narrow, often unstable trail, bringing you to the east tip of Shadow Lake and the only established campsite.

Despite its 14-foot depth, Shadow Lake is still too shallow for its eastern brook trout, which occasionally suffer winterkill. So while fishermen may be disappointed, swimmers won't, since the rocky north shore provides excellent swimming. However, this lake's premier attraction is its setting. Sunk in a glacier-chiseled bench in the north face of Peak 6817, the lake is perched on the brink of a 650-foot cliff that drops precipitously to Sky High Valley. From the lake you have a sweeping view northwest to Marble and Black mountains.

From the Shadow Lake Trail junction, the Pacific Crest Trail ascends west-southwest easily through the forest of red firs, whose lichened trunks indicate a winter snowpack of 5 to 8 feet. The climb tops out as the trail leaves the forest and immediately comes to a junction with the spur to Soft Water Spring (0.5, 6600). This left-forking trail gently descends 75 yards to the seeping spring, encompassed by aging cowpies. Contouring along the grassy slopes, the Crest Trail also takes 75 yards to reach an almost nonexistent junction—just above the spring—with a second trail to Shadow Lake. If you were coming from the west, this would be the shorter route to the lake. Although a sketchy tread can be found, it might be easier to simply head roughly north up the ridge, reaching the crest 10-20 yards east of the line of firs that also ascends the ridge. Just off the ridgecrest, you'll pick up a narrow trail that traverses the north slope of Peak 6817. This 1/3-mile spur then drops obscurely along the west side of the cirque, which contains the meager inlet creek, and it ends at the lake's southwest tip.

Beyond the second Shadow Lake trail, you descend moderately, taking in the expansive views of the Wooley Creek watershed below. The Mt. Thompson complex in the distant Trinity Alps is just visible to the south through a notch in Wooley Creek canyon's far wall. As the trail momentarily regains the crest in a small saddle above Sky High Valley, the descent levels out. Shortly beyond a patch of metavolcanic rock piles laced with thimbleberry and fireweed, the heavily brushed-in trail drops moderately to a junction with the Sky High Valley Trail (1.0, 6410). This trail swings around Peak 6615, then descends steeply, reaching Frying Pan Lake in one mile. Just 130 yards past the junction you meet a second, unsigned path in a rocky rubble patch. This trail, used by travelers from the west, connects with the main Sky High Valley Trail in 120 yards.

One hundred yards farther, the trail regains the crest, approaching a saddle with a stunning view of Black and Marble mountains. On a clear day, as you continue along the crest, you might be able to make out Mt. McLoughlin, in the southern Oregon Cascades, by looking north-northeast down Can-

yon Creek valley. The ridgecrest descent ends in a narrow saddle, among a veritable convention of trail-junction signs (0.5, 6232). To the left (west-southwest) you can descend, then climb, to Big Elk Lake (1.6 miles). Straight ahead (west-northwest) is the Marble Rim Trail, signed for foot traffic only. If you won't have time to take the more exhausting Marble Gap Trail and would like a glimpse of the striking west escarpment of Marble Mountain, then walk 1.2 miles along this trail to a saddle on the rim itself, southwest of Peak 6880.

Taking the Crest Trail toward Marble Valley, you branch right (north-northwest) and follow a couple of switchbacks steeply down the lushly gardened slopes to the head of Little Marble Valley. Just as the trail begins to curve out of the valley toward the forest, you pass a remnant of the Little Marble Valley Trail branching off on the right, which descends along the forest perimeter for 0.2 mile to a grassy meadow with a spring.

Black Mountain rising above Sky High Valley

Once in the forest, the path quickly reaches and briefly descends along a spur ridge. Then it follows a rolling descent through extensive marble outcrops and intermediate gullies to a step-across creek. Uphill, 80 yards beyond the creek crossing, you reach the Marble Valley Guard Station and a junction with the Canyon Creek Trail (1.0, 5700).

In its role as an easily accessible jumpoff point for hikers wishing to explore the geologic wonders of Black and Marble mountains, and as first stop on the "Horsepacker Express," the flat by the guard station hosts a sprawling campsite beneath a truly impressive grove of red firs. The guard station, used by trail crews and backcountry rangers, is not open to public use. The considerable traffic through the area has necessitated the installation of a pit toilet, located just off the northwest corner of the guard station.

The trail disintegrates as you reach the flat, and the trail-junction sign indicating Lovers Camp simply points off into the underbrush. To head back to the trailhead, go past the Lovers Camp sign 15 yards to the guard station's flagstone walkway, then bear east-southeast.

The moderate descent soon reaches and travels briefly alongside a meadow-bound brook before arriving at a junction with the trail to Sky High Valley (0.2, 5600), which climbs nearly 2 miles to the lakes at the head of Sky High Valley. The Canyon Creek Trail meanders through several gullies, some filled with trickling, undependable flows, as it descends steeply to a junction with the Sky High Valley Trail (0.4, 5300). This trail unites with the higher spur trail in 0.4 mile. The Canyon Creek Trail's remaining 4.1 miles back to the Lovers Camp trailhead is described in detail, albeit in reverse, in Hike 23. Briefly, it quickly crosses Canyon Creek at a magnificent cascade, then descends extremely steeply down the "marble staircase" to the broad valley bottom of Canyon Creek. Meandering along the richly forested canyon floor, the trail then descends easily to the trailhead.

Marble Gap Trail

You may think your views of Black and Marble mountains as you travel this loop are not half bad, but they are nothing like what you can see *from* Black and Marble mountains, specifically from Marble Gap.

To reach the gap, follow the Pacific Crest Trail which winds generally northwest from the Marble Valley Guard Station 0.3 mile to the junction with the Marble Gap Trail. This trail starts west-southwest and climbs moderately through an angelica-dotted meadow, then steeply through a forest, and turns abruptly south-southwest just after entering a meadow along the bed of an intermittent stream. A few ducks help you across a stretch of gravelly, dry meadow, in which the trail fades, and then you locate a more obvious tread again, curving back toward the gap into denser vegetation. The lay of the land, with small bulges and hollows, has different sun-exposure and snow-retention qualities, and these have created a striking juxtaposition of wet and dry floral communities.

The climb eases momentarily to pass through a couple of small gullies, then resumes its strenuous course. Hauling yourself up an excessively steep final ¼ mile, you arrive at Marble Gap amid wind-whipped foxtail pines and stunning vistas (1.3, 6830).

Marble Mountain rises above you, then stretches off to the south in a commanding arc above the awesome drop to Rainy Valley's east fork. The distant prominences include Medicine Mountain (230°) and, down the valleys of Rainy and Elk creeks and across the Klamath River to the High Siskiyous, Preston Peak (310°). The summit due west across Rainy Valley is Elk Peak, whose metasedimentary earth tones contrast sharply with the light granitic rock of the Wooley Creek pluton, exposed in the ridges farther west.

Swinging your focus back toward the way you came, your eye might first be caught by the mammoth bulk of Red Mountain in the east, with the significant bumps including Boulder Peak (85°) and Peak 7735 (95°), and neighboring Peak 7636 (110°). To the east-southeast, above the defile of Canyon Creek, you can just see the upper meadow of Sky High Valley before it disappears behind the north-northeast-trending spur that separates it from Marble Valley. And to the southeast lies the great arc of Salmon Mountains peaks that tower above Man Eaten Lake and the headwaters of Wooley Creek.

Hike 23

Sky High Valley

Distance: 5.8 miles, one way
Low elevation: 4220'
High elevation: 5860'
Suited for: weekend
Usage: extremely high
Difficulty: moderate

Directions to trailhead: Same as on page 129.

Trail description: The slightly rolling Canyon Creek Trail goes ¼ mile to a map kiosk, then continues on a semilevel course to a junction with the Red Rock Valley Trail (0.9, 4300). From here, the Canyon Creek Trail climbs moderately, then drops briefly to a scrub-bordered creeklet (0.6, 4500), up whose course you'd find the site of Grindstone Camp. You repeat the up-down pattern to a crossing of Death Valley Creek (0.4, 4510), then follow a gently rolling, imperceptibly ascending trail to intermittent Big Rock Fork (0.9, 4570). During the periods of local glaciation, the valley of Canyon Creek was considerably affected; glaciers extended as far down the valley as Lovers Camp. The glacial till left after their departure is the foundation of a highly fertile bottomland, producing prodigious growth in the mixed-conifer forest you walk through.

Beyond Big Rock Fork, the route begins a more obvious ascent, then climbs still more rigorously as it approaches the base of the "marble staircase." For 1/3 mile you labor up the rocky, marble-lined path, perhaps pausing near the midpoint to refresh yourself with the fragrance of mock-orange blossoms. The climb moderates as it approaches a crossing of narrow Canyon Creek, which immediately below falls off in a grand, crashing cascade. After three more switchbacks up through a richly flowered creekside meadow, you arrive at a junction with the Sky High Valley Trail just inside the forest perimeter (1.3, 5300). The right fork continues ascending 0.6 mile to a junction with the Pacific Crest Trail in Marble Valley.

For Sky High Valley, take the left fork along the rim of a deeply incised gully, crossing a burbling creeklet in 110 yards amid a thick undergrowth of the deep-green, heart-shaped leaves of wild ginger. After swinging into the main gully to cross another intermittent flow, climb moderately to a junction with the upper Sky High Valley spur trail (0.4, 5460). This trail climbs northwest 0.3 mile to meet the Canyon Creek Trail 0.4 mile above where you left it.

At the edge of a meadow just beyond the trail junction, turn sharply east-southeast to climb steeply onto a flat and into its patchy meadow. The respite from climbing is short-lived, however, as the path quickly heads up a moderate grade along the precipitous wall of a northeast-trending ridge that separates Sky High Valley from Little Marble Valley.

Bending south-southeast around the nose of the ridge, the climb eases as you approach a stock gate (0.5, 5640). Sky High Valley is perhaps the most visited area in the entire wilderness, so its meadows are only opened for cattle during the first two weeks of October. The stock gate serves as the door to Sky High Valley as the forest quickly parts and the semilevel trail arrives at a switchback beneath a western white pine, from which you get your best view of tiny Gate Lake, swallowed up by willows.

Using two quick switchbacks, the trail descends to meadow level, and soon crosses a muted creek before bending back to a trail junction (0.2, 5540). While the main trail, signed for *Sky High Lakes*, continues straight ahead, the unsigned left fork passes quickly through an open campsite and climbs briefly into lushly flowered meadows. After rolling along this overgrown trail for ¼ mile, one makes a short, steep descent to the banks of the Sky High Lakes outlet creek, which has fir-canopied campsites on its east bank. From the Sky High suburbs here, one can easily commute to a hard day's play at the lakes and return to relative solitude in the evening.

From the trail junction, climb moderately through clumps of black cottonwoods and quaking aspens standing in the varicolored wildflower garden, then level off to cross a grassy flat before climbing steeply through an open forest to an upper meadow (0.4, 5720). The upper meadow contains a maze of usage trails and erosion channels from abused former trails. Following the most obvious path that isn't blocked, bend south and head across the pasturelike meadow toward a patch of quaking aspens and willows (0.2, 5770) growing along the lip of the bowl that holds the Sky High Lakes.

After the trail curls around the corner of the willow-aspen thicket, you come to a trail intersection. The well-worn trail to the right heads into the brush to a concealed pit toilet. The trail to the left is the major arterial to the network of usage paths that lead to the network of campsites on either side of Lower Sky High Lake's outlet creek and, ultimately, to the open-faced Adirondack shelter. Predating the CCC projects of the 1930s, the shelter stands a chance of receiving historical-monument status and remaining available for public use instead of being dismantled after the 1980 hiking season as originally intended.

From the willow-aspen thicket, the trail climbs the upper meadow's central knoll, whose top has a virtual city of campsites. After dropping of the knoll, the path quickly arrives at the shores of aptly named Frying Pan Lake (0.3, 5830), once known by the equally appropriate name of Banjo Lake. Resulting from a mere abrasion of the valley floor by the resident glacier, rather than from major surgery, Frying Pan Lake is too shallow to offer anything more than cosmetic appeal.

Frying Pan Lake

Marble Valley Loop

To add some Salmon Mountains ridge-crest scenery to your Sky High Valley experience, you can fashion a loop route through Marble Valley. Continue on the Sky High Valley Trail northwest from Frying Pan Lake, and begin climbing steeply out of the valley. The trail follows the timbered crest of one spur ridge, then angles up an open flat to an even steeper crest ascent of a second spur. Shifting back and forth between open forest and scrub garden, it climbs above the north side of an upper meadow, then turns to the northwest to finally reach the ridgecrest in a shallow saddle (0.8, 6420).

From the saddle, you traverse just below the timbered crest, whose forest opens to reveal stunning exposures of Black and Marble mountains as you approach a trail junction (1.0, 6430). The left trail, for eastbound travelers, meets the Pacific Crest Trail in 55 yards. The right fork heads 120 yards west to a junction with the PCT.

For a complete description of the loop from here, refer to the Red Rock Valley-Marble Valley Loop, Hike 22. Roughly, the loop continues northwest along the Crest Trail for ½ mile to a junction with trails to Big Elk Lake and Marble Rim. From here the Crest Trail traverses one mile north, crossing Little Marble Valley before reaching Marble Valley and a junction with the Canyon Creek Trail. By descending 0.2 mile along this trail, you'll reach the upper access trail to Sky High Valley.

Hike 24   Rye Patch Trail, to Paradise Lake

Distance: 2.1 miles, one way
Low elevation: 4900'
High elevation: 6240'
Suited for: day trip
Usage: high
Difficulty: strenuous

Directions to trailhead: Leaving the Scott River Road at its junction with FS 44N45, 14 miles west of State Highway 3 and 16.5 miles south of State Highway 96, you follow FS 44N45 for 8.8 miles to a signed left fork onto FS 44N44. The trailhead is 3.5 miles up FS 44N44, at the far end of a small parking area on the left. A rustic, Forest Service notice board marks the spot. Unless you own a 4-wheel drive vehicle, it will be a somewhat longer walk in the early season since there is a bridgeless ford of Kelsey Creek's South Fork just under 0.3 mile from the trailhead.

Trail description: Following first an earth-barred skid road, then a single-lane trail, climb through a cutblock and into forest at a wilderness-border sign (0.2, 4950). The climb quickly steepens through the mixed-conifer forest, then abates above an open stand of Douglas-firs and white firs. Your gentle grade is a short-lived pleasure for the trail steepens once more and, aided by a series of sporadic switchbacks, climbs into ceanothus scrub (1.0, 5680).

After a few more switchbacks and twistings that crisscross a minor ridgelet, the trail gradient moderates as you move into a steady west-southwest heading up toward the crest of Cayenne Ridge. Just before curving west at the ridgecrest (0.7, 6240), you get a fascinating view of the metasedimentary strata in the cliff face south of Paradise Lake.

Shortly after dropping off the crest of the ridge, the trail becomes sketchy to nonexistent. You have three options for completing your hike to Paradise Lake. If you plan to camp at Paradise Lake (0.2, 6120) and wish

to respect the 200-foot camping restrictions (all the lakeside campsites are right on the shoreline), you can head roughly north 110 yards along a pussypaw-carpeted minor crest, down to a few small-to-tiny campsites in and around a cluster of red firs. The lake is then 160 yards west across the meadow. Or you can follow what appears to be the intended trail by curving sharply south through a slight depression for 125 yards to a junction with the Pacific Crest Trail. The cool, brush-enshrouded spring on the far side of the Crest Trail makes the large, trailside campsite here the most inviting of the legitimate camping spots, since the lake and its outlet creek are lukewarm to the taste by midsummer. From the campsite, Paradise Lake is little more than a football field away. Finally, if campsites are not a consideration, you can continue straight ahead about 50 yards to the lip of the glacial bowl containing Paradise Lake, then drop directly west through the meadow to the lake.

Paradise Lake was named by a Forest Service employee for the atmosphere created by the great numbers of butterflies that grace its shores and the surrounding meadow during the summer. He certainly wasn't remarking on the lake itself, whose shallow shoreline waters and mucky bottom are an acquired taste for those wishing to be refreshed by an afternoon swim. Perhaps it's the captivating view of Kings Castle's marble cap on the ridge west of the lake, that makes it so popular.

Kings Castle

For a captivating view *from* the top of Kings Castle, there's a strenuous, though oft-used, bushwhack route. It begins by climbing almost due west above the lake's south shore, on the brushy slopes beneath the magnificent metasedimentary cliffs. After reaching the ridgecrest saddle southeast of Kings Castle, follow the ridgeline to the castle top.

Hike 25   Kelsey Creek Trail, to Paradise Lake

Distance: 7.6 miles, one way

Low elevation: 2380'

High elevation: 6120'

Suited for: weekend

Usage: low up Kelsey Creek; high at Paradise Lake

Difficulty: moderate

Directions to trailhead: Take the Scott River Road 16.9 miles west from State Highway 3, or 13.6 miles south from State Highway 96, to an unsigned dirt road immediately north of a bridge across the Scott River. Turn west onto the dirt road and follow it 2/3 mile to the trailhead on the right.

Trail description: After an initial, moderate ascent, the trail eases into a gently ascending westward climb high above Kelsey Creek. The elevation gain is unfortunate since the cascades and deep, eddying pools of Kelsey Creek, so seductive on a baking midsummer day, are inaccessible. If the clifflike, dark gray outcrop that the trail swerves beneath looks distinctly granitic, it's because the trail crosses a large gabbro-diorite intrusion for the first few miles.

As you skip through the litter of autumn's pale yellow and pink madrone leaves, you arrive at an unsigned trail junction (0.7, 2640) with a 0.1-mile path that descends to a creekside gravel terrace. Beyond the trail junction, the trail continues climbing and soon follows a right-hand bend in the creek to curve onto a sparsely forested slope.

Just before a short descent, you dip briefly into a gully, whose red soil indicates a "window" of ultramfic rock from the extensive mass to the west. Having curved to a generally northwest heading, the trail resumes a moderate climb through a heavy concentration of madrone, noted by its smooth green-peeling-tc-red bark. If its glossy foliage and smooth red bark remind you of manzanita, it's because both are closely related members of the heath family.

Climbing sporadically now, you make a brief descent to the edge of Kelsey Creek. Then, 0.2 mile farther, the trail comes creekside again. Here a short path leads down to an elaborate, bench-and-tabled campsite on a sandy flat beside a narrow minigorge with small but accessible pools and cascades (1.6, 3220). Just past the campsite, four switchbacks climb alongside a major gully in the slopes, which you eventually cross to make a gentle-becoming-steep climb high above the creek. Your westward ascent eases as the trail bends into the gully of a stream that dries up by midsummer, then continues on to a crossing of the alder-choked, ever flowing North Fork (1.5, 3820).

Having paralleled Kelsey Creek's bend to the southwest, the trail now climbs moderately, crossing an insignificant intermittent stream as it heads toward the full-bodied cataract of Maple Falls. A *Marble Mountain Wilderness* sign announces the wilderness perhaps ½ mile prematurely, and the trail becomes quite steep as it climbs through the

Kings Castle

fireweed and thimbleberry of a rocky, scrub-covered slope. Although the vegetation doesn't bear the distinctive stamp of ultra-mafic soil—Jeffrey pines—the red earth occasionally underfoot is a sign that you've crossed over the eastern edge of a broad, ultramafic mass, which spreads west across the Marble Mountains. The ascent continues to quick flowing Packers Valley creek (1.9, 4950) then, on the north side of a stock gate just beyond the creek, you reach a fine, roomy campsite on the Kelsey Creek side of the trail.

Beyond the campsite the canyon loses its narrow, stream-cut aspect and broadens its bottom. On this more-level bottom the incense-cedar-bordered path gently ascends toward the meadows of upper Kelsey Creek canyon. You pass through small open areas that provide views up toward the head of the canyon and the craggy ridgecrest above Paradise Lake. The trail steepens, crossing several seeps and miniature creeks before entering a large meadow. You cut through a line of black cottonwoods, which appear silver-spangled in the slightest breeze due to the rustling of their silvery bottomed leaves. Past the trees, angle up the meadow and past a junction with the Big Ridge Cutoff Trail (0.5, 5280), which goes to shallow, moderately visited Turk Lake.

Turk Lake

To reach Turk Lake, head west-southwest up this right fork and climb strenuously through the forest for 0.4 mile. As the ascent eases, the trail enters a rocky meadow and fades away. Your route angles west-southwest across the meadow, then follows its south edge to a campsite 50 yards short of Turk Lake's brush-bounded east shore (0.6, 5820). Just 35 yards northwest of the campsite a large, sign-bedecked fir marks the faint beginnings of a north-northwest-heading spur trail which climbs 0.7 mile to the Pacific Crest Trail, and also the continuation of the north-heading Big Ridge Cutoff Trail, which climbs through Packers Valley to the Tyler Meadows Trail.

Beyond the junction, the Kelsey Creek Trail becomes thicker flowered along a moderate ascent. Having crossed two more small flows, the second in a west-climbing gully,

Morning calm over Turk Lake

the trail gradually steepens again, passing through a veritable jungle of flora and an open stand of firs. Into meadow again, you climb away from Kelsey Creek and cross two closely spaced intermittent streams, then start an arc across the valley headwall back toward Kelsey Creek. Midway along this strenuous climb you meet a trickling creek-let enlivened with purple spikes of tower delphineum. You then struggle up to a crossing of Kelsey Creek (1.3, 6060).

Just beyond an isolated switchback, the climb eases as you enter a meadow flanking the east side of Paradise Lake. After hiking 50 yards southwest across the meadow on the ill-defined trail, you come to a junction with the Pacific Crest Trail, near the lake's outlet (0.1, 6120). Although there are large, inviting campsites along the lake's north shore, they are obviously within the 200-foot no-camping zone. More appropriate sites can be found in a grove of young red firs, 160 yards east across the meadow, or by heading up the Pacific Crest Trail 0.1 mile to a trailside site next to a brush-hidden spring.

Chapter 10

Crest Trails

Introduction: There are times when a loop or out-and-back trip is simply not enough. When something inside you craves a more obvious feeling of having traversed *space,* of being able to look at the map and say "I went from here to there." For those times when you've got to put your travelin' shoes on, nothing but an end-to-end trail will do.

An end-to-end trail provides a "survey course" approach to an area: you explore nothing in depth, for the subject's so broad and the time for study so limited. Yet you have an opportunity to sample selected tidbits that are representative of the whole, the choice portions of a given wilderness. An end-to-end hike is like a Sunday buffet brunch: You pick and choose from the overburdened tables, perhaps taking a little extra of some rare delicacy, and leave the meal pleasantly sated, rested, and prepared to enjoy the remainder of the day.

If you scan the maps of the Marble Mountain Wilderness, you'll see two end-to-end routes that readily suggest themselves: the Pacific Crest Trail, which traverses the Salmon and Marble mountains in a south-north direction from Etna Summit to Grider Creek, and what the author calls the Salmon Mountains Crest Trail, a west-east route from Haypress Meadows to Shackleford Creek along the middle portion of the horseshoe-shaped Salmon Mountains range. These two routes provide a cornucopia of high-country vistas, ready access to many lakes, kaleidoscopic color in multiflowered meadows, and the sheltered closeness of heavily forested, deeply stream-cut valleys. These two trails present the Marble Mountains area in microcosm, for almost everything the Marbles has to offer is available to the crest-trail traveler.

These two hikes are recommended not only by their natural attractions, but also by historical significance in one case, and Congressional edict in the other. The route of the Salmon Mountains Crest Trail roughly follows that of the old Kelsey Trail, built in Gold Rush days. The Pacific Crest Trail is of more recent vintage, born of the impetus provided by a few active dreamers and, later, the passage of the National Trails System Act.

The Salmon Mountains Crest Trail

When gold fever overran the banks of the Klamath and Salmon rivers in the early 1850s, one of the most pressing problems was keeping the miners provisioned. Ranching in Scott Valley was a burgeoning industry, but there was a need for flour, salt, and general merchandise. The most efficient means of reaching far northern California was by sailing ship up the coast. But the river routes inland from the northern California coast were hampered by sporadic Indian conflict and by the length and difficulty of the trails.

In 1855 Tom Kelsey was commissioned to build a trail from Crescent City to Yreka. The total cost of his route over the Coast Ranges and the Salmon and Marble mountains: $4200.

There appear to have been two distinct routes crossing the Salmon and Marble mountains from the Klamath River to Scott Valley. There is still some debate as to which route was the original. The northern route climbed up Titus Creek from Ferry Point, and over into the Elk Creek drainage. Here it headed down Elk Creek to its confluence with East Fork Elk Creek, then went up the East Fork to Buckhorn Mountain. It then followed Big Ridge southeast to where it would drop through Packers Valley and follow Kelsey Creek out to the Scott River, and thence lead to Fort Jones in Scott Valley.

The more southern route is essentially that of the Salmon Mountains Crest Trail. In the Siskiyou County Historical Society's 1950 yearbook, there's a description of this section of a 19-day round trip from Scott Valley to Crescent City. After climbing the length of Shackleford Creek, the packtrain spent its first night at the head of the creek. The second day finished the climb to the crest and traversed it to Whisky Camp. There was a small blacksmith shop maintained at Whisky Camp, for it was a common stopover point; also common was the keg of whisky the packers would bring with them with which to pass the evening there. The third day continued along the crest to Cuddihy Valley, although it was reached by dropping down Franks Valley, just past Spirit Lake, then traveling up Cuddihy Valley. On the fourth day, they returned to the ridge and followed it to Haypress Meadows. The trail forked at Haypress Meadows, the left fork heading for the Stanshaws, a Klamath River family for whom Stanshaw Creek and meadows were named. The pack train took the right fork, which descended to the Klamath River at the Coon Creek Ford near Cottage Grove (about midway between Happy Camp and Somes bar).

As for the present-day route, the Ten Bear Trail has been chosen as the route into (or out of) Haypress Meadows for, although it is longer than any of the other Haypress Meadows trails and not so well maintained as some, it appears to best represent the route of the old Kelsey Trail. A trail no longer drops steeply through Cuddihy Valley and then climbs tortuously up Franks Valley, so you'll have to be satisfied with ambling easily along the semilevel crest trail.

The decision to describe the hike from west to east was largely arbitrary. However, if you wish to go easy at the beginning of your hike in order to eat into your packweight and reaccustom yourself to backcountry life, your trek will be more pleasurable in the relatively lightly used Ukonom district than among the hordes pouring into the Shackleford Creek area.

Two final notes on the Salmon Mountains Crest Trail: For one thing, it's called the Salmon Mountains Crest Trail only in this book, since the name is the author's creation. It's actually a chain of several trails, known to the Forest Service as, (reading from west to east:) Ten Bear Trail, Haypress Trail, Shackleford Trail, Pacific Crest Trail, and Shackleford Creek Trail. You'll need to keep that in mind should you have specific questions to ask at a ranger station.

The second item has to do with the recommended hiking season for this trail. This is not an early-season hike. Although most of the route is along windswept ridges and treeless south slopes that are soon free of winter snowpack, virtually every lake easily accessible by the trail is snug up against a north face. Hence you can expect to find these lakes remaining ice-cold, if not ice-covered, well into summer. Even if chill waters are no deterrent, you'll find that snow lingers on these north slopes, obscuring the often already obscure lake trails. It's best to hike this trail after the Fourth of July, although the extent and duration of winter snowpack will, of course, vary each year.

The Pacific Crest Trail

The concept of a Pacific Crest Trail dates back to the 1920s, and perhaps earlier. However, it was not until 1968, after years of lobbying by private individuals, that Congress recognized the burgeoning popularity of backpacking and related outdoor activities, and passed the National Trails System Act, in which the Pacific Crest Trail was named, along with the Appalachian Trail in the east, as a National Scenic Trail.

Through a long, involved process, the Forest Service developed a route incorporating existing trails, abandoned trails, and twinkle-in-the-cartographer's-eye trails. Although the proposed route received final approval in 1972, the Forest Service is still engaged in the laborious task of turning ink into 24"-wide, less-than-15°-grade tread. In the Marbles area, this has almost meant starting from scratch. Trail existed from the head of Kidder Lake canyon to the wilderness boundary at the north end of Big Ridge. In order to meet the required specifications, however, much of the trail had to be reconstructed, and often rerouted, a process still in progress.

The requirement that the trail stay as faithful as possible to crest-travel resulted in a new section of trail built from above Kidder Lake south to Etna Summit. Although this segment was open for use by late 1978, difficulties in obtaining easement to or ownership of some tracts of private land in the Russian Peak area has left a gap in the permanent Pacific Crest Trail south of Etna Summit. For a Crest Trail hiker starting anywhere south of the Marbles to make the connection, a temporary route was created using existing trails and roads. It enters the Marbles via the Mule Bridge trailhead on the North Fork Salmon River, then climbs the Shelly Meadows Trail up the Right Hand Fork and onto the ridgecrest saddle above the Shelly Fork. In 1979, the Forest Service obtained the last stretch of private land it needed to complete the permanent Crest Trail south of Etna Summit. By 1981 perhaps, certainly by 1982, the Etna Summit-to-Shelly Meadows section of the Pacific Crest Trail will be baptised by the Mexico-to-Canada speedburners.

The Forest Service faces a greater problem at the northern end of the Marbles. It must deal with the stipulation that the Pacific Crest Trail should not use any roadway open to motor traffic. This stipulation has few exceptions, the most notable one perhaps being the use of the Bridge of the Gods to cross the half-mile span of the Columbia River between Oregon and Washington. The Klamath River presents a similar situation. The route between the lower trailhead of the Grider Creek Trail—now part of the Crest Trail—and the resumption of the permanent Crest Trail west of Seiad Valley currently follows roads to a Highway 96 bridge over the Klamath. In order to build the remaining few miles of permanent Pacific Crest Trail between these two points, the Forest Service will also have to build an extravagantly expensive hiker/horse crossing. Of the 10 proposals being considered in the summer of 1979, there were none less costly than $340,000—that's 1978 dollars, folks—except for an eleventh proposal, which would be to petition Congress to pass an amendment allowing another exception to the rules.

The Pacific Crest Trail is described here from south to north. The bulk of the trail hovers around 6000 feet, but the north trailhead at Grider Creek is 1700 feet. Hence you have a choice of beginning your hike, under full pack, with a climb of 4400 vertical feet, or finishing your trip, with light pack and with 4400 feet of descent. The choice is yours; the direction of the trail description just gives you a little hint.

Hike 26   Salmon Mountains Crest Trail

Distance: 31.7 miles, one way
Low elevation: 4600'
High elevation: 6610'
Suited for: 4-6 days
Usage: moderate-to-high
Difficulty: moderate

Directions to trailheads:
East trailhead is same as on page 119.
West trailhead is same as on page 68.

Trail description: The first 4.7 miles of this hike are described as the Ten Bear Trail, whose description starts on page 68. The following 7.1 miles along the Haypress Trail to its junction with the Cuddihy Lakes Trail are discussed in Hike 9, whose description starts on page 72. You should note that the small spring on the Haypress Trail, 0.4 mile above the spur trail to Round Meadow, is the last trailside water until Spirit Lake, 9.5 miles beyond.

Beyond the Cuddihy Lakes Trail, the Salmon Mountains Crest Trail begins a level traverse across the predominantly scrub-covered south slope of Peak 6864, on which greenleaf manzanita together with Sadler and huckleberry oak join the more familiar tobacco brush and bitter cherry. Cuddihy Valley opens below you and its creek bends south toward its appointment with Wooley Creek's North Fork. Above the North Fork a sea of ridges and canyons swells to the southeast. The path climbs gently for a short while as you pass beyond 6864, then levels off, and then climbs again as you leave the south slope to bend sharply north into a side canyon cut by a Cuddihy Fork tributary. The climb steepens as you pass through an open stand of red firs and come out at a narrow saddle (1.8, 6300).

Arcing away from the saddle, the trail climbs gently in stages through a patchy forest, then descends easily through the re-emergent scrub to the saddle west of Pigeon Roost. As you climb gently along Pigeon Roost's south slope, you might be surprised to see a handful of knobcone pines scattered among the isolated red firs, since they are about 1000 feet above their recognized upper-elevation range. After turning sharply onto Pigeon Roost's east slope, with Elk Peak coming into view to the east-northeast and Black Mountain beyond it, you begin a moderate, quite rocky descent to a junction with the Burney Lake Trail (1.0, 6180).

Burney Lake

For most people it is more than a day's hike from the trailhead to Burney Lake, so hikers usually stop at one of the inviting lakes that are reached before Burney. As a result, Burney Lake is probably the least used lake along this entire trail. To reach it, scramble 300 yards up through rubble on a sometimes indistinct path to the Salmon Mountains' crest, then wind 0.6 mile down a bone-racking, steep trail to the southeast shore of this sizable lake. A large east-shore campsite near the lake's outlet creek is the least abusive of the 100-foot no-camping regulation.

From the Burney Lake Trail junction, the Salmon Mountains Crest Trail continues its descent to a narrow saddle above the head of Franks Valley, leaving the region of the Wooley Creek pluton's granitic rock in the process. You climb steeply from the saddle, forsaking the crest for the north slope and its cool, lushly understoried forest. After the climb tops out in a saddle on a north-south-trending ridge, the path begins to descend through scrub toward Spirit Lake. Above the scrub, you can see Black and Marble mountains, reigning imperiously in the east-north-east. The descending trail curves down to a slight spur ridge above the northwest shore of Spirit Lake, then arcs above the lake's east shore to reach a spur trail (1.4, 6030).

Spirit Lake

The spur trail leads 0.1 mile down to the north shore, which is one extended camp-site that ignores the 100-foot no-camping guideline. Other campsites are found on its west side. Regardless of where you settle, this brushy-shored, deep lake provides fine swimming and tasty fishing.

Leaving Spirit Lake behind, you begin a rolling, almost imperceptible descent along the narrow ridgecrest, its forest opening occasionally to provide a glimpse of nearing Elk Peak to the northeast. Then the trail leaves the crest to begin a level traverse along Elk Peak's scrub-robed south slope. Shortly before passing off the face of Elk Peak, the path returns to the forest and soon comes to a junction with the Marble Gap Trail to Rainy Lake (1.0, 5980).

Rainy Lake

A torturously steep ½-mile descent brings you into the upper reaches of Rainy Valley, and here, by a stand of red firs, you meet a path that turns to the right to curve 0.1 mile around the fir grove to Rainy Lake. This moderately used lake looks better than it plays: its setting against the valley's cliff-like headwall is picturesque, but the opportunities for water sports are minimal.

Beyond the Marble Gap Trail junction, the Salmon Mountains Crest Trail climbs gently through the welcome shade of the fir forest. Soon it bends south and climbs more noticeably up to a slight depression in a south-trending spur. As the trail bends east across the nose of this spur, you return to south-slope scrub and an easy stroll along level trail. Curving east-northeast, the route begins a long arc above the headwaters of North Fork Wooley Creek. The metasediments take on a more specific definition now: above you, the least glamorous face of the Marble Rim presents its pale visage, and marble outcrops occasionally appear at trailside. The patchy forest and rock-garden scrub, dry and hot enough to contain a scattering of sagebrush, give way to a uniform forest through which the path climbs briefly to a junction with the Marble Rim Trail (1.4, 6150).

Marble Rim Trail

Although this 2.3-mile-long trail is 0.7 mile shorter to the four-way junction with the Pacific Crest Trail than is the Salmon Mountains Crest Trail via Big Elk Lake, one might not save time by taking it. For once you reached the broad saddle on the rim itself, with its breathtaking exposure and stunning perspective of the marble escarpment, you might sit there for the rest of the day in order the catch the evening sun's bold brushstrokes on the canvas of the precipitous rim.

The Marble Rim Trail is not maintained very often, which can make the 0.6-mile, switchbacking climb through the burgeoning, moist-gully vegetation an act of mental, as well as physical, concentration. Once across the saddle just south of Peak 6665, the

Burney Lake

trail's ensuing ½-mile traverse is generally uneventful until it reaches the rim saddle, with a view that is an event in itself. Beyond the rim, you contour along an extremely rocky trail beneath the summit of Peak 6880, then descend steeply along the crest of its southeast ridge to a junction with the Pacific Crest and Salmon Mountains Crest trails.

Whisky Camp

Five yards northwest of the junction with the Marble Rim Trail, a sketchy trail leaves the Salmon Mountains Crest Trail and drops steeply 0.1 mile to beautifully secluded Whisky Camp, with undependable water in a neighboring gully and a trickling spring 75 yards farther south in a more significant watercourse. If you intend to follow the Marble Rim Trail as an alternative to the Crest Trail's route by way of Big Elk Lake, you might want to visit Whisky Camp, since the next source of trailside water will be Summit Lake, 7.6 miles away.

Beyond the Marble Rim Trail junction, the Salmon Mountains Crest Trail continues its gentle, curving ascent, dipping briefly into a small gully filled with mountain ash, then into a major gully with an intermittent creeklet, before gradually mounting a richly flowered northwest slope. As you approach the nose of a spur, then bend around it, the floral coat of many colors gives way to thin

forest and thick shrubbery. As the trail gains a bit more southern exposure and levels off completely, the common south-slope scrub becomes dominant.

After crossing a forested saddle north of Peak 6640, you descend steeply, switchbacking out onto an open slope with impressive views ranging from the craggy headwall of Wooley Creek east to the continuation of the Salmon Mountains crest and its outlier, Peak 7636. Beyond it, Red Mountain tails off to the northeast. In the midst of the trail's curve to the northeast, you pass a junction with an abandoned trail to Dads Pocket. Shortly beyond this junction Big Elk Lake comes into view and, after bending down toward its south shore, you reach the lake at its outlet creek (1.4, 5970).

Big Elk Lake is a horsepackers' lake, surrounded by great meadowed fields ideal for forage. The abundant lake-bottom vegetation in this 10-foot-deep lake severely decreases its effective depth, making it too shallow for good swimming but keeping the trout within biting distance of the surface. The east end of the lake is thick with campsites, but the only spot that acknowledges the 200-foot limitation is beneath a small stand of firs on a knoll above the lake's south shore.

Before leaving Big Elk Lake, be sure to fill your water bottles since the next trailside source of water, Summit Lake, is 6.9 miles away. The path climbs briefly away from the

Big Elk Lake

lake, through a field of aster, Bigelow sneeze-weed and goldenrod, then descends steeply through a more lush and varied garden, and then more gently into a dense fir forest. The silence of the forest is extraordinary as you descend quietly to a junction with the Wooley Creek Trail (0.9, 5620).

Ananias Camp

Although the trail junction is quite obvious and the trail appears substantial, the Wooley Creek Trail is "maintained" as a primitive trail between here and the Big Meadows Trail junction, several trail miles downstream. Perhaps two or three parties a year beat their way down the length of the Wooley Creek Trail, but their challenge doesn't begin until they get below Ananias Camp. Just enough people are attracted by an evening amid the inimate splendor of the forest-deep, to keep the one-mile path to Ananias Camp relatively open.

The Wooley Creek Trail begins by descending moderately along a well-forested hillside 0.2 mile to a trail junction at the edge of a long, linear meadow. Follow the more worn left fork and continue the descent just inside the forest's edge, eventually entering a great meadow. Wading through the waist-deep wildflowers, follow the overgrown path down the meadow's length.

Shortly after bending down toward the Big Elk Fork of Wooley Creek to begin rounding a bulge in the hillside, you come to a trail junction (0.9, 5040). The brushbound path descending south-southwest 40 yards to the creek is the continuation of the Wooley Creek Trail. Taking the left fork, you descend through a thicket of American dogwood and soon come to Ananias Camp, perched on a small island of land between Ananias spring and a dry gully. Spelunkers mapping the caves in the Marbles believe that Ananias spring issues from a subterranean reservoir in the caves, which would account for its remarkable chilliness.

One may wonder at the origin of the name "Ananias Camp," as Ananias was an early Christian who was struck dead for lying to the Apostle Peter. It seems that a group of local folks were gathered at the campsite by the spring one evening, sharing hunting tales around the campfire. As the evening wore on, the veracity of the stories told became so supect as to bring Ananias to mind.

From the Wooley Creek Trail junction you climb moderately, curving around a bulge in the slopes and up into a major gully lined with marble outcrops. Leaving the gully, the trail steepens, arcing to the east and leaving the forest for south-slope scrub. This climb tops out at a narrow saddle, at which you meet a multisigned junction (0.7, 6232) with the Marble Rim and Pacific Crest trails (see page 153).

For the next 4.3 miles the Salmon Mountains and Pacific Crest trails are one and the same. You can find this section described, in reverse direction in Hike 27, beginning at the junction of the PCT with the Shackleford Creek Trail (see page 152).

Upon reaching the junction with the Shackleford Creek Trail, you leave the Pacific Crest Trail, which continues straight ahead along the ridge while you turn north-northwest around a hefty boulder of ultramafic rock and onto the Shackleford Creek Trail (4.3, 6590). In 200 yards, the initially semi-level trail comes to a usage path on the right that quickly reaches a rocky point with expansive views out over the Shackleford Creek drainage. Summit Lake sparkles invitingly below, but Cliff and Campbell lakes lie hidden behind a median ridge that once bisected the glacier that carved out the head of Shackleford Creek.

Take a look at the postage-stamp meadow, your next goal, which lies 400 feet directly below you. Back on the Shackleford Creek Trail your descent starts slowly, then picks up speed as the gradient increases, curving down to a meadowed cirque, then switch-backing to head down a broad ridgecrest. Several switchbacks through ceanothus scrub on the ridge's southeast slope bring you down to the small meadow you saw from above. You skirt its northern edge, then cross its burbling creeklet, along which you continue the switchbacking descent to a junction with the Campbell Lake Trail (1.0, 6020), a few moments walk from the shores of Summit Lake.

The remaining 5.0 miles of this hike follow the Shackleford Creek Trail down to its trailhead. The description can be found, in reverse direction, in Hike 19, starting on page 119.

Hike 27

Pacific Crest Trail

Distance: 49.4 miles, one way
Low elevation: 1700'
High elevation: 7210'
Suited for: 5-7 days
Usage: high
Difficulty: moderate

Directions to trailheads:

South trailhead: Thirteen miles north of the Callahan F.S. work center, or 10.7 miles south of the Scott River Ranger Station, leave State Highway 3 on the turn-off for Etna. In 0.5 mile, turn west on Etna's Main Street, following it out of town and up 10.3 miles to Etna Summit. The trail takes off from the west side of the road, contouring along the south side of the ridge. In 1979 this trailhead was still unsigned. However, the Forest Service intends not only to put up a sign, but to create a camping area with packstock facilities. Not only is the summit, and the prospective camping area, without water, but there is no permanent water along

the trail until you reach the creek at Shelly Meadows, 10.7 miles distant.

North trailhead: Same as on page 47.

Trail description: On a clinkery trail blasted out of the metavolcanic ridge, head west on a gentle ascent. The climb stiffens for a while after you round a south-trending spur, then it resumes a gentle-to-moderate grade through a mixture of fir forest and rock garden. The trail leaves the forest at a narrow, wind-whipped crest saddle (1.0, 6350), where the Mill Creek watershed spills away on the right and the Russian Creek drainage drops off on the left. After traversing the saddle, climb briefly up the crest, then leave it to contour through south-slope scrub. To the south, the powdered faces of Mt. Thompson and the Trinity Alps come into view.

The route leaves the south slopes after descending briefly to another ridgecrest saddle, overlooking the main branch of Mill Creek, then enters the wilderness as it climbs variably along the crest. The trail follows the

Mt. Shasta, from ridge north of Etna Summit

ridgecrest's bend to the southwest and soon moves off the crest to the south slope. After a variegated stand of timber gives way to rock and sparse scrub, Mt. Shasta can be seen over your left shoulder, rising grandly in the east.

A single switchback returns you to the crest (1.8, 6640), from which you make an arcing traverse along north and east slopes, above the head of Mill Creek, to a ridgecrest saddle. To the southwest the crumbling summit of Yellow Dog Peak rises at the head of a long, exposed ridge. To the west, below the valley of Big Creek, the Salmon River's North Fork slices deeper into its canyon.

Past the saddle, the trail contours along west slopes, then descends gently into a nearly pure stand of red firs and on down to a saddle at the southeast end of Razor Ridge (0.9, 6670). Turning east-northeast at the saddle, you descend moderately through north-slope forest. In it you might be able to wet your lips at the seep dripping from a massive, mossy outcrop above the trail. Curving out of the forest, you gradually descend, then ascend, along open, rocky slopes, crossing an early-season trickle at the low point. Then, after turning east into a bouldery amphitheater, cross a slightly more durable flow (1.0, 6450), and bend back to the north.

Ever so gently, the trail loses elevation as it continues to contour above Pointers Gulch, twice dipping east into depressions that might stay moist through midsummer. The route curves around a southwest-trending bulge and climbs north momentarily to a small, rocky freshet (2.0, 6170), which offers the first real possibility for late-season water. You curve west-northwest, then north again to a second small flow with questionable staying power, in the midst of a bouldery, sparsely forested slope.

From this second intermittent stream, one climbs moderately into a young stand of red firs and western white pines, then arcs gently up to a ridgecrest saddle overlooking Babs Fork to the north-northeast (0.9, 6290). This saddle marks a transition from a region of metavolcanic rock to a narrow band of metasediments.

The trail levels as you approach and round a southwest-trending spur, then resumes a gentle gradient as you curve up onto the south slopes of Peak 6667. After rounding its southwest spur, you descend steeply to a ridgecrest saddle above the head of the Glendenning Fork (1.4, 6430). The path contours, then climbs gently toward the saddle east of Peak 7219's south summit. As you have just reached the granitic Shelly Lake pluton, notice how the vernally moist meadow of lupine and grasses you pass through on the approach to the saddle is similar to some of the well-drained meadows in the area of the Wooley Creek pluton.

Now you bend west-southwest beneath the saddle and begin descending. The "rusty" rock you see after turning north is not some mysterious shingling of metavolcanics, but is that same, once-shining granitic rock you've been walking through. The coloration is a part of the weathering process, most likely the oxidation of iron-rich minerals in the rock. The descent eases, and you traverse the scrubby slopes below unseen Shelly Lake on semilevel trail. There is no constructed trail to Shelly Lake, but you will notice several apparent "paths" heading upslope as you descend along a northwest-trending spur.

After rounding the spur—a glacial moraine —you drop quickly to the outlet creek from Shelly Lake (1.7, 6170), the first assuredly permanent water along the trail. Here you might notice a couple of small, creekside sleeping spaces tucked into the trees above the trail. For more spacious accomodations, climb briefly from the creek, following the trail 115 yards to a campsite on your right, in the forest strip bordering bilberry-filled Shelly Meadows. Shelly Meadows is part of a summer-range allocation. However, the cattle generally begin their summer in Cabin and Bug gulches to the west, and come to Shelly Meadows only toward the end of their stay.

Near the north tip of the meadows, one passes the remnants of Wilson Cabin, on the left. Its state of disrepair is a function of campers who viewed it as a source of firewood rather than a site of potential archeological significance. In 1978 the few remaining logs were "protected" by a historical-site preservation notice.

The next trail segment, 0.1 mile long, climbs gently from the ruins, passing a large, developed campsite on your right at the meadow's edge before reaching a trail junction. The left fork starts north, then bends westward for a 1/3-mile descent to a junction with the Shelly Meadows Trail, which in turn descends to Bug Gulch and the Right Hand Fork. We keep to the right fork, which begins its gentle ascent to the northeast. The climb steepens somewhat, passes an unofficial trail junction with the Shelly Fork Trail, then eases up a final 115 yards to a trail junction in the ridgecrest saddle above the Shelly Fork (0.5, 6380). The 2.3-mile Shelly Meadows Trail descends to the west-southwest. A trail sign indicates the Shelly Fork Trail to be descending to the east, but the trail you see down the headwall below you actually comes out at the unsigned trail junction you recently passed. The Pacific Crest Trail continues northwest through the saddle.

Shelly Fork Trail

If, for some reason, you wish to save yourself 8.9 miles of walking, but add 1470 feet of vertical climb, you can begin your Crest Trail outing with the Shelly Fork Trail. In some respects, the most difficult part of this route is finding the trailhead. Follow the "directions to trailhead" for the Kidder Creek-Kidder Lake Hike, 18, to the 8.4-mile point along Kidder Creek road. There take the left fork, which curves to a bridge over Kidder Creek. Across the creek 0.1 mile, you take the right turn at a road junction and follow this sometimes rough, steep, dirt road. You pass a left turn at 0.9 mile, and cross a bridgeless Shelly Fork, before reaching another unsigned road junction 0.2 mile beyond the Shelly Fork crossing. Turn left and follow this road upslope 0.3 mile to a road-end parking area and corral.

The Shelly Fork Trail begins as a blocked-off jeep road, climbing at an excessively steep clip. The ascent eases to merely steep, crossing an intermittent stream in 1/3 mile. After a brief, forested descent brings you beside the Shelly Fork, you follow a bend in the creek into a broad, rocky, scrub-garden flat (1.0, 5240). You meander with the creek through the flat, then climb moderately around an east-trending spur to a meadow-edge campsite. Although the creek has moved to the far side of this meadow, there is accessible water less than 30 yards into the meadow. You should probably consider filling your water bottles here, for it is another

1.1 extremely steep miles to the ridgetop, then 2.5 miles along the Pacific Crest Trail to the next trailside water.

Leaving the campsite and meadow, you begin the steep ascent through sheltering forest, then move out into the scrub as you climb above the head of the creek. As your rocky switchbacks bring you near the ridgecrest, the trail begins breaking into a number of separate paths. The trail receives little use except by ranchands driving their cattle, who are notoriously bad switchback-cutters. The most obvious path traverses roughly south 230 yards from a final switchback, climbing up and over the ridge to drop quickly to the unofficial trail junction (1.3, 6370) 115 yards short of the junction saddle.

After leaving the trail junction above the Shelly Fork, climb briefly into a forest of white and red firs, then begin a level traverse of the south slopes of Peak 7085. After crossing a multiflowered meadow, you return to forest and metasedimentary rock, leaving the Shelly Lake pluton behind. As you approach the southwest spur of Peak 7085, the trail comes out onto open, scrub slopes, and you see the high peaks of the Trinity Alps rising in the south. As you round the spur, the high peaks of the Salmon Mountains which separate the drainages of Kidder and Wooley creeks can be seen rising to the west-northwest.

Heading north-northeast now, you begin a long, curving, semilevel traverse above the deeply cut defile of Timothy Gulch. The traverse ends in a gentle descent to the ridgecrest saddle west-southwest of Peak 7109 (2.2, 6410). The trail crosses to the north slope and descends through an open forest of weeping spruce, mountain hemlock, red fir and western white pine to a series of terraced, trailside campsites on the edge of a pocket-sized cirque with a permanent brook (0.3, 6260).

Beyond the campsites, the path quickly descends to cross the brook. You then contour along rocky, open slopes to the outlet creek of Fisher Lake (0.4, 6170). After climbing above the grassy peninsula extending from the tarn's northwest shore, the route continues to ascend to somewhat smaller Marten Lake (0.3, 6340).

Peak 7646 above PCT and Kidder Creek's Hayes fork

The rolling, rocky traverse above the Hayes fork of Kidder Creek canyon continues through patchy scrub, crossing numerous seeps and boggy meadowlets. Near the head of the Hayes fork you come alongside a cluster of small campsites on the left, near a small tarn (1.1, 6450). Beyond the campsite, the path curls quickly down to the head-waters of the Hayes fork. This is the last trailside water of any dependability until you reach Marble Valley, 8.1 miles ahead; although Cold Springs, 0.3 mile below the trail, is only 5.1 miles away.

From this creek you climb, steeply at times, through the ruddy, weathered granitic rock of the western edge of the Heather Lake pluton, to a ridgecrest switchback at a junction with the new Kidder Lake Trail (0.5, 6600), which drops 1.1 miles down to that cozy little lake. Only 110 yards beyond the switchback, the PCT passes a junction with the abandoned Kidder Lake Trail. As you climb steeply up the rock-gardened, crestline trail, Kidder Lake comes into view below, tucked in at the foot of Peak 6554.

The ascent becomes uncommonly steep as you traverse the subalpine meadowed east slope of Peak 7550. The mop-headed west-ern pasqueflower, scarce in the Marbles, sways in the breeze as you push toward the ridge overlooking Cliff and Campbell lakes and the Shackleford Creek canyon. At the narrow crest, you get your first view of Black and Marble mountains, framed by the saddle to the northwest. Across the lakes basin stands the ultramafic Red Mountain massif. Peaks 7401 and 7636 flank the deep saddle to the north, and Boulder Peak swells to a point in the north-northeast.

At the crest you turn southwest to contour around the cirque in Peak 7550's north face; this trail segment often remains snow-bound late into the summer. The trail returns to the crest at the high point of the Pacific Crest Trail in the Marbles (0.9, 7210), then drops to the west slope, along which it works its way back to the crest at a rocky, open saddle that provides a broader perspective of Black and Marble mountains in the northwest. Across the sweep of Wooley Creek canyon, Medicine Mountain stands high in the west.

Moving onto the west slope again, the rock-rubble trail descends moderately into heavy forest, then regains the crest in a less forested saddle. Beyond the saddle you turn west to climb gently through an open field, yellowed with sulphur eriogonum and woolly sunflower above the reddish undertones of Davis' knotweed. After curling back into the forest and up to the crest, the trail begins a steep, switchbacking descent, during which it twice brings you to the edge of the precipitous cliff above Summit Lake; from the brink you can see where rock has sheared away, avalanching to a rubble-pile halt along the southwest shore of the lake.

The descent eases as you come into a saddle and a junction with the Shackleford Creek Trail (1.8, 6590). This trail heads north-northeast, past a huge ultramafic boulder, descending in 1.0 mile to a junction with the Campbell Lake Trail near the north shore of Summit Lake. The Pacific Crest Trail leaves the saddle heading northwest in a gentle descent. Ever since the junction with the Kidder Lake Trail, you have been walking over metavolcanic rock. Now you enter the realm of the ultramafics, as you travel along the edge of the vast body of serpentinized peridotite that forms Red Mountain. If the ruddy color of the rock and soil isn't a giveaway, there is more evidence as the path

suddenly drops steeply out of the largely fir forest onto the sparsely forested southwest slopes of Peak 7636. The vegetation here is a classic, ultramafic-soil community: scattered Jeffrey pines, western white pines and incense-cedars above great patches of huckleberry oaks, greenleaf manzanitas and serviceberries.

The PCT maintains a level grade across the face of Peak 7636, then returns to the crest for a short, gentle descent through thick forest to a junction with the Cold Springs Trail, on the left (1.6, 6300); an unofficial shortcut down into Red Rock Valley takes off on the right. The steep 0.3-mile path to Cold Springs is seldom maintained, and the campsite there lies within the vandalized shell of an old cabin. But the water, my god, the water—you'd sign away your first-born for a drink of this water. (The campsite is 120 yards west of the main spring.)

In another 0.3 mile along the ridge, you reach a second double trail junction. This time the official, signed trail is on the right, bound for Red Rock Valley, and the unofficial trail is a western route to Cold Springs.

Cliff Lake and partly hidden Campbell Lake, from PCT

Shadow Lake

You ascend gently from the junction 1/3 mile to another junction, this one with the Shadow Lake Trail, just inside a dense stand of firs. This 0.4-mile spur trail climbs steeply to a small meadow on the east slope of Peak 6817, then descends steeply to the lake. The trail through the meadow is obscure and following it requires some attention, but this small lake overlooking Sky High Valley is certainly worth the trouble to reach it.

Beyond the Shadow Lake Trail you climb gently around the forested south slopes of Peak 6817, then exit the forest on level trail, passing at once a 75-yard spur trail to seeping, generally cattle-polluted Soft Water Spring. An equal 75 yards along the Crest Trail brings you to a semihidden sign marking an entirely hidden junction with a secondary spur trail to Shadow Lake. Here too, you are but a few yards above Soft Water Spring.

From the second Shadow Lake trail, you descend moderately through the grassy fields, looking out over the high-relief handiwork of Wooley Creek, then return briefly to the crest at a saddle overlooking Sky High Valley. The trail levels somewhat as it passes through patchy south-slope scrub and forest, then drops gently to a junction with the Sky High Valley Trail (2.2, 6410). This trail swings around Peak 6615, then descends steeply to reach Frying Pan Lake in one mile. Hiking 130 yards down the Crest Trail, you reach a patch of rubble with a second, unsigned junction, which connects with the main Sky High Valley Trail 120 yards to the east.

Beyond the Sky High Valley Trail the PCT soon regains the crest in a saddle that presents a full frontal close-up of Black and Marble mountains. Following the ridgecrest now, the descent bottoms out at a multi-signed trail junction (0.5, 6232). Descending onto the south slope is the trail to Big Elk Lake and points west. Straight ahead, the Marble Rim Trail climbs along the crest, reaching in 1.2 miles a rimside seat overlooking Rainy Valley and the awesome west face of Marble Mountain.

From the saddle, the PCT descends steeply along thickly flowered slopes to the head of Little Marble Valley. As you approach the forest on the north side of the valley, a remnant of the abandoned Little Marble Valley Trail can be seen slipping down the edge of the meadow. In 0.2 mile this path fades at the edge of a silent spring.

Soon after entering the forest, you descend briefly along a spur ridge, then leave it to undulate through the gleaming outcrops along Marble Mountain's flanks. Beyond a shallow creek the trail climbs 80 yards to a red-fir flat where you find the Marble Valley Guard Station and a junction with the Canyon Creek Trail (1.0, 5700). The pit toilet behind the guard station is a valuable addition to the heavily used camping area on the flat.

Descending north-northwest from the flat, the PCT quickly crosses a sluggish brook, then climbs steeply through the forest and across a strip of meadow to a forested spur. You climb through the forest perimeter, and soon reach a junction with the Marble Gap Trail (0.3, 5840). If you think the view of Marble Gap for the last few minutes has been pleasurable, the view *from* the gap is damn near orgasmic. It is only a sometimes staggeringly steep mile away.

The Crest Trail bends northwest, skirting the bottom of a meadow before crossing the variably flowing headwaters of Canyon Creek. Beyond the creek you switchback steeply into forest, then ascend more easily into a small field of wildflowers. The trail rounds a small point and descends briefly to contour through several gullies before climbing again beneath the metasedimentary cap of Black Mountain.

After rounding the east nose of Black Mountain (1.2, 6390), you climb onward beneath hulking marble cliffs. The path crosses a marble bench, with intricately fluted and fissured openings, then descends briefly to a generally dry campsite beneath a sparse canopy of red firs and mountain hemlocks. Level now, you arc above the head of Big Rock Fork through an extraordinarily diverse garden, then begin climbing gently away from Black Mountain.

The easy ascent becomes a slight descent to the meadow beneath Big Rock. There is a half-buried sign at the meadow edge indicating a trail climbing over into Elk Valley. However, this trail is sufficiently abandoned to have been excluded from all maps since before the 1955 USGS topo maps. Beyond the meadow the trail climbs into forest, then out again onto open slopes as it nears a ridgecrest. After a final look over your shoulder at the marbled cliffs, you curl down to the broad saddle of the Jumpoff (1.4, 6640).

After an initial steep descent from the Jumpoff, the trail eases into a level contour above the head of Kelsey Creek. After rounding a bulge in the hillside, you walk a few moments up a steep grade, then contour through a broad, dry-meadowed depression to the northeast spur of Peak 7162 (1.7, 6480).

From the spur, the trail bends initially into north-slope forest, descending briefly, then follows a semilevel course through a rocky gully before descending steeply to Paradise Lake (0.7, 6120). This beautifully situated but somewhat shallow and mucky-bottomed lake is bordered by illegal campsites on its north shore. For a more ecologically sound campsite with added privacy, look to a small stand of red firs 160 yards east across the meadow from the lake's outlet creek. A trailside flat, passed just before entering the lake-bordering meadow, is a bit public but the brush-encased spring just behind it is a welcome alternative to the summer-warmed water of the lake and its outlet creek.

From Paradise Lake the PCT heads northwest, traversing a knotweed-laced meadow before crossing a small brook and beginning to climb along the heavily vegetated hillside beneath the marble citadel of Kings Castle. The path curves into a northeast-facing cirque, crossing its freshet, which is so chill it cramps your throat. This is the last trailside water until Buckhorn Spring, 5.4 miles hence.

After meandering through the cirque's brushy bowl, you switchback up into a redfir forest, then climb extremely steeply up to the ridgecrest and out into outcroppings of the ultramafic body of Red Rock and its environs. The trail then descends moderately along the crest to a four-way trail junction in a saddle (1.6, 6580). To the east, a 0.7-mile trail drops to shallow Turk Lake; to the west, a slightly shorter trail descends just as steeply to Bear Lake, which has greater waterplay potential yet no greater usage.

Kings Castle above Paradise Lake

From the saddle the Crest Trail switchbacks steeply up the rocky south slope of Peak 6923 nearly to its broad summit before moving over to the west slope. The view behind you is exceptional: the deeply dished-out head of Kelsey Creek canyon, the fair, marbled crags of the ridge north of Kings Castle and the glistening pool of Bear Lake beneath ruddy-complexioned Red Rock. You descend gently along the west slope to a shallow, ridgecrest saddle, then contour through an open stand of red firs to a multi-signed trail junction (0.8, 6790). The Tyler Meadows Trail bends to the north, and a seldom-maintained spur trail heads east to drop into Packers Valley, connecting with the Big Ridge Cutoff Trail in just over ½ mile.

The Pacific Crest Trail leaves the crest to contour northwest, revealing vistas of the Coast Ranges to the west and High Siskiyous to the northwest. After a few stretches of gentle climbing, you reach a saddle above the head of Stones Valley (1.6, 6920). Our trail now contours beneath the rounded summit of Peak 7036, descending in stages to just beneath the saddle above the head of Cliff Valley, then it curves west-northwest to traverse the south slopes of Buckhorn Mountain.

Shortly after climbing briefly to surmount the southwest spur of Buckhorn Mountain, the trail disappears as it descends into a meadow of corn lilies. In 1979 you simply pointed yourself west-northwest toward the signpost at Buckhorn Spring, 75 yards off in the middle of the meadow (1.6, 6610). However, survey stakes are already in place to slightly relocate the trail above the fragile springs area (probably during 1980). A cozy campsite beneath the sheltering limbs of a gargantuan, triple-trunked red fir lies 10 yards to the left of the trail just as the trail enters the meadow. It allows you to scramble up to the nearby top of Buckhorn Mountain (6908) for a front-row seat on the sunset and the sunrise. The panorama from Buckhorn is an inspiration regardless of the time of day.

Beyond Buckhorn Spring continue west-northwest across the meadow, picking up distinct tread again as you approach the forest. In the forest, the trail continues de-

Bear Valley, from PCT near Peak 7036

scending steeply down to and around Buckhorn Mountain's west spur. After a brief respite to curl through a depression and climb around a rocky bulge in the hillside, it resumes the steep descent to a tiny spring (0.8, 6130), near the top of a narrow meadow.

In 0.2 mile you contour past another small spring, 25 yards below the trail, at the north edge of another meadow of corn lilies, then roll across a forested spur and into a sprawling meadow. Near the northeast corner of the meadow, you come to signs marking the junction with the 2.5-mile Huckleberry Mountain Trail (0.5, 6060).

Beyond the junction, a few minutes' moderate climbing brings you up to a ridgecrest saddle at a wilderness boundary sign. From here, the route descends into dense, north-slope forest as it arcs above the head of a branch of Cliff Valley creek. The trail returns briefly to the crest at a saddle, amid a scattering of marble rubble. You move off the ridge again to continue the arc to the north-northeast, returning to it again just before coming into the open at the edge of a cutblock. The remainder of the route is displayed before you as you can see the deep gash cut by Grider Creek to the north-northeast, and beyond it, the Klamath River valley at the base of the Siskiyou Mountains.

The ridgecrest serves as the cutblock border and, though you occasionally travel through standing timber of white fir, red fir, Douglas-fir and sugar pine on the east slope, the trail spends much of its time descending moderately through the cutblock.

The trail drops off the crest just as it reaches a logging road (1.6, 5350). Going north on the road for 25 yards returns one to the ridgeline where the "trail"—now a blocked-off former logging road—starts descending north-northwest. You almost immediately curve off the ridgecrest and walk down a roadbed, leveling off as you near the head of the main tributary to Cliff Valley creek, which you parallel northward. The "trail" descends moderately-to-steeply again through a continuation of the cutblock until, 90 yards short of another still serviceable logging road, you bear north onto forested trail. This trail undulates along the west slope, then bends through a gap in the ridge to descend southeast to a crossing of a passable road (1.2, 4770).

Across the road you arc along the upper edge of another cutblock on a trail lined with great patches of thimbleberry. After 0.3 mile the trail curves north onto another blocked-off logging road, which then winds down through a young ponderosa-pine plantation to yet another still-active road (0.9, 4250). Angle north across the road to where a duck marks the nearly hidden trail heading north-northwest.

Beyond this road, you curve clockwise very gradually to a generally southward heading, gently descending through a mixed-conifer forest. After coming out into the last clearcut on your route, you soon switchback north-northeast and quickly re-enter the forest. The descent steepens as a couple of switchbacks cross back and forth through a shallow, seeping depression on the steep hillside above Cliff Valley creek.

Curling to the west, the path crosses an intermittent trickle and, a couple of hundred yards farther, crosses a somewhat stronger flow gliding out from beneath the delicate fronds of five-finger fern. By early August you can help the bears and birds harvest the prolific thimbleberry crop that lines the trail as you continue the descent northward to a boulder ford of a vigorous tributary of Cliff Valley creek (2.1, 3220). Beyond it you walk through scrub 0.1 mile to a dirt road, then north along the road another 0.1 mile, past a creekside car-camping area, to the upper trailhead of the Grider Creek Trail.

The last 7.4 miles of this hike are described in detail, albeit with a north-to-south orientation, in the Grider Creek Trail, Hike 2. In brief, it descends along Cliff Valley creek 0.8 mile to a bridge over Grider Creek and a marvelous cascade and pool, just below its confluence with Cliff Valley creek. Generally staying well above Grider Creek, but crossing enough tributary streams to keep your whistle wetted, the well-forested trail bridges the creek three more times along its descent before coming to a halt at the west-bank trailhead. There are two camping possibilities along this stretch. The first is partly hidden on Grider Creek's west bank below the trail, some 75 yards before you reach the first bridge; the second site is also concealed, tucked into the east-bank shrubbery about 30 yards before the second bridge, which is 1.9 miles down-trail from the upper trailhead.

Recommended Reading and Source Books

Geology

Alt, David D., and Donald W. Hyndman, *Roadside Geology of Northern California*, Missoula, MT: Mountain Press, 1975.

Davis, Gregory A., "Metamorphic and granitic history of the Klamath Mountains." In *Geology of Northern California* (Edgar H. Bailey, ed.), Sacramento: California Division of Mines and Geology Bulletin 190, 1966.

Diller, Joseph S., *Topographic Development of the Klamath Mountains*, Washington: U.S. Geological Survey Bulletin 196, 1902.

Hotz, P.E., *Plutonic Rocks of the Klamath Mountains, California and Oregon*, Washington: U.S. Geological Survey Professional Paper 684-B, 1971.

Hotz, P.E., *Geology of Lode Gold Districts in the Klamath Mountains, California and Oregon*, Washington: U.S. Geological Survey Bulletin 1290, 1971.

Irwin, William P., "Geology of the Klamath Mountains province," In *Geology of Northern California* (Edgar H. Bailey, ed.), Sacramento: California Division of Mines and Geology Bulletin 190, 1966.

Pough, Frederick H., *A Field Guide to Rocks and Minerals*, 4th ed., Boston: Houghton Mifflin, 1976.

Shelton, John S., *Geology Illustrated*, San Francisco: W.H. Freeman, 1966.

Botany

Arno, Stephen F., and Ramona P. Hammerly, *Northwest Trees*, Seattle: The Mountaineers, 1977.

Crittenden, Mabel, *Trees of the West*, Millbrae, CA: Celestial Arts, 1977.

Ferlatte, William J., *A Flora of the Trinity Alps of Northern California*, Berkeley: University of California Press, 1974.

Franklin, Jerry F., and C.T. Dyrness, *Natural Vegetation of Oregon* and *Washington* (Chapter VI: Forest Zones of Southwestern Oregon), Portland: U.S. Forest Service, Pacific Northwest Forest and Range Experiment Station, 1973.

Griffin, James R., and William B. Critchfield, *The Distribution of Forest Trees in California*, Berkeley: U.S. Forest Service, Pacific Southwest Forest and Range Experiment Station, 1972.

Grillos, Steve J., *Ferns and Fern Allies of California* (California Natural History Guide 16), Berkeley: University of California Press, 1966.

Horn, Elizabeth L., *Wildflowers 1: The Cascades*, Beaverton, OR: Touchstone Press, 1972.

Horn, Elizabeth L., *Wildflowers 3: The Sierra Nevada*, Beaverton, OR: Touchstone Press, 1976.

Munz, Phillip A., and David D. Keck, *A California Flora and Supplement*, Berkeley: University of California Press, 1968.

Niehaus, Theodore F., and Charles L. Ripper, *A Field Guide to Pacific States Wildflowers*, Boston: Houghton Mifflin, 1976.

Palmer, George, and Martha Stuckey, *Western Tree Book*, Portland: Victoria House, 1977.

Sudworth, George B., *Forest Trees of the Pacific Slope*, New York: Dover, 1967 (1908 reprint with new Foreword and Table of Changes in Nomenclature).

Thompson, Mary, and Steven Thompson, *Huckleberry Country: Wild Food Plants of the Pacific Northwest*, Berkeley: Wilderness Press, 1977.

Thompson, Steven, and Mary Thompson, *Wild Food Plants of the Sierra*, Berkeley, Wilderness Press, 1972.

Watts, Tom, *Pacific Coast Tree Finder*, Berkeley: Nature Study Guild, 1973.

Zoology

Ingles, Lloyd G., *Mammals of the Pacific States*, Stanford: Stanford University Press, 1965.

Kirtzman, Ellen B., *Little Mammals of the Pacific Northwest*, Seattle: Pacific Search Press, 1977.

Larrison, Earl J., *Mammals of the Northwest*, Seattle: Seattle Audubon Society, 1976.

Lederer, Roger J., *Pacific Coast Bird Finder*, Berkeley: Nature Study Guild, 1977.

Murie, Olaus J., *A Field Guide to Animal Tracks*, Boston: Houghton Mifflin, 1975.

Peterson, Roger Tory, *A Field Guide to Western Birds*, Boston: Houghton Mifflin, 1961.

Robbins, Chandler S., Bertel Bruun, Herbert S. Zim, Arthur Singer, *Birds of North America*, New York: Golden Press, 1966.

Stebbins, Robert C., *Amphibians and Reptiles of California* (California Natural History Guide 31), Berkeley: University of California Press, 1972.

Ulvardy, Miklos D.F., *The Audubon Society Field Guide to North American Birds*, New York: Alfred A. Knopf, 1977.

Index

(Where more than one feature has the same name, the ranger
district in which each is located is given in parentheses.)